Moses

Moses

Man among Men?

Anthony Rees

LEXINGTON BOOKS
Lanham • Boulder • New York • London

Published by Lexington Books
An imprint of The Rowman & Littlefield Publishing Group, Inc.
4501 Forbes Boulevard, Suite 200, Lanham, Maryland 20706
www.rowman.com

86-90 Paul Street, London EC2A 4NE

British Library Cataloguing in Publication Information Available

Library of Congress Cataloging-in-Publication Data

ISBN 978-1-4985-6130-3 (cloth)
ISBN 978-1-4985-6131-0 (e-book)

∞™ The paper used in this publication meets the minimum requirements of American National Standard for Information Sciences—Permanence of Paper for Printed Library Materials, ANSI/NISO Z39.48-1992.

Contents

Acknowledgments

Books take time. This one is no different. For what seems like a lot of years I have been thinking about, talking about, and at times, actually writing, this book. I am grateful to many colleagues who have generously engaged me as I have worked on this book. My first public outing of any of these ideas came at a seminar held at St Mark's in Canberra, an event coordinated by David Neville. I am grateful to David for the opportunity to speak there and for his ongoing support of my work over some fifteen years. In October 2018, Nasili Vaka'uta and Emily Colgan hosted a public lecture on this topic at Trinity Theological College in Auckland. Their hospitality to me and my family over numerous visits to Aotearoa has always been warm and generous. I am grateful to you both, and to the Trinity College community. *Nga Mihi.*

Closer to home, I have been fortunate to work amongst wonderful colleagues at United Theological College in Sydney who have engaged with me on these chapters over a number of years. Your questions and challenges have helped me sharpen ideas and to clarify aspects which were poorly developed. I am always grateful for your warmth and kindness and for the truly collegial spirit we have developed. In particular, my thanks go to Jeffrey Aernie whose support and encouragement over years has far exceeded what might be normally considered collegial relations. Jeff, you are a true friend and I will always be thankful for the years we worked together.

Alongside wonderful colleagues, I have also been fortunate enough to be surrounded by enquiring, talented students. I wish to express my thanks to the many students who have listened to me talk about these matters, pressing me to explain things better, and broadening my cultural view. This book is better considered because of you.

The staff at Lexington have always been a pleasure to work with. This project has come to its close with the assistance of Megan White, but over the years I have worked with a number of editors who have all been unerringly patient and kind. Megan facilitated two reviews of the manuscript, and I am grateful to those two readers whose questions and suggestions pushed me to go further than I thought I would or could. Like all books, this one says both too much and too little. Both are my doing.

Finally, to my family. Kohen and Summer have grown up alongside this book. Jesse and Nelly have asked tricky questions about it. Maybe one day one of you might read it. I hope so. And if you do, I hope you think that it matters. And to Natalie (whose artwork is on the cover): you have ridden the highs and lows of this book, and of me. Your support, even in the most difficult times, is a source of wonder and strength. My love is always for you.

January 2023, Darug land

Introduction

LOCATING MOSES

Moses is synonymous with biblical tradition. It is impossible to imagine the bible without him. From his miraculous emergence in the early moments of the book of Exodus, through to his stirring final addresses in the book of Deuteronomy Moses is the central human character in the bible's foundational partition. The law, or more accurately *Torah*, is intractably linked to him, and through that association the shadow of Moses looms large over the rest of the Old Testament materials and into the New Testament as well. Mosaic tradition is strong in the presentation of Jesus, to the point where the gospel of Matthew clearly presents Jesus as a type of new Moses.

Not surprisingly then, much has been written about Moses, reflecting a wide variety of concerns. In the first century, in the face of anti-semitic sentiment, Philo of Alexandria wrote his *De Vita Mosis*,[1] an account of the central figure of Judaism set in the biographical style so popular at the time. Essentially an *apologia* for Judaism, Philo presents Moses as a figure demonstrating many of the virtues prized in Greek culture as a way of defending his religion from its detractors. As he writes, "I have conceived the idea of writing the life of Moses . . . the greatest and most perfect man that ever lived, having a desire to make his character fully known to those who ought not remain in ignorance respecting him."[2] Philo's account of Moses' life rarely if ever departs from this lofty view, creatively rendering those parts of his life which are unknown (most specifically, his upbringing in Egypt), and retelling his story in a fashion that uniformly paints Moses as a hero. For example, his slaying of the Egyptian in Exodus 2 is regarded as a pious action, "destroy[ing] one who lived solely for the destruction of others."[3]

1

More recently, Jonathan Kirsch has written a biography of Moses' life with a similar intent, though perhaps not quite so politically motivated. Kirsch's book on Moses draws on a range of literary material unavailable to Philo in order to uncover "The Moses No One Knows."[4] Kirsch's study is imaginative and wide-ranging in its scope, though in the end falls short of identifying an historical figure that lies behind these stories. Instead, Kirsch concludes that the "real" Moses is the one whose example inspires us in the day-to-day living of our own lives. To his credit, Kirsch recognizes that the so-called "ideal-Moses" is a troubling man, and the discerning reader has choices to make regarding the ways in which they will follow this towering figure.[5] More recently again, Avivah Gottleib Zornberg has reconstructed the "human" Moses through recourse to Jewish tradition and contemporary psychoanalysis. In doing so, her biography becomes more a study of the reception of Moses, but it nonetheless contributes to the building up of Moses' character for those who would read it.[6] These treatments of Moses' life have an historical aspect to them, though they tend to have a more overtly religious tone, encouraging their readers to learn something from the story they are being told, or as Kirsch explicitly suggests, to find inspiration from Moses. These three treatments are not of a piece. Clearly, Philo assumes the biblical data to be a record of actual history, his task being to bring that history to a new audience. It appears that Zornberg too most commonly assumes a historical Moses, though her motivation is not to defend Moses or her faith, but to reimagine the life of Moses in light of tradition and contemporary theories of the mind. Amongst a broader set of goals, Kirsch searches for a historical Moses, but is ultimately frustrated in that effort. However, despite these differences, the three accounts end up with a similar result: that there is something enduring in the stories of Moses that continue to speak to the world despite the enormous contextual distances that separate us from them, and that despite some of the challenges inherent in the character of Moses, he remains a model towards which what we do well to aspire.

Such treatments are not the normal *modus operandi* of the biblical scholar, whose work is traditionally meant to be more detached than these three examples. Historical or theological questions tend to dominate the discourse, rather than the more homiletical tone of the works cited thus far. So, for example, the short work by German scholar Gerhard von Rad offers a brief sketch of the life of Moses as found within the biblical materials, using this as a way of examining the revelation of God associated with his name.[7] It is worth noting, however, that his own positioning makes this a remarkable work, in so far as it was written in the context of the Third Reich where anything Jewish was met with hostility and violence. As Walter Brueggemann points out in the Foreward to a new edition of this work, Nazism was making an idol of the state, and so von Rad's emphasis on the first two commandments in this context was an act of uncommon courage.[8] George Coats turns to the traditions about Moses and finds them to present a picture of Moses as a heroic figure, and a man of God. He contends that a heroic saga centred on the life of Moses is drawn together with a narrative tradition regarding Yhwh's mighty acts in history. Incidentally, Coats finishes his book with a reflection that there is something about Moses that should inspire us to try and emulate him, an unusual exhortation at the end of a scholarly work. Finally, a recent work by Jeffrey Stackert[9] argues that Moses is presented as a prophet in each of the traditions which make up the Pentateuch. Ultimately, Stackert's book is not so much about Moses, as it is about demonstrating the ongoing relevance of the documentary hypothesis for reconstructing our understanding of Israelite religion.[10] In demonstrating the prophetic function of Moses across the strata, Stackert is able to show the parochialism of the early formulations of the documentary hypothesis which sought to separate these two aspects of Israelite religion.[11] The figure of Moses, as embodiment of both law and prophecy, becomes a crucial aspect in his investigation.

These three works then, differ sharply from the first three considered, offering not a reconstruction of the life of Moses, but rather demonstrating a greater level of interest in the historical and theological dimensions of the text's claims. They do not seek to present Moses as a model for contemporary living (Coats' brief comments aside), but instead are more concerned with the matter of the text, rather than the subjects within it. They are not apologetic nor homiletic in tone, but rather sober investigations into matters of theology and history. These are not works written for a popular audience, but rather for a more formal academic readership.

IMAG[IN]ING MOSES

Not surprisingly, the figure of Moses is better known through more accessible imaginings of him. Popular recognition of Moses is driven by the classic cinematic portrayals of him: the iconic Moses of Charlton Heston, and more recently, the more muscular portrayal given by Christian Bale. As Murphy comments, ask someone to close their eyes and imagine Moses, and almost certainly Charlton Heston appears in their mind's eye.[12] The images of Moses in these two films have become authoritative in public understanding of who Moses is, the two cinematic Moses' giving the Moses of the bible a new life, or perhaps better, new lives,[13] lives which differ from the biblical telling, and yet which are connected in significant ways. For example, it is clear that the writers of *Exodus: Gods and Kings* went to some effort to

understand Moses. Early on in the film we hear Moses complain about the
influence of a Priestess who utilizes the types of divinatory techniques leg-
islated against in Deuteronomy 18:9–13. In a similar fashion, we see Moses
speak against the flogging of a slave, in a fashion which shows familiarity
with Deuteronomy 15:12–17. While some may raise objections regarding the
historical questions such a characterization ignores, it seems to me to suggest
that the cinematic Moses of Christian Bale may well be a little more biblical than some of his detractors have realized. Murphy suggests that Scott's
Moses demonstrates an overt rationality in his shunning of superstition and
the prophecies of Pharaoh's Priestess.[14] But is this not a play with the Deuteronomy legislation Moses will later speak? Likewise, Hays overstates his case
in his playful rendering of Scott's Moses as "MovieMoses™." Yes, aspects
of Moses' story, including the substitution of Moses' staff for a sword are
non-biblical. And yes, the Moses of Torah raises no ethical objection to Yahweh's plagues. But Hays' final assessment of Scott's Moses is problematic:
"The filmmakers took Israel's reluctant, stammering, paradigmatic prophet,
who needed human help and understood his God's dark side, and turned him
into MovieMoses™, a handsome, silver-tongued general who bravely and
heroically leads his people, and even argues with God about the harshness of
his justice, like Abraham."[15] This description fits Scott's Moses, but is it not
largely true also of the Bible's Moses? The stuttering and stammering Moses
disappears as quickly as he appears. There is no sense of a stutter or uncer-
tainty in the Moses who stares down the shepherds at the well in Exodus 2,
or in the early exchanges with Yahweh at the bush, or in any other moment.
Aaron's appointment as Moses' prophet seems largely to be symbolic. Moses
speaks continually throughout the Torah, his claims more likely an excuse,
or perhaps related to issues of language. The biblical Moses needed help, but
so too Scott's Moses, who begs Zipporah to help him understand the nature
and person of God and is nursed back to health following his injuries in a
horrific landslide. Scott's Moses, Hays states, is a heroic leader, but is that
really a point of departure from the bible's Moses? Indeed, if Moses' disability of speech is taken at face value, we might even argue that Scott's Moses,
equipped as he is with sword and military training, is by comparison, not
heroic enough! And while the biblical Moses may not confront Yahweh over
the destructive violence wreaked on Egypt, he does confront God on other
matters in ways which go beyond Abraham's bargaining with God. In short,
Hays seems upset that the film departs in ways from the biblical "script," and
for some that may well be a fair enough complaint. But his analysis of the two
different portrayals of Moses seems overstated in both cases.

The cinema is not the only place where one finds portrayals of the life of
Moses. Composers of opera have long found in the story of Moses a drama

fitting for the stage.[16] The operatic stage gives a space for an even more dramatic telling of the story than the cinema; opera does not concern itself with the type of age-restrictions common to more digital media like television or cinema. Theatre goers know that depictions of sex and violence, carefully controlled on the screen, are a part and parcel of the theatre going experience! No surprise then, that the opera widely regarded as the greatest of the twentieth century is *Moses ünd Aron*[17] by the leader of the second Viennese school, Arnold Schoenberg.[18] Schoenberg's opera far exceeds the cinema in terms of what might be regarded as adult-only appropriate content.

These dramatic portrayals, as well as the range of paintings, murals, sculptures and all other manner of representations all serve to build up an image of who Moses is. Each attempt at imag[in]ing Moses draws on understood aspects of Moses as well as ignoring others. As we know, no single photo, video or painting of ourselves fully does justice to our own complexity, and neither should we expect the same of attempts to render biblical characters, particularly those with such a strong presence as Moses.

MASCULINITY STUDIES

In the 1980s a wave of studies into masculinity began to emerge in critique of "male sex role" literature.[19] Resisting the notion that anatomy was in some way determinative of identity, scholars interrogated the "centrality of male power to dominant ways of being a man."[20] This work resulted in the development of the important concept of *hegemonic masculinity* which served to give the field direction in its formative years. The concept posits that hegemonic masculinity is normative, embodying the most culturally honored ways of being a man.[21] Drawing on the Gramscian formulation, hegemony, "refers to the cultural dynamic by which a group claims and sustains a leading position in social life,"[22] in this instance, men, and more specifically, a particular imagination of what it is to be a man. In becoming normative it presents itself as the model that all men are measured against, even while very few men might attain it. As Brittan somewhat flatly suggests, "[m]ost discussions of masculinity tend to treat it as if it is measurable. Some men have more of it, others less."[23] Such men are not necessarily the bearers of powerful office, and indeed, this myth of masculinity may well be propagated through fictional characters, such as James Bond, Jason Bourne, Frank Underwood, Harvey Spectre, Don Draper, and so on.[24] On this point, it is important to note the hegemonic masculinities can be constructed that bear little to no resemblance to the lives of real men. However, this does little to harm the theory precisely because these remain ideals, fantasies and desires that *do* bear on real men.[25]

However, as Connell notes, hegemony is unlikely to be achieved without a correspondence between cultural ideals (even those based in fictional representations) and institutional power, so that in our world, top level corporate, business, and military demonstrations of masculinity necessarily play into the construction of the idealized type.[26]

The existence of an "ideal type" assumes that other expressions of masculinity are possible, and these types are also categorized in the theoretical literature. Connell refers to subordinated, complicit masculinities, and marginalized masculinities,[27] the descriptors themselves pointing to their definition relative to the exalted norm. By extension, the theory of hegemonic masculinity also serves to subordinate all women to men. As such, even men who do not attain the hegemonic ideal benefit in some way from the gender hierarchy, enjoy what Connell refers to as the "gender dividend."[28]

Despite a surprising lack of reference to Judith Butler in the seminal works, it is clear that this developing understanding of masculinity is closely related to the notion of gender performance. In her classic work *Gender Trouble,*[29] Butler contends that gender is not to be understood as a stable identity marker which gives rise to performed acts, but rather that repeated acts give rise to the gendered identity.[30] These actions are understood within cultural and social contexts and so gender is understood as a socially-constructed reality. It also serves to demonstrate that gender is not to be thought of in an essentialist way. That is, differing social contexts provide the possibility for differing performances of gender. Speaking specifically of masculinity, Connell and Messerschmidt comment "Masculinity is not a fixed entity embedded in the body or personality traits of individuals. Masculinities are configurations of practice that are accomplished in social action and, therefore, can differ according to the gender relations in a particular social setting."[31] Further, gender hierarchies are subject to challenge and change and so demonstrations of hegemonic masculinity are (re)produced in particular social locations.

Having assessed the emergence and successes of the concept of hegemonic masculinity, Connell and Messerschmidt conclude:

> From the mid-1980s to the early 2000s, the concept of hegemonic masculinity thus passed from a conceptual model with a fairly narrow empirical base to a widely used framework for research and debate about men and masculinities. The concept was applied in diverse cultural contexts and to a considerable range of practical issues.[32]

HEGEMONIC MASCULINITY AND HEBREW BIBLE STUDIES

Amongst that range of diverse cultural contexts and academic discourses identified by Connell and Messerschmidt was the study of the Hebrew Bible.

Because of the capacity of hegemonic masculinity to interrogate a variety of social constructions, the very concept serves as a defense against claims of homogenizing or essentializing of masculinity. It is the performance of particular actions in cultural context that define masculinities. These actions can be observed in real people but can also be analyzed through the literary output of a particular cultural group. Not surprisingly, given the way in which hegemonic masculinity highlights the patriarchal nature of a society, it has proven a fruitful tool in studying the constructions of masculinity in the Hebrew Bible. As Haddox notes, "[t]he play between the hegemonic and subordinate variants of masculinity is particularly active in the biblical texts."[33]

A seminal moment in the development of masculinity studies in the Hebrew Bible came with the 1995 publication of a paper by David Clines.[34] In an attempt to analyze the construction of masculinity in the Hebrew bible, Clines lays out a typology of biblical masculinity under six categories:

1. The fighting male, by which is meant strength and the ability to be active in the killing of other men.
2. The persuasive male, which relates to the skill of speaking, both publicly and privately, recognizing here that words can be understood as instruments of control. In this sense, persuasion is a further extension of the physical power manifest in the first category.
3. The beautiful male, manifest in good looks and bodily ability.
4. The bonding male, relating to a particular type of male-male relationship that brings with it particular forms of exclusive commitment and a valuing of this relationship above other relationships.
5. The womanless male, which refers to emotional attachment. Women are present, of course, but women are not *owed* anything and play an instrumental rather than engaged role.
6. The musical male, which refers to David's noted skill as a lyre player, but also the sonorous nature of his singing voice.

While these categories come from a reading of David and not the whole Hebrew Bible canon, Clines asserts his view that the myth of masculinity enshrined in the David story was potent amongst Israelite men and must have been influential in the ongoing perception of masculinity within that culture.[35] Clines' subsequent work on Moses saw a subtle shift in the terminology he employed, driven largely by nuanced differences between Moses' and David's social role. In a chapter on Exodus 32–34,[36] Clines examines aspects of Moses' masculinity though here his nomenclature has moved from "the fighting male" to "the warrior male" suggesting that "killing is the quintessential male characteristic in the Hebrew bible"[37] and pointing to Moses' role as the head of the chain of command. Wilson notes that Clines does not utilize the term "hegemonic masculinity" in his article on David,[38] a pattern that continues in his work on Moses and again on a more recent paper on divine masculinity.[39] Nonetheless, his 1995 paper works with categories he identifies as "cultural norms,"[40] norms which he continues to develop and refine in subsequent work, so while the nomenclature that Clines deploys departs from that which is widely accepted, it is clear that his project is concerning itself with the same phenomenon.

Scholars have wrestled with Clines' ideas, accepting the validity of some categories, rejecting others, and proposing alternate schemes. For example, Susan Haddox develops her own typology and speaks of three broadly conceived components: honor, potency, and wisdom.[41] These broader categories draw in aspects of Clines' schema but also point in different directions. Honor relates to provision and protection for the man's family, practices of hospitality and forthright and honest speech.[42] Clines considers honor in a later piece on the divine masculinity,[43] noting that honor is a recognition of society regarding the status of a man. It is in flux, subject to challenge, and so needs to be protected.

Haddox utilizes "potency" across a number of domains: skill in warfare (drawing close here to Clines' fighting male), in leadership, in the sexual realm, and in "physical wholeness and autonomy."[44] The raising of sexual potency here comes close to a category developed by Wilson, that of "fertility and marriage" which marks a developmental category, particularly in the production of legitimate heirs.[45] In so far as this relates to kinship and family matters we can see how this also relates to notions of honor.

Finally, in "wisdom" Haddox refers to decision making and appropriate action in various circumstances. Interestingly, Haddox three-part scheme overlooks a category from a previous article in which she notes the imperative for the hegemonic male to avoid appearing feminine, with a particular emphasis on avoiding excessive attachments with women and women's activities.[46] In Haddox's three-part scheme, relationships and dealing with women has been folded into the concept of honor. For the hegemonic male, provision for and control over his family is central. Wives and daughters bear upon his honor in different ways, and so Haddox's move to consolidate relations with women in this fashion is constructive, allowing a consideration of the different types of relationships men hold with women.

The issue of relations between men and women, or masculinity and femininity has also been addressed by Moore. For him, the issue is not solely about emotional detachment, but association. Simply put, a man is a man and acts like one, which is to say, does not act like a woman. Masculinity acts on a binary logic: to be a man is to not be a woman. Clines' notion of avoiding un-necessary attachment *with* women is coupled with an injunction against performing *as* a woman.[47] Wilson reminds us, though, that other categories of hegemonic masculinity are frequently associated with women, most notably, wisdom. Further, Yahweh is often described in terms that are overtly feminine.[48] We need to carefully distinguish then between a conceptual category, such as "wisdom," and feminization, or acting "as a woman."

In a study on masculinity as it is imagined in Deuteronomy, Mark George concludes that "to be a man in Israel is perhaps encapsulated in the concern with having a name in Israel."[49] A key aspect for this, in George's view, is the exercise of self-control. He notes this in relation to his discussion of behaviour in warfare,[50] though as Wilson notes, the broader regimentation of masculinity laid-out in the book of Deuteronomy is such that self-control may well be considered a category in its own right in so far as it guards excesses in relation to food consumption and sexual expression,[51] as well as some of the other concerns taken up by George, including place in society (by which is meant the exercise of appropriate social roles) as well asmovement through time and space in relation to religious practice, and the divine ordering of the created order. In addition to these categories, Wilson identifies the significance of children (as noted above) and the related issue of kinship solidarity. That is, proper exercise of manhood involves both procreation and solidarity within a kinship network.

The development of Clines' ideas, both in his own work and the contribution of others, is reflective of two realities: that multiple masculine performances always exist within cultures, and that the Hebrew Bible itself is a product not of a single moment in time and unfolds over centuries. Not surprisingly, the diversity of texts reveals different ideas and ideals concerning the performance of masculinity and the (competitive) relationship between them.[52] Some analyses of masculinity have focused on these various texts, so that Rhiannon Graybill speaks of "prophetic" masculinity,[53] characterising it as inherently unstable. Brian DiPalma has sketched out ideas concerning "scribal" masculinity with an emphasis on the stories of Daniel.[54] As we have seen, George speaks of a "regimented" masculinity through an examination of Deuteronomy. While drawn from specific texts, each of these newly defined masculinities continue to relate to the hegemonic masculinity of their time and find their points of comparison against that cultural ideal.

These developments of Clines' initial formulation have served to strengthen studies in biblical masculinity and have opened up new areas for inquiry. In doing so, they help resist the danger identified by Moore in 2010 of generalization,[55] a concern echoed by Nissinen in 2014.[56] Nissinen expresses a satisfaction regarding the theorization of the hierarchy of gender, noting the way in which these are related to relationality, a point which will become significant in this study. So while an "identikit profile of the ideal Israelite"[57] may well emerge and be beneficial across a range of biblical texts, it is important not to assume this to be the case and to be aware of ways in which the categories are being subverted and alternate masculinities being foregrounded. As Graybill notes, subsequent scholarship has issued a challenge to what she calls "easy assertions of hegemonic masculinity."[58] Given the reality that gender is a social construction, and performed socially, we can only understand it in the context of relationships.[59] These alternate performances of masculinity demonstrate that gender inequality exists not just between men and women, but also between men and men, as well as women and women. In order to distinguish between these competing masculinities we will also consider the issue of homosociality.

HOMOSOCIALITY

Homosociality refers to non-sexual relationships between members of the same sex. Bird argues that it is homosociality that allows the distinction to be drawn between hegemonic and nonhegemonic performances of masculinity. In doing so she identifies three key meanings which contribute to the way in which hegemonic masculinity is buttressed by homosociality: Emotional detachment, referring to the process of boys distancing themselves from their mother and developing their identity in relation to what they are not; competitiveness, by which relationship with other men becomes not a matter of individuality, but rather competitive individuality; sexual objectification of women, a notion developed amongst other men and designed to understand male identity over and above female identity.[60] These three meanings confirm Flood's assertion: "men's lives are said to be highly organized by relations between men . . . Males seek the approval of other males, both identifying with and competing against them. They attempt to improve their position in masculine social hierarchies . . ."[61] and that of Kimmel: "We are under the constant careful scrutiny of other men. Other men watch us, rank us, grant us acceptance into the realm of manhood. . . . Masculinity is a *homosocial* enactment. We test ourselves, perform heroic feats, take enormous risks, all because we want other men to grant us our manhood."[62]

It is precisely this aspect of competition and prestige in relation to masculinity that buttresses hegemonic masculinity's place in the cultural order. The categories we have considered above, what Stone refers to as cultural expectation,[63] allow for testing and comparison, for the validation of others and the possibility of being charged as inadequate. This sense of competition among men crosses the cultural divide between our world and that of the Hebrew Bible. As Kelly Murphy notes, in the Hebrew Bible "there are men and women, but there are also men and other men, and it is the differences *between men* that sometimes matter most for others to consider someone a real man."[64]

Studies in homosociality in biblical studies have often revolved around questions of sex.[65] While homosocial relations are understood as non-sexual, shared sexual activity with others is often a part of homosocial relations. An insightful book by Barbara Thiede[66] has recently made this reality visible. She notes: " . . . shared sexual experience is a pivotal part of male homosocial relationships in the Hebrew Bible. The men in question may not be having sex with one another, but sex with women serves both to create opportunities for men to bond and maintain alliances and friendships." I have no wish to minimize the truth of this claim, which Thiede forcefully demonstrates throughout her book. Nonetheless, in the story of Moses, sex is almost entirely absent, especially the kind to which Thiede refers. If her claims that "Sex and sexual acts with women underly proof of manhood in the Hebrew Bible" and that such acts "generate" male-male relationships,[67] are true—and in general terms I am convinced they are—Moses has bypassed one of the most powerful tools for the establishment of hegemonic masculinity. Yes, Moses has two sons, but no sexual act is recorded. Zipporah is given in marriage and bears a son (Exod. 2:21–22). The second son appears in the story without warning. As such, while the present study will pay attention to the dynamics of homosociality and its competitive, dangerous effects, it makes a departure from those studies focussed towards sexual expression and domination, particularly, though not exclusively, of women.

MASCULINITY AND CHARACTERIZATION IN THE MOSES NARRATIVE

By foregrounding the categories of masculinity surveyed above and taking the insights of homosociality seriously, this book will focus on the relationships that Moses shares with other male characters. In doing so, it will make an evaluation of the ways in which Moses' superior performance of masculinity is evident in the way these relationships are relayed to us through the biblical materials. Hegemonic masculinity, then, provides a type of organizing principle for the exploration of its constituent categories, demonstrated through the competitive nature of male-male homosociality. The study also takes seriously the notion that gender is socially constructed and so performed through relation to others. In relation to this, an understanding of the socially-constructed relationships will also be in view. That is, what does it mean to be a brother? Or a son-in-law? And how does appropriate performance within these relationships intersect with notions of masculinity?

Given that this is a literary task, the observation of masculine traits and performance of Moses and the other characters within the narrative will proceed utilizing the gains of narrative criticism. As such, the study is attentive to both direct and indirect means of characterization,[68] recognizing that aspects of masculine performance will be present through both means of description. It is important to note here that not all characters in this book are "equal," by which I mean there are differing depths of relationship considered here. For example, while the relationship between Moses and Yahweh essentially spans the entirety of the material we will cover, the relation between Moses and his father-in-law—as significant as it is—is far more episodic in nature. The encounters with Korah and Phinehas are briefer again, and while they are key aspects laid out in those singular stories, we simply can't expect the same depth of characterization in these instances. In contrast, the amount of material shared between Moses and Pharaoh, or Moses and Aaron, and finally Moses and Yahweh allows for a far rounder picture of these characters.

Given that this is a literary task, the book is not concerned with the type of historical-critical methods which are often characteristic of Pentateuch studies. As such there is no attempt to posit a date for these events; no effort to interrogate the reality of an historical Moses; no attempt to explain the mystery at the sea, the identity of the Pharaoh or issues surrounding the development of the textual strata present in the final form of the text as we have it. Much valuable work has been done in regard to each of these questions and more besides.[69] However, those interrogations make little to no contribution to the type of investigation being made here and so are left aside. Instead, the analysis here sticks close to the text as it is received, essentially being an exercise in close-reading. Moses is understood here as a literary figure, a figure of memory, rather than investigated as a figure of history.[70]

HEGEMONY, IDEALS, AND THE PAPER PERSON

The discussion to this point highlights a number of complexities that bear on this work in different ways. Firstly, while the theory of hegemonic masculinity continues to occupy an important place within masculinities studies, it is true to say that the theory and its subject share a certain slipperiness. While certain categories may possess a universality about them, the cultural production of these types is such that we are likely speaking too boldly to speak of a singular biblical hegemonic masculinity. The proliferation of studies on masculinity in the Hebrew Bible is evidence of such dynamism. The work of Clines and Haddox—seminal as it is—continues to be refined in the subsequent work which has followed. The story of Moses and the scholarship which surrounds it may well be a banner example of this type of issue. It is widely held that that Pentateuch is comprised of range of literary strata composed, compiled and redacted over hundreds of years.[71] These strata hold within them particular views of masculinity held in their own specific locations. Perhaps there is similarity between them: indeed, that is most likely the case. But if we take seriously the idea that gender ideals are shaped by time and place we cannot assume complete congruency. Stories about Moses were told in different places to different audiences which held nuanced, particular ways of understanding the world and human relations. Within them we would have found, presumably, nuanced understandings of masculinity demonstrated in the character of Moses and the men around him.

The scholarly material around Moses and masculinity demonstrates such diversity. In the work of Graybill we have work which concentrates on the vulnerability on Moses' body,[72] while Wilson considers coming-of-age questions.[73] Both begin with the concept of hegemonic masculinity and utilize particular categories as the means of pursuing their own readings. The approach here is broader, thinking through a wider range of masculine categories with an attention to homosocial relationality. This emphasis on characterization means the final form of the text is the one under examination, without consideration of the historical development of the texts themselves.

The second issue also relates to hegemony and the reality that hegemony presents an ideal type. That which is ideal is rarely, if ever real, so the presentation of hegemonic models always carries a degree of fantasy to it. Given the destructive picture of masculinity painted thus far, perhaps we should take some relief at that. This issue also points to a key point of differentiation regarding this study and others which have centred on the person of Moses. Previous studies have been concerned with particular historical priorities which have each in their own way been concerned with real, living people, whether that be the author of the literary strata—or perhaps more accurately, an understanding of the historical location of that real persona—or the historical Moses himself. This phenomenon was identified by Barthes[74] and gave rise to his notion of the "paper being." Bal explains it thus:

> . . . [T]he people with whom literature is concerned are not real people. They are fabricated creatures made up from imagination, memory: paper people, without flesh and blood. . . . The character is not a human being, but it resembles one. . . . It is fair to say that characters don't exist. Yet narratives produce 'character-effects.' The character-effect occurs when the resemblance between human beings and fabricated figures is so great that we forget the fundamental difference: we even go so far as to identify with the character, to cry, to laugh, and to search for or with it. . . .[75]

Such a view does not disqualify the notion of an historical Moses, but recognizes that these stories, by necessity, create a different type of Moses, one reduced to words on a page. Indeed, we might say that the reduction of Moses is the reduction of multiple paper-Moseses. That is true of Moses and is true of the other characters considered within this project. It is the notion of character-effect which is significant here. No one could deny the significance of Moses in the religious traditions in which he is revered. Indeed, the scriptures of each hold this literary figure as a model, a symbol of the power of character effect. And again, that is true of the other characters as well. If the other characters are considered antagonists of Moses, there is also a character-effect at work in their presentation. It is the interaction between the characters—the homosocial relationships—that give articulation to the understanding of masculinity within the story and the structure of these relationships.[76] Part of the close-reading strategy employed here then is to be attentive to the ways in which this effect is deployed, particularly in relation to questions of gender and homosociality.

UNFOLDING THE BOOK

The primary focus of this work is the relationships Moses shares with other male characters within the narrative. This serves two purposes: it responds to the reality that gender is socially-constructed and so examines masculinity within the social relations constructed in the story-world. Second, it allows the concept of hegemonic masculinity to be foregrounded, assessing character through relation to the range of categories understood to exemplify this idealized type.

However, before that work begins, the first chapter considers the characterization of Moses beyond those social relationships. This allows consideration of some of the aspects of masculinity not so easily discernible within those male-male relationships. As such, this chapter considers aspects of Moses' characterization that lie beyond the relationships covered elsewhere. We have seen that women play a significant role in the performance of masculinity and in the development of homosocial relationships. Moses is an ambiguous figure in this regard: while women play significant roles in his life, these do not revolve around the types of sexual domination that characterizes particular types of masculine performance. In large part Moses embodies the emotional indifference characteristic of the hegemonic male, without the sexual conquest that is often coupled with it. We will consider, then, the way in which Moses' life is borne upon by the women who are a part of his story. The final category considered here will be that of Moses' appearance. The bible is well-known for the lack of physical description of its characters, and so certain aspects related to Moses' appearance are considered.

Following the initial chapter focused on the character of Moses, a series of studies follows which investigate Moses' homosocial relationships with the following characters: his brother, Aaron, his father-in-law, the Pharaohs of Egypt, his cousin Korah and his nephew, Phinehas. The chapter on Aaron will focus on issues of bonding, persuasion and wisdom. While the idea that Aaron would serve as Moses' prophet never seems to materialize, it is true that their relationship is the closest that Moses experiences, forged by a common objective and at times, being targeted as a pair. Chapter three, which centres on Moses' father-in-law engages the categories of honor, wisdom and potency. The fourth chapter focuses on one of the key relationships within the Exodus narrative, namely, Moses' relationship with the two Pharaohs. While these are distinct characters within the story there is a narrative strategy of collapse as both characters exhibit similar tendencies. The discussion circles around issues of wisdom and potency while also considering notions of violence and honor. The chapter on Korah considers wisdom, honor, potency and also beauty, picking up ancient ideas regarding baldness. Chapter six considers the episode of Numbers 25 and the actions of Moses' nephew Phinehas. It engages potency, violence, honor and wisdom. In each of these human relationships, as assessment is made regarding the relative success of each in relation to masculine performance.

In each case it will be seen that a dynamic of the presentation of the relationship is the way in which Moses is presented as a superior male, and so in these relationships, the concept of hegemonic masculinity is clearly evident. The intersection of masculinity with the social construction of these relationships, as previously mentioned, also informs aspects of these studies. There is an exception to this broad rule and that comes in the relationship between Moses and his father-in-law, variously named Jethro, Reuel and Hobab. In a fashion quite unlike any of his other relationships, Moses relies on Jethro. Early on in their relationship that reliance was largely physical. It is Jethro that welcomes Moses into his home, provides a daughter as a wife, and allows Moses to contribute to their families' well-being. Later in the story, after Moses essentially abandons his wife and sons, it is Jethro who reunites them, and it is Jethro who counsels Moses regarding the difficulty of his responsibilities. In each instance Moses honors him in a way that is unique. So while Moses may not emerge as the "better" man in his relationship with Jethro, it is accurate to say that he is made better by Jethro and that more than any other human character, it is Jethro who exerts the greatest influence on him.

The final chapter considers the most significant relationship in Moses' life, that with Yahweh. Not surprisingly, the masculinity of Moses is less influential in this relationship, and while at points Moses exerts himself and is able to have an influence on Yahweh's actions, ultimately this is seen to be a momentary aberration. While he emerges as "the man, Moses" in his dealings with the other human characters, his relationship with Yahweh has the opposite effect. This does nothing to diminish Moses in the story-world. Indeed, it is in large part due to his special relationship with Yahweh that Moses holds such a significant place in both the story world and memory. Despite his short-comings, which are amplified in comparison to Yahweh, the memory of Moses is as the ultimate prophet, the earth's meekest man, servant of Yahweh. In this we may see a subversion of the concept, whereby it is the performance of masculinity in the public sphere coupled with a posture of humility before Yahweh that enshrines Moses' place as "the man."

A concluding reflection will look back on the ground covered and see to what extent the concept of hegemonic masculinity has allowed an examination of these relationships. In doing so we will know Moses better, as well as the characters that surround him. We will then point towards future possibilities in the engagement of masculinity studies with sacred texts. But now we turn to our primary protagonist, the man, Moses.

NOTES

1. Philo, *The Works of Philo: Complete and Unabridged*, trans. Charles Duke Yonge, New Updated ed. (Peabody: Hendrickson, 1993). Josephus follows a similar route in his own reworking of the Torah narrative, describing Moses in the same triumphalist way. See, Flavius Josephus, "The Antiquities of the Jews," in *Complete Works of Flavius Josephus* (Grand Rapids: Kregel, 1960).

2. Philo, "On the Life of Moses, I," in *The Works of Philo: Complete and Unabridged* (Peabody: Hendrickson, 1993), 459.

3. Ibid., 463.

4. Jonathan Kirsch, *Moses: A Life*, 1st ed. (New York: Ballantine Books, 1998). This is the title of the first chapter of the book.

5. Ibid., 361.

6. Avivah Gottlieb Zornberg, *Moses: A Human Life*, Jewish Lives (New Haven: Yale University Press, 2016).

7. Gerhard von Rad, *Moses*, trans. Stephen Neill, 2nd ed. (Eugene: Wipf and Stock, 2012).

8. Walter Brueggemann, in ibid., xi. While it is true that all scholarly work is driven by the particular circumstances of the interpreter, it is interesting that the work of Philo and von Rad come together on this point, both providing a response to the scourge of anti-Semitic thought and practice.

9. Jeffrey Stackert, *A Prophet Like Moses: Prophecy, Law, and Israelite Religion* (Oxford: Oxford University Press, 2014).

10. Ibid., 1.

11. Ibid., 69.

12. Kelly J. Murphy, *Rewriting Masculinity: Gideon, Men, and Might* (Oxford: Oxford University Press, 2019), 45.

13. For a more extended discussion of Moses' cinematic portrayals, see Brian M. Britt, *Rewriting Moses: The Narrative Eclipse of the Text*, Journal for the Study of the Old Testament Supplement Series (London: T & T Clark, 2004), 40–58.

14. Murphy, *Rewriting Masculinity: Gideon, Men, and Might*, 45.

15. Christopher Hays, "Live by the Sword, Die by the Sword: The Reinvention of the Reluctant Prophet as Moviemoses," https://www.academia.edu/10037402/Live_By_the_Sword_Die_By_the_Sword_The_Reinvention_of_the_Reluctant_Prophet_as_MovieMoses_.

16. For an extensive review of the life of Moses in Opera see Helen Leneman, *Moses: The Man and the Myth in Music* (Sheffield: Sheffield Phoenix Press, 2014).

17. Arnold Schoenberg, "Moses Und Aron: Oper in Drei Akten" (Mainz: B. Schott's Söhne, 1957); *Moses Und Aron* (Munich: Art Haus Musik, 2006), videografación, 1 videodisco (134 min.): son., col. ; 4 3/4 plg. + 1 folleto (37 p.); 18 cm., 101259 Arthaus Musik.

18. See, Anthony Rees, "What Gleams Must Be Good: Reading Arnold Schoenberg's Moses Und Aron," *The Bible and Critical Theory* 15, no. 2 (2019).

19. On the "male sex role" see, James B. Harrison, "Men's Roles and Men's Lives," *Signs* 4, no. 2 (1978); Joseph Pleck, "The Theory of Male Sex-Role Identity: Its Rise and Fall,1936 to the Present," in *In the Shadow of the Past: Psychology Views the Sexes*, ed. Miriam Lewin (New York: Columbia University Press, 1983).

20. Stephen M. Whitehead and Frank J. Barrett, "The Sociology of Masculinity," in *The Masculinities Reader*, ed. Stephen M. Whitehead and Frank J. Barrett (Cambridge: Polity Press, 2001), 15.

21. R. W. Connell and James W. Messerschmidt, "Hegemonic Masculinity: Rethinking the Concept," *Gender & Society* 19, no. 6 (2005): 832.

22. R. W. Connell, *Masculinities*, 2nd ed. (Cambridge: Polity Press, 2005), 77.

23. Arthur Brittan, "Masculinities and Masculinism," in *The Masculinities Reader*, ed. Stephen M. Whitehead and Frank J. Barrett (Cambridge: Polity Press, 2001), 51.

24. These three final figures are characters on House of Cards, Suits, and Mad Men (dealing with Government, Law, and Business, respectively). In each of these fictional cases, the hegemonic ideal is contrasted against a range of other men who demonstrate a less-than-ideal masculinity. In each instance, the failings of the idealized figure pale in comparison to their positively-received traits.

25. Connell and Messerschmidt, "Hegemonic Masculinity: Rethinking the Concept," 838.

26. Connell, *Masculinities*, 77.

27. Ibid., 78–80. See also, Frank J. Barrett, "The Organizational Construction of Hegemonic Masculinity: The Case of the Us Navy," in *The Masculinities Reader*, ed. Stephen M. Whitehead and Frank J. Barrett (Cambridge: Polity Press, 2001), 78ff.

28. Connell, *Masculinities*, 79.

29. Judith Butler, *Gender Trouble: Feminism and the Subversion of Identity*, Routledge Classics (New York: Routledge, 2006).

30. Ibid., 191.

31. Connell and Messerschmidt, "Hegemonic Masculinity: Rethinking the Concept," 836.

32. Ibid., 835.

33. Susan E. Haddox, "Favoured Sons and Subordinate Masculinities," in *Men and Masculinity in the Hebrew Bible and Beyond*, ed. Ovidiu Creangă (Sheffield: Sheffield Phoenix Press, 2010), 3.

34. David J.A. Clines, "David the Man: The Construction of Masculinity in the Hebrew Bible," in *Interested Parties: The Ideology of Writers and Readers of the Hebrew Bible* (Sheffield: Sheffield Academic Press, 1995).

35. Ibid., 216.

36. David J.A. Clines, "Dancing and Shining at Sinai: Playing the Man in Exodus 32–34," in *Men and Masculinity in the Hebrew Bible and Beyond*, ed. Ovidiu Creangă, The Bible in the Modern World (Sheffield: Sheffield Phoenix Press, 2010).

37. Ibid., 55.

38. Stephen Wilson, "Biblical Masculinities and Multiple Masculinities Theory: Past, Present and Future," in *Hebrew Masculinities Anew*, ed. Ovidiu Creangă (Sheffield: Sheffield Phoenix Press, 2019), 24.

39. David J.A. Clines, "The Most High Male: Divine Masculinity in the Bible," ibid.

40. "David the Man: The Construction of Masculinity in the Hebrew Bible."

41. Susan E Haddox, 'Is There a "Biblical Masculinity"? Masculinities in the Hebrew Bible', *Word & World*, 36 (2016): 5–14.

42. For a fuller discussion on the aspect of honor in Hebrew Bible masculinity see, Stephen M. Wilson, *Making Men: The Male Coming-of-Age Theme in the Hebrew Bible* (New York: Oxford University Press, 2015), 42–44.

43. Clines, "The Most High Male: Divine Masculinity in the Bible," 72.

44. Susan E. Haddox, "Is There a 'Biblical Masculinity'? Masculinities in the Hebrew Bible," *Word & World* 36, no. 1 (2016): 6.

45. Wilson, *Making Men: The Male Coming-of-Age Theme in the Hebrew Bible*, 40.

46. Haddox, "Favoured Sons and Subordinate Masculinities," 4.

47. Stephen D. Moore, "Final Reflections on Biblical Masculinity," in *Men and Masculinity in the Hebrew Bibla and Beyond*, ed. Ovidiu Creangă (Sheffield: Sheffield Phoenix, 2010), 246.

48. Wilson, *Making Men: The Male Coming-of-Age Theme in the Hebrew Bible*, 38. For a study on feminine imagery for God see L. Juliana M. Claassens, *Mourner, Mother, Midwife: Reimagining God's Delivering Presence in the Old Testament* (Louisville: Westminster John Knox, 2012).

49. Mark George, "Masculinity and Its Regimentation in Deuteronomy," in *Men and Masculinity in the Hebrew Bible and Beyond*, ed. Ovidiu Creangă (Sheffield: Sheffield Phoenix Press, 2010), 67.

50. Ibid., 73.

51. Wilson, *Making Men: The Male Coming-of-Age Theme in the Hebrew Bible*, 39.

52. Murphy, *Rewriting Masculinity: Gideon, Men, and Might*, 42.

53. Rhiannon Graybill, *Are We Not Men?: Unstable Masculinity in the Hebrew Prophets* (New York: Oxford University Press, 2016).

54. Brian Charles DiPalma, "Scribal Masculinity and the Court Tales of Daniel," in *Hebrew Masculinities Anew*, ed. Ovidiu Creangă (Sheffield: Sheffield Phoenix, 2019).

55. Moore, "Final Reflections on Biblical Masculinity," 246.

56. Marti Nissinen, "Biblical Masculinities: Musings on Theory and Agenda," in *Biblical Masculinities Foregrounded*, ed. Ovidiu Creangă and Peter-Ben Smit (Sheffield: Sheffield Phoenix, 2014), 274.

57. Moore, "Final Reflections on Biblical Masculinity," 246.

58. Rhiannon Graybill, "Jonah 'between Men': The Prophet in Critical Homosocial Perspective," in *Hebrew Masculinities Anew*, ed. Ovidiu Creangă (Sheffield: Sheffield Phoenx, 2019), 212.

59. Sharon R. Bird, "Welcome to the Men's Club: Homosociality and the Maintenance of Hegemonic Masculinity," *Gender and Society* 10, no. 2 (1996): 122.

60. Ibid., 121.

61. Michael Flood, "Men, Sex, and Homosociality How Bonds between Men Shape Their Sexual Relations with Women," *Men and Masculinities* 10, no. 3 (2008): 341.

62. Michael S. Kimmel, "Masculinity as Homophobia: Fear, Shame and Silence in the Construction of Gender Identity," in *The Masculinities Reader*, ed. Frank J. Barrett and Stephen M. Whitehead (Cambridge: Polity Press, 2001), 275.

63. Ken Stone, *Sex, Honor, and Power in the Deuteronomistic History*, Journal for the Study of the Old Testament Supplement Series (Sheffield: Sheffield Academic Press, 1996), 39.

64. Murphy, *Rewriting Masculinity: Gideon, Men, and Might*, 42.

65. See, Stone, *Sex, Honor, and Power in the Deuteronomistic History*, 136.

66. Barbara Thiede, *Male Friendship, Homosociality, and Women in the Hebrew Bible: Malignant Fraternities*, Routledge Studies in the Biblical World (London: Routledge, 2021).

67. Ibid., 8.

68. See, Uri Margolin, "Character," in *The Cambridge Companion to Narrative*, ed. David Herman (Cambridge: Cambridge University Press, 2007).

69. For a brief overview of the current state of complexity within Pentateuchal studies using the book of Numbers as an exemplar see, Christian Frevel, *Desert Transformations: Studies in the Book of Numbers*, Forschungen Zum Alten Testament (Tübingen, Germany: Mohr Siebeck, 2020).

70. Jan Assmann, *From Akhenaten to Moses: Ancient Egypt and Religious Change* (Cairo: American University in Cairo Press, 2014).

71. See, Stackert, *A Prophet Like Moses: Prophecy, Law, and Israelite Religion*.

72. Graybill, *Are We Not Men?: Unstable Masculinity in the Hebrew Prophets*.

73. Wilson, *Making Men: The Male Coming-of-Age Theme in the Hebrew Bible*.

74. Roland Barthes, *Image, Music, Text*, trans. Stephen Heath (New York: Hill and Wang, 1977), 111.

75. Mieke Bal, *Narratology: Introduction to the Theory of Narrative*, 3rd ed. (Toronto: University of Toronto Press, 2009), 113.

76. See, Graybill, "Jonah 'between Men': The Prophet in Critical Homosocial Perspective."

Chapter One

Moses the Man

The main purpose of this book is to study the ways in which masculinity is configured in Moses' homosocial relationships with other male characters. However, the characterization of Moses includes more than just relationships with other males, and these aspects provide information regarding the person of Moses and a means by which to consider the ways in which he may be presented as a hegemonic male in other homosocial settings. In this chapter then, we will consider characterization of Moses that takes place beyond the confines of individual relationships with other male characters but which still serve to build up our image of him as a man.

Firstly, Moses' characterization as a violent man is not adequately represented in the relationships that will be examined later, and so will be considered more intentionally here. Also under consideration here is the category of the womanless male. An examination of Moses' attitudes towards the women in his life reveals the unrecognized significance of women in Moses' life and reveals him a paradigmatic example of the way in which this category is understood. The third category is that of the beautiful male. Nothing is said of Moses' appearance in the scriptures, and so here we consider beauty language from other parts of the canon and how it might inform an understanding of the physical appearance of Moses. Likewise, the musical nature of Moses does not feature in the context of personal relations, and so will be considered here. Beyond these categories, we will consider other elements of Moses' character which do find expression in his relationships with other men but which also are developed in particular ways outside of the relationships. These categories enable Moses to perform aspects of his masculinity in arenas that are beyond the level of individual relationships: most importantly, his role as the leader of the people of Israel. This fuller picture of Moses then informs our understanding of him as we read these other relationships and consider the ways in which Moses moves and is received within the broader story.

MOSES AND THE EXECUTION OF VIOLENCE

Scholars are agreed that a primary marker of ideal biblical masculinity is the execution of violence. As Thiede succinctly puts it, such a man "[k]ill[s] well."[1] Violence is a trait we easily associate with figures such as David, which is perhaps why Clines places violence in first in his list of masculine traits.[2] We might readily associate violence with the portrayal of Saul, Samson and Joshua, other significant military leaders from Israel's history. What though of Moses' own execution of violence?

In a later work[3] Clines speaks of the violence of Moses in the wake of the episode of the golden calf (Exod. 32), so it is clear that he sees violence as a key masculine trait extending beyond the story of David into other parts of the biblical materials. In the article on Moses, Clines has moved away from the language of the fighting male, to "The Warrior Male." Warriors fight on battlefields and demonstrate their masculinity in their military prowess. This is the David who returns from battle to the songs of women singing of his extraordinary performances, slaying tens of thousands by contrast to Saul's singular thousands (1 Sam 18:8). The women see Saul as a great warrior, but significantly inferior to David on this count. But is the notion of the warrior consistent with the ways in which Moses is engaged in acts of violence?[4]

Like David, Moses is not always engaged directly in fighting, or personally responsible for acts of violence. What is clear is that Moses understands the importance of violence, or perhaps, the necessity of violence in the performance of his masculinity. As Lemos has recently argued, the practice of violence in the contextual world of the bible was a crucial factor in the establishment and maintenance of personhood, a practice even more prominent in the establishment of masculinity. Violence was a means of marking and reinforcing relations of social dominance,[5] and so a crucial tool of the socially dominant male. Indeed, the socially dominant male seem not only entitled to exercise such violence but were expected to in order to abrogate the personhood of others.[6]

Socially entitled violence forms the context of the first mention of Moses. A Pharaoh, curiously paranoid, orders a purge of all new-born Hebrew baby boys (Exod. 1:22). It is, of course, a classic colonial move intended to eliminate a group of people by the theft of their identity in the space of a single generation. Controlling the birth of children is a way in which the politically powerful create their desired society.[7] Moses, famously, avoids the fate of the other Hebrew boys, but the dangerous circumstances of his birth, and the preceding story of the increasingly callous Pharaoh (whose house he will soon inhabit), gives an indication of the way in which executive exercise of violence permeates the world into which he is born.

The first recorded act of Moses' adult life is his murder of an Egyptian man. That is, Moses' first adult introduction is that he is a man of violence. Wilson[8] sees Moses' actions here as an exhibition of a fundamental aspect of masculinity, namely, strength enacted as violence committed against another man. This is of great significance. The building of a literary character begins from the first moments of their entry into the story.[9] What happens in those early moments sets a trajectory of inferences which inform the way we evaluate subsequent actions and reports. And so it seems quite clear: the world of violence which Moses is born into, and in particular, the world of entitled violence, seems to have shaped him in predictable ways. Moses does not transcend this world. He is simply a part of it. The hierarchy of entitlement highlighted by Lemos almost immediately makes itself known. The Pharaoh hears of Moses' actions and seeks to have him killed (Exod. 2:15). There are two elements to this which are of interest. Firstly, it is significant that the Pharaoh hears of it, in so far as it seems unlikely that the Pharaoh would be made aware of every murder that happens in Egypt. There is something particular about this one. Two things, in fact. The first is that it is close to home, having been committed by one of his own house. That in itself is unlikely to be the reason for the Pharaoh's decision to try to kill Moses. Rather, Pharaoh's response is likely to be motivated by his own anxiety regarding the Hebrews. Would Moses have been endangered had he killed a Hebrew slave? That seems unlikely. Moses' victim was in the process of beating a Hebrew. Given the Pharaoh's previous attempts at afflicting the Hebrews, it seems unlikely that the beating of a Hebrew would be sanctioned. The murder of one beating a Hebrew though represents a different type of crime, in that it symbolically resists the Pharaoh's desire to eliminate the Hebrews. In a particular way Moses becomes guilty of treason and so becomes a target of Pharaoh's wrath.

Having fled from Egypt, Moses quickly finds himself in a confrontation. Shepherds interrupt a group of women as they attempt to water their father's flock (Exod. 2:16–17). Moses is described as "coming to their defense" after the shepherds had driven the women away. How are we to imagine this as anything other than a violent encounter? The shepherds drive the women away. The root *garash* is used elsewhere to refer to the driving out of the inhabitants from the land, and so it is most commonly used in a fashion that implies extreme force and violence. Moses stands against that effort. We must assume that men who are not above aggression towards women are equally likely to kill a man and so Moses put himself in harm's way. But how does a single man repel a group of shepherds? Perhaps the social hierarchy gives us a way of understanding this. Moses has grown up in the court of the Pharaoh. Even exiled from that social position, he would wear the entitlement that accompanies that in his being. While this is no lasting homosocial relationship, what it does demonstrate is the competitive nature of masculinity. The shepherds would no doubt recognise the social *gravitas* of their opponent. In Ridley Scott's version of the story, Moses reveals a remarkable sword, a gift from Pharaoh, the effect of which is to have the shepherds back down immediately. It is the biblical version of the flashing of a gun, only with an ancient twist. To own such a sword, one is likely to have a history of military training, and the accumulation of great skill in the enactment of violence. One has either earned it, or stolen it, and having stolen such a thing, it is unlikely that one would openly advertise the crime for fear of recriminations. It is important to note here that Scott's telling is extra-biblical. The Moses of Exodus isn't said to brandish a sword, as Hays points out.[10] Moses comes to the defense of the women and the shepherds back off, presumably recognizing they are no match for Moses. Perhaps he uses violence. It is unclear. DiPalma notes that the verbs used in the daughters report to their father do not *require* violent action.[11] One can be saved or delivered without the execution of violence, though most commonly these verbs are associated with violent conduct. DiPalma wonders if the obscuring of Moses' actions is an attempt to imagine a masculinity which is not dominated by violent conflict between men, a change from his earlier, more physical means of conflict resolution.[12] His point is well made. Nonetheless, we must also bear in mind the context: a group of shepherds drive young women away and Moses comes and saves them. In the absence of any dialogue, it is difficult to imagine how this might occur without at least the threat of violence. Wilson connects Moses' slaying of the Egyptian with his actions at the well. For Wilson, Moses' action in killing the Egyptian serves as an indication of his maturation: where no other man was present to act, Moses acts and so becomes that man.[13] His actions at the well are a natural continuation of that trajectory. Having slayed the Egyptian, Moses now demonstrates courage in confronting the "hostile shepherds."[14] Rather than separating the violence of the first episode from the ambiguity of the second, Wilson prefers an integrated approach, one which seems to hint at the threat of violence, if not the execution thereof.

In the aftermath of the Golden Calf incident in Exod. 32, Moses commands a purge of the camp. While he is not involved in the executions, he certainly commissions them, and the sons of Levi summarily execute approximately 3000 people (Exod. 32:38). While Moses is not responsible for their killing, he certainly does not hesitate in ordering their killing, exercising his social entitlement to make such actions a reality. A similar result ensues in Numbers

25. After the sons of Israel provoked the wrath of God on account of their dalliances with the daughters of Moab, Yhwh commands the impalement of the chiefs. Moses, the recipient of this command, makes an alteration, ordering the chiefs to execute those from amongst their tribes who had transgressed. In a later chapter we will examine the actions of Moses in altering divine commands, but here we note that Moses has the authority to command executions and anticipates that they will be carried out. He might not engage in the violence directly, but he certainly is not shy about it taking place. His command to violence reinforces his status as the authoritative figure in the community; the one with the entitlement to execute violence in the maintenance of the social order.

These four examples demonstrate that the execution of violence is a central aspect of the characterization of Moses, either by his own hand or in command of others. In light of them, the claims that Moses was the most meek or humble man to walk the earth (Num. 12:3) meet some difficulty. It would seem more accurate to say that Moses was a man of considerable violence, though with the caveat that such violence was, as Lemos has pointed out, perhaps even expected for an individual of his social distinction. Killing is, in the thought of Clines, the quintessential male characteristic in the Hebrew Bible,[15] so it should be no surprise to find it closely attached to one of the towering figures of the tradition.

MOSES AND WOMEN

As we have seen, a key aspect to the performance of masculinity is tied both to the management of relationships with women and avoiding circumstances whereby one may become feminized. While Clines' language of the "womanless" male may over-state the case, it remains true that for masculine performance, women play an instrumental role. They provide status, sex and offspring.[16] No life is lived without women. Masculine performance is concerned with how one engages with women, or as Măcelaru suggests, the way in which women are used to one's personal advantage.[17]

The early characters in Moses' story are women. He is born to a man and woman from the tribe of Levi (Exod. 2:1), but after that brief announcement, the characters are exclusively female. For the first months of his life it is his mother who cares for him, hides him, and who executes her plan in the hope that he may float to safety. It is an unnamed sister who watches him float into the presence of the Pharaoh's daughter, and then dupes the Egyptian princess into having the child nursed by his own mother. Very quickly, three women have become a part of Moses' story, ensuring his survival, providing an environment of shelter, protection and privilege, and so allowing him to develop in a safe, nurturing environment. Brenner-Idan notes, "Moses himself, the axis around which all action revolves, is only a pawn . . . the actual heroines are the three anonymous women who attend Moses."[18] Typically for a baby and young boy then, Moses' early life is one lived in the presence of, and reliant upon, women. None of this could conceivably understood as a sleight on Moses' masculinity. It was simply the normal way children were socialized.[19] Part of the maturation process is the differentiation of the son from the mother, though in this instance we have no record of that development in Moses' life.

The narrative quickly moves to Moses as an adult and his exile on account of his murder of the Egyptian man. Moses flees and settles in Midian and sits by a well. The root for settle and sit is the same and so getting a sense of time here is not possible. But immediately on his "settling," more female characters arrive in the shape of seven sisters who are identified as the daughters of a Midianite priest. As a result of his assistance to them, this Priest, named here as Reuel, invites Moses to stay with the family and offers one of the daughters, Zipporah, in marriage (Exod. 2:18–21). And so alongside the two mothers of Moses and the sister who played a crucial role in Moses' early life, another woman is added, a wife.[20] Zipporah also has a son with Moses,[21] and so we are to assume that Moses lives with his father-in-law and family for a length of time, surrounded, it would appear, by sisters-in-law! This is borne out in 2:23 when it is reported that the oppressive Pharaoh dies after a long time.

Zipporah is an enigmatic figure in the narrative. While Moses' story is told over the books of Exodus-Deuteronomy, Zipporah appears on only two more occasions. The first is one of the more inexplicable passages in the entire biblical tradition. In Exod. 4, she famously saves Moses from an unexplainable divine attack, thereby joining the group of women who at various points in time save Moses' life. Issues of masculinity permeate this story. Having set out with his family for confrontation with Pharaoh, Moses is attacked by Yahweh in the dark of the night (Exod. 4:24). No rationale is given for this attack. So confusing is this passage, Shectman notes "[m]any have tried and failed to explain this bizarre story."[22] The events and their implications are telling in relation to masculinity. Recognizing the danger, it is Zipporah who responds to protect her family. She takes a knife in hand and circumcises her son, exercising what is both a fatherly[23] and distinctly Priestly role.[24] The Priestly role is emphasized by the dabbing of the blood on "his feet" and the retreat of Yahweh as a result of Zipporah's blood ritual. The circumcized son is referred to as "her son" (Exod. 4:25), further highlighting the dynamic role of Zipporah in this scene,[25] and conversely, Moses' passivity, a reversal of normal masculine expectation.[26]

And then in chapter 18, Jethro contacts Moses to tell him he is coming to visit, bringing Zipporah and the two sons with him (Exod. 18:6). Moses' reception of his family is curious. He kisses his father-in-law (here named Jethro, rather than Reuel as before), enters a tent with him, and begins speaking to him about Yhwh's deliverance of the people from the hardship of Pharaoh and Egypt, much to the delight of Jethro. And yet there is no mention at all of Moses greeting Zipporah, Gershom, or Eliezer. As Propp asks: "Is Moses glad to see them? Is Zipporah immediately set to cooking?"[27] The reporting makes a number of things clear. Firstly, Moses has left his family on his return to Egypt to take up his divine commission. In 4:18, it seems that Zipporah and the sons are accompanying Moses back to Egypt with the blessing of Jethro. However, having saved his life, Zipporah is immediately removed from the story. We have no sense at all that she played any role in the decision to be separated from her husband with their children.[28] Secondly, she again seems to have no say in the decision to come and visit Moses, along with her two children. Is this a reunion she is happy about, given Moses' abandonment of them and indifference towards them? Either way, as wife, daughter or mother, Zipporah has lost the agency she so forcefully demonstrated in saving Moses' life. Thirdly, Moses appears to have no significant emotional attachment to his wife or children, and so this seems to make it clear that in the category of the womanless male, Moses is a banner example. And yet to say that is to ignore the reality that Moses' life is punctuated by women who allow his story to progress. Without a mother willing to risk her own life for the sake of her son, a sister who skilfully negotiated his care with an enemy princess who was moved with compassion for a baby floating alone on the river, and a foreign wife who put herself in harm's way to rescue him, Moses' story would have never made it to the little ark on the river let alone the Pharonic palace or the steppes of Moab. In contrast to the homosocial relations demonstrated by men which are concerned with contest and domination, the women in Moses' story demonstrate the advantage of organization and cooperation in ways that make Moses' survival possible.[29] Moses is not a womanless man. He is a man who does not recognise the significance of women in his life.

MOSES THE BEAUTIFUL?

The bible is notorious for the lack of description of its characters. Despite this, Clines is adamant about the ancient ideal of masculine beauty, which he finds in the David story[30] and again in the description of men in Exodus 32–34.[31] Clines' argument, particularly in relation to the Exodus chapters, rests not on the use of vocabulary of beauty, but on the ways in which the characters behave. For example, Clines sees the wearing of jewellery by men as being indicative of a sense of their own regard for their appearance. That is, you don't wear adornments unless you think there is something worth enhancing.[32] Further, Clines investigates the "shining face" of Moses through an examination of other instances of the mention of shining faces through the Old Testament, faces both divine and human. Throughout this investigation, Clines concludes that a shining face is an attractive face, and so is related to beauty, even when beauty vocabulary is absent.

Wilson is not convinced by Clines' arguments, suggesting that the words traditionally associated with beauty are more likely references to stature or youthfulness.[33] Saul is described as good, and this has traditionally been understood as a comment on his handsomeness. But the text stresses that Saul's defining characteristic is his height. Adonijah is described using the same word, suggesting that it is something of his physicality which is impressive, but this is not the same as beauty. The word *yapheh* is the most commonly used word for beauty in the Old Testament and used explicitly of three men: David, Absalom and Joseph. Macwilliam notes that this word commonly speaks of the sexual attractiveness of its subject[34] and shows how it has often been linked with notions of power and strength. However, Macwilliam carefully examines the three individuals and demonstrates how beauty in each of their cases serves not as a symbol of power, but something far more vulnerable or tragic.

The word used to describe Saul and Adonijah (*tob*) is used to describe Moses' appearance as a baby. Saul and Adonijah are both men when the epithet is used of them, so it may be out of place to make a direct link between the use of a word in relation to a baby and an adult. Nonetheless, in relation to the category of beauty a brief examination will be useful. Macwilliam notes that *tob* can be used in a similar way to *yafah*, but most commonly does so when used within a larger phrase.[35] That is, to call one "good" does not carry with it the same sense of desirability that comes with calling one a "beauty" but can still speak of some elevated physical appearance. Saul is a case in point. In 1 Samuel 9:2, Saul is described as *tob* twice. NRSV renders this as handsome on both occasions. But the further description of Saul, as the one who stood head and shoulders above everyone else seems to suggest that *tob* here points not to Saul's beauty or handsomeness, but rather to his height. The point is reinforced in 1 Sam 10:24 when his height is used as an explanation as to why he had been chosen to be King.

Adonijah, the son of David, presents himself as successor during David's decline in 1 Kings 1. The description of him as *tob-ta'r me'od* is rendered as "very handsome" in the NRSV, which seems reasonable given the construction.[36] Adonijah has aspiration to be King, an aspiration in no way thwarted by his father (1 Kings 1:6). Aside from his aspiration, his strongest attribute appears to be his good looks, which is mentioned even before we discover he is actually the most likely successor following the death of his older brother Absalom. The mention of Absalom here, a man described as beautiful, seems to subvert Adonijah's aspiration: the older, better looking brother had failed. Why would the younger brother fare any better? Adonijah's good looks seem to serve him well as he recruits charioteers and foot-soldiers to proclaim his approach (1 Kings 1:5) as well as the support of military man Joab and priest, Abiathar. But his grasp for power fails. Indeed, his attempt at the throne leads directly to Nathan's intervention and the appointment of Solomon as David's successor and to the fracturing of his relationship with the court. His subsequent request for Abishag as a wife (1 Kings 2:17) is interpreted by Solomon as an attack on his own legitimacy and leads to Adonijah's execution. So while Solomon is not described as being physically pleasing in the way Adonijah is, good looks are not enough to spare Adonijah from Solomon's purge of potential threats. Physical attractiveness might be a part of the hegemonic ideal but is revealed here as less important than other characteristics. In Saul's case, his physical stature does not overcome the raft of other characteristics displayed in the person of David. Adonijah is noted for his appearance, but in a way that is lesser than his older brother Absalom, and in a way that does not protect him from the potency of his younger brother, Solomon.

How might this inform our understanding of the description of Moses as *tob*? His mother looks at him and sees that he is a fine baby, and this is used as the rationale for attempting to save him. But as we have seen, the meaning of the word is ambiguous. It might relate to his appearance, though it hardly marks Moses out as special that his mother had a high regard for her baby son's looks! Graybill suggests that *tob* might relate to ethical or moral goodness,[37] though that might be saying too much for an infant and would certainly be difficult to ascertain through her looking at him! The daughter of the Pharaoh sees the basket Moses is floating in, opens it and sees the baby, but the primary motivation for rescuing Moses is not his appearance, but his crying (Exod. 2:6). It his crying which moves the Princess to pity, not a regard for the way he looks. The appearance of Moses leads her to assume he is a Hebrew child, though the reasons for this are not made clear.[38] Certainly a mother's view of her child is qualitatively different to that of another person and we are right to hold a degree of suspicion regarding a parent's assessment of their own child. Nonetheless, parental assessments of children are rare in the scriptures, and any information given around births tend to point to a greater narrative significance.[39] Moses' mother looks at him and *sees* something. Perhaps this is the thing that all parents see when they look at their children, the dreams and hopes that they hold and that are in some way made real by the embodiment of the child. While we might not be able to say anything about the specifics of Moses' appearance, it is clear that the narrator wants to mark something about the life of this baby in the designation of him as *tob*. That these ideas are held by his mother might at once seem obvious, and yet given the tragic circumstances in which she gazes on her child, the significance of them are heightened.

What do we know of Moses' appearance as an adult? Our imagination of Moses is driven largely by the cinematic portrayals of him: the tall and elegantly bearded Charlton Heston, or the muscular and more youthful Christian Bale inform the way countless millions imagine him. The sisters he meets at the well in Midian report to their father that an Egyptian had helped them, suggesting that by manner of dress, physical appearance or speech Moses appeared to be an Egyptian. This echoes the earlier episode when an Egyptian princess sees Moses and understands him to be Hebrew. Aside from that, we have no information to guide our thinking. Moses may have been *tob* in his mother's eyes, and foreign-looking in the eyes of his wife, but none of this serves to differentiate him in any useful way from the other men in his life.

POTENT OF BODY

The category of potency relates to a number of areas of the male life. One is to do with violence, which we have noted already. A second is to do with potency of speech, or persuasion, which will be dealt with separately given the significant place speech plays in the story of Moses. A third is to do with the production of children, most valuably sons.[40] On this point, Moses is a success. In Exodus 2:22 we read of the birth of Gershom. In 18:6 we learn of the imminent visit of Moses' father-in-law who is bringing with him Zipporah and Moses' two sons, the second of which is named Eliezer. While two sons is far from a prodigious family in biblical terms, they do represent a potency in reproduction. That is, at the very least we can say that Moses is not deficient in this area.

A further aspect of potency which requires examination in relation to Moses has to do with bodily integrity.[41] As Graybill notes, the hegemonic ideal brings notions of dominance, virility, strength and agility. These all demand what we might call an "abled" body.[42] If we understand Moses' heavy tongue as a type of disability, then Moses' body demonstrates a weakness or vulnerability against those norms.[43] Similarly, the skin affliction Moses suffers during his dialogue with Yahweh in Exod. 4:6 constitutes a significant—albeit temporary—impairment which calls for exclusion from the community in other parts of the biblical materials (Lev 14).[44] It points also to the ongoing characterization of Moses' body (and for that matter, all bodies) as vulnerable. It is for this reason that Kalmanofsky speaks of Moses' "compromised" masculinity.[45] Indeed, Kalmanofsky pushes this point further, arguing that the impairments of Moses' body are a means of feminising him in order to position him more appropriately as God's prophet.[46] Nothing is less masculine than feminization.

Graybill identifies a further instance of Moses' body failing him, high-lighting his inability to hold his arms up unassisted during the battle with the Amalekites in Exodus 17. The heaviness of his arms is described using the same word used to describe the heaviness of his tongue, drawing the two corporeal failures together and reinforcing the weak and yet extraordinary nature of Moses' body.[47] Junior and Schipper note that the use of this word, כבד, when used in relation to bodily organs, indicates a failure in normal function, arguing that this suggests some type of physical disability.[48] That is, his arms are capable of remarkable feats, but need the support of others. His tongue is capable of remarkable feats but relies on the support of others. This type of physical reliance on others tears at the ideal of the independent, virile, physically competent male and so this series of bodily failures certainly does fracture views of Moses as the idealized male figure.

Related to this issue of potency is the reality of Moses' elderly body. In Deuteronomy 31 Moses tells the people of Israel that at 120 years old he can't get around very well anymore. We are left to imagine a bent over, largely immobile Moses, despite the eulogy in Deut. 34:7 which says that Moses died without losing vigor and retained perfect vision! This comment is im-mensely significant. Long life is a way of affirming divine favor. As Kirova has recently demonstrated, the ever-decreasing lifespan of men in the early chapters of the scriptures speak to the increasing gap between the divine and human worlds. Beyond the mythological age in which characters lived hundreds of years, the lifespan of ordinary people, or characters presented in worlds that more closely resemble our own experience becomes a marker of special favor. Or perhaps another way, old age is a marker of righteousness.[49] The report of Moses' possession of good sight and vigor then is an ideologi-cal ploy to set him apart from the normal processes of aging, whereby sight and vigor are natural losses in the process of aging.[50] Kirova notes that the synecdoche of weakened vision is that sight is often metaphorically linked with the mind and so is closely related to intellectual *and* spiritual power.[51] In relation to the characterization of Moses, this serves as a way of buttress-ing his authority. Not only does Moses live to old age, signifying both divine favor and unusual personal righteousness, but he is remembered doing so in a fashion that avoids the normal travails of human deterioration.

PERSUASIVE OF TONGUE

A significant aspect of the early characterization of Moses is his inability to speak, or more precisely, his insistence that he lacks the ability to speak. Any understanding of Moses as the hegemonic male runs into a problem here in so far as potency of speech appears to be a key characteristic of biblical mas-culinity. Clines identifies it as a characteristic in its own right[52] while Wilson ties it to the demonstration of wisdom.[53] Haddox does not mention skill in speech explicitly, though perhaps it is implied in her sub-category of "leadership" within a broader category of "potency."[54] Moses is a curious case here, because as Haddox notes, biblical masculinity is hindered by disability,[55] so if Moses does suffer the type of affliction he claims, then this would certainly impede his ability to demonstrate this particular characteristic.

However, Moses' claims seem to be without warrant. Despite the appointment of Aaron as Moses' spokesperson, it quickly becomes clear that it is Moses who does his own speaking: to Pharaoh, to the people of Israel, to Yhwh, and to whoever else it is who seeks to engage him. The most powerful example is the book of Deuteronomy, presented as a series of speeches given by Moses, exhorting them to abide by the commitments they have made and in doing so, making a choice of life over death.

Despite the challenges Moses claims to experience in relation to speech his power as a communicator is central to his characterization, both in relation to groups (primarily the people of Israel, but often sub-sets within that larger group), but also in relation to communication with individuals. This is one of the primary means by which Moses' masculinity is established and maintained as will be explored throughout several of the chapters that follow.

SINGING MOSES

The book of Psalms and the Song of Solomon aside, the Old Testament is not a series of books that we might readily imagine as being particularly musical. And yet throughout the sweep of its pages, music is found. Given that the scriptures are reflective of a social group's experience of the world, this is not so surprising. As Burgh notes, one would be hard pressed to find a cultural group for which music does not play some role in day-to-day life.[56] In the scriptures, this is most commonly expressed through songs. Or more accurately, through words which are called songs, with the sad reality that musical actualization of these compositions is lost to us. So we have the song of Miriam at the crossing of the sea, the song of Hannah, the song of Deborah, the singing of David at the death of Saul and Jonathan, the servant songs of Isaiah and so on. We also have references to the use of musical instruments: trumpets, though not always used for musical purposes; various percussion instruments; stringed instruments; flutes and pipes; and of course, the human voice. It is important to note that while the great majority of music seems to be religiously motivated, this is not exclusively so. The women of Israel sing songs about their military heroes on their return from battle, as we have noted above. Singing can also be dangerous. Or rather, singers can be dangerous, and in particular, one type of singer poses a great threat. The deutero-canonical book, Sirach warns men: "Do not dally with a singing girl, or you will be caught by her tricks" (Sir. 9:4). The singing girl is synonymous with the strange women and harlots that lurk in every dark corner, waiting to ruin the reputation of the innocent young man so precariously imagined in the bible's wisdom literature. It seems clear that the singing girl is singing a different kind of song, and so singing cannot uniformly be considered a good thing.

But returning to religiously motivated singing: Song is used to express both praise and lament and so stands at both ends of the human experience. It is a corporate activity, such as in the context of the worshipping community, and as such, involves men and women performing together.[57] Singing can also be done individually. Famously, David is brought to the court on account of his singing voice which calms the increasingly erratic Saul. Most commonly, it appears that songs, even when reported as being performed spontaneously, have a sense of order to them, and that they are led by a particular figure. An emblematic example of this is Moses' song in Exodus 15, the song offered as a response of praise to the destruction of the Egyptian army at the sea of reeds. The text reports that Moses and the sons of Israel[58] sang this particular song to the Lord. Such a performance is only possible when the song is known, and even better, rehearsed. On the death of Saul, David commands that the people be taught a particular song in order to be able to join in a communal lament over the loss of these two heroes of Israel. So it appears that music played a major role in the life of Israel, particularly in key aspects such as communal worship, celebration of victories and in times of lament and sorrow. The case of David shows that skill in music was highly valued.[59] But is it a marker of masculinity? That seems more difficult to verify. As we have noted, singing is an activity of both men and women. Deborah sings, Hannah sings, Miriam sings. But what is noteworthy is that their songs are individual songs, in the case of Hannah and Deborah, and for Miriam, her leadership is of other women singers. It appears that the leadership of musical performance that is inclusive of all people is reserved for men, and at least in terms of the biblical witness, prominent men.

But the song of the sea is not Moses' only engagement with music. In Deut. 31, Yhwh instructs Moses to write down a song and teach it to the Israelites. They are to learn it by heart, using the idiomatic "put it in their mouth." That song forms the substance of chapter 32. There are some issues around this, though. Deut. 31:30 reports that Moses "speaks" the words of the song, the regular translation of *dabar* (NRSV suggest "recites").[60] How are we to think of this material? To call it song is to suggest music: a melody, rhythm and so on. These are the rudimentary elements that shift poetic words into the arena of music, of song, and this is how it is referred to internally. That is, in contrast to the words which the Israel are to remember (a reference to the spoken discourse which precedes the song), the song is mentioned explicitly five times: In 31:19 Moses is commanded to write the *song*, in order that the *song* may act as a witness. In verse 21, the conditions are given for its use. That is, when troubles come on them on account of their inevitable wayward-ness, the *song* will confront them. In verse 22 Moses is reported as writing the *song* that very day, and finally in verse 30, we have the report that Moses speaks the words of the *song*. Given the repeated nature of this usage, I think it is reasonable to assume that what Moses teaches is a song: that is, that there is music involved. So while Moses speaks the words of the song, it is right to imagine he also teaches the tune. In the same way that psalms often have a didactic purpose, a purpose which is aided by their singing, so too this song of Moses. The musical nature of this material is largely overlooked by commentators who refer to the song without reference to the reality that a song is a musical form. In contrast to this is Duane Christensen, who notes that text set to music is the most effective means of having that text etched indelibly into our hearts and mind.[61] Given that the purpose of this song is remembrance to elicit repentance,[62] it seems reasonable to assume that it is just that: a song, music and all.

On balance, we might say that Moses' leadership of the song at the sea and the song which concludes his farewell discourse are manly things, though we might not want to push the consequences of it too far in terms of it being a categorical display of masculinity. This isn't a category in which Moses dem-onstrates a superior or trumping masculinity in relation to other male figures. David is lauded for his musical talents: they play a significant role in the narra-tive of his rise and through his patronage of the psalms, they play a prominent role in religious memory of him. For Moses, musical performance seems to be a function of his particular office in Israelite history. When the next great leaders of Israel, Joshua and Samuel address the people, it is not in song. That practice seems reserved for Moses. These episodes, particularly the song of Deuteronomy 32 are unique within the canon. But so too, is Moses.

This discussion has revealed much about the way in which Moses' character is established within the biblical narrative. In relation to masculinity we have already noted that there are categories in which Moses demonstrates particular strengths but others which show certain vulnerabilities. However, much of this characterization has dealt with Moses' private world rather than his performance as a man in the context of homosocial relationships. Understanding gender as a social phenomenon means that we need to consider the relational aspect of gender performance, to which we now turn.

NOTES

1. Barbara Thiede, *Male Friendship, Homosociality, and Women in the Hebrew Bible: Malignant Fraternities*, Routledge Studies in the Biblical World (London: Routledge, 2021), 6.

2. David J.A. Clines, "David the Man: The Construction of Masculinity in the Hebrew Bible," in *Interested Parties: The Ideology of Writers and Readers of the Hebrew Bible* (Sheffield: Sheffield Academic Press, 1995).

3. "Dancing and Shining at Sinai: Playing the Man in Exodus 32–34," in *Men and Masculinity in the Hebrew Bible and Beyond*, ed. Ovidiu Creangă, The Bible in the Modern World (Sheffield: Sheffield Phoenix Press, 2010).

4. It should be noted here that David the warrior seems to lie behind certain attitudes towards him even though in terms of the biblical materials this is a far less prominent aspect of his life. David is far more likely to command others to commit acts of violence rather than engaging in them himself. Likewise, his successor Solomon seems more comfortable having his killing done for him rather than carrying it out himself, as we will see in the story of Adonijah.

5. T. M. Lemos, *Violence and Personhood in Ancient Israel and Comparative Contexts* (Oxford: Oxford University Press, 2017), 172.

6. Ibid., 27.

7. For an example of this practice in the Australian context, see Anthony Rees, "Numbers 25 and Beyond: Phinehas and Other Detestable Practice(r)s," in *Leviticus-Numbers*, ed. Athalya Brenner and Archie C.C. Lee, Texts@Contexts (Minneapolis: Fortress 2013). The use of such practices, as these two examples suggest, have long been a part of Imperial projects.

8. Stephen M. Wilson, *Making Men: The Male Coming-of-Age Theme in the Hebrew Bible* (New York: Oxford University Press, 2015), 80.

9. Alan Palmer, *Fictional Minds*, Frontiers of Narrative (Lincoln: University of Nebraska Press, 2004), 40.

10. Christopher Hays, "Live by the Sword, Die by the Sword: The Reinvention of the Reluctant Prophet as Moviemoses," https://www.academia.edu/10037402/Live_By_the_Sword_Die_By_the_Sword_The_Reinvention_of_the_Reluctant_Prophet_as_MovieMoses_.

11. Brian DiPalma, "De/Constructing Masculinity in Exodus 1–4," in *Men and Masculinity in the Hebrew Bible and Beyond*, ed. Ovidiu Creangă (Sheffield: Sheffield Phoenix Press, 2010), 47.

12. Ibid.

13. Wilson, *Making Men: The Male Coming-of-Age Theme in the Hebrew Bible*, 81.

14. Ibid., 83.

15. Clines, "Dancing and Shining at Sinai: Playing the Man in Exodus 32–34," 55.

16. Thiede, *Male Friendship, Homosociality, and Women in the Hebrew Bible: Malignant Fraternities*, 6.

17. Marcel V. Măcelaru, "Saul in the Company of Men: (De)Constructing Masculinity in 1 Samuel 9–31," in *Biblical Masculinities Foregrounded*, ed. Ovidiu Creangă and Peter-Ben Smit (Sheffield: Sheffield Phoenix, 2014), 55.

18. Athalya Brenner-Idan, *The Israelite Woman: Social Role and Literary Type in Biblical Narrative*, 2nd ed., Cornerstones (London: Bloomsbury, 2015), 98.

19. For an overview of the role of the mother in ancient Israel, see chapter 2 of Victor Harold Matthews and Don C. Benjamin, *Social World of Ancient Israel, 1250–587 Bce* (Peabody: Hendrickson, 1993). It is worth noting here that Moses does not grow up in Israel, though we might assume cultural similarities in practice.

20. Wilson notes that marriage is a significant feature of "manliness" in the Old Testament. Wilson, *Making Men: The Male Coming-of-Age Theme in the Hebrew Bible*, 40–42.

21. Propp notes that Torah is largely indifferent to Moses' role as procreator. William Henry Propp, *Exodus 1–18: A New Translation with Introduction and Commentary*, 1st ed., 2 vols., The Anchor Bible (New York: Doubleday, 1999), 635.

22. Sarah Shectman, *Women in the Pentateuch: A Feminst and Source-Critical Analysis* (Sheffield: Sheffield Phoenix Press, 2009), 111.

23. Susan Ackerman, "Why Is Miriam Also among the Prophets? (and Is Zipporah among the Priests?)," *Journal of Biblical Literature* 121, no. 1 (2002): 74.

24. Ursula Rapp, "Zipporah: The Vanishing of a Wife," in *Torah*, ed. Imtraud Fischer, Mercedes Navarro Puerto, and Andrea Taschel-Erber, Bible and Women (Atlanta: SBL Press, 2011), 320.

25. Propp, *Exodus 1–18: A New Translation with Introduction and Commentary*, 234ff.

26. Rhiannon Graybill, *Are We Not Men?: Unstable Masculinity in the Hebrew Prophets* (New York: Oxford University Press, 2016), 40.

27. Propp, *Exodus 1–18: A New Translation with Introduction and Commentary*, 635.

28. In chapter 4 there is only one son. In chapter 18 on her return to the story, Zipporah has another of Moses' children, suggesting that she was pregnant at the time of their separation, and that Moses has not yet seen Eliezer. This makes his indifference to them all the more shocking.

29. Elyse Goldstein, *Revisions: Seeing Torah through a Feminist Lens* (Toronto: Key Porter, 1998), 82.

30. Clines, "David the Man: The Construction of Masculinity in the Hebrew Bible," 221.

31. "Dancing and Shining at Sinai: Playing the Man in Exodus 32–34," 59.

32. Ibid.

33. Wilson, *Making Men: The Male Coming-of-Age Theme in the Hebrew Bible*, 34–5.

34. Stuart Macwilliam, "Ideologies of Male Beauty and the Hebrew Bible," *Biblical Interpretation* 17 (2009): 267.

35. Ibid., 278.

36. Rachel is described as *yapha to'ar yapha mar'eh* (beautiful of form, beautiful to look at), a construction that is very similar to this description of Adonijah. The

substitution of "good" for "beautifl" is telling and cannot be dismissed on the basis of gender given the use of yapha for other male characters.

37. Graybill, *Are We Not Men?: Unstable Masculinity in the Hebrew Prophets*, 27.

38. Kalmanofsky wonders if this may be related to Moses being circumcized, creating a physical differentiation between Hebrew and Egyptian boys. See, Amy Kalmanofsky, "Moses and His Problematic Masculinity," in *Hebrew Masculinities Anew*, ed. Ovidiu Creangă (Sheffield: Sheffield Phoenix Press, 2019), 176, n4.

39. Graybill, *Are We Not Men?: Unstable Masculinity in the Hebrew Prophets*, 27.

40. Susan E. Haddox, "Is There a 'Biblical Masculinity'? Masculinities in the Hebrew Bible," *Word & World* 36, no. 1 (2016); "Masculinity Studies of the Hebrew Bible: The First Two Decades," *Currents in Biblical Research* 14, no. 2 (2016). In the first article listed here Haddox subsumes sexual potency with a larger category of potency. In the second article she addressed the same notion as virility, which she sees as a vital aspect in the conceptualization of hegemonic masculinity.

41. Haddox uses the terminology of bodily integrity solely in reference to penetration. That is, the hegemonic male resists being penetrated, whether in sexual relations or violent combat. Instead, the dominant male is always the penetrator. See "Masculinity Studies of the Hebrew Bible: The First Two Decades," 180.

42. Graybill, *Are We Not Men?: Unstable Masculinity in the Hebrew Prophets*, 25.

43. It is worth noting here that for Graybill, the unstable nature of Moses' body is symbolic of a wider phenomenon present in the bible's representation of masculinity. While the text may promote an ideal form, that form is always under pressure. See ibid., 26.

44. For a further example of skin disease undermining notions of masculinity, see the story of the famed Aramean General, Namaan, in 2 Kings 5. There, the skin affliction of a foreign General, healed by the Israelite Prophet Elisha, seems to play into a type of nationalistic trope whereby all Israelite things (men included) trump all Aramean things: the Israelite slave girl sets the healing into motion, the Israelite Kings appears a far for sombre leader than the powerful Aramean King, the Israelite river provides the healing required despite Namaan's insistence that the Aramean rivers are superior, and finally, the healed Namaan vows to worship the God of Israel.

45. Kalmanofsky, "Moses and His Problematic Masculinity," 181.

46. Ibid.

47. Graybill, *Are We Not Men?: Unstable Masculinity in the Hebrew Prophets*, 30.

48. Nyasha Junior and Jeremy Schipper, "Mosaic Disability and Identity in Exodus 4:10; 6:12, 30," *Biblical Interpretation* 16 (2008): 429. They note that this view cuts against the position of Coats. See, George W. Coats, *Moses: Heroic Man, Man of God*, Journal for the Study of the Old Testament Supplement Series (Sheffield: JSOT Press, 1988), 68–9.

49. Milena Kirova, *Performing Masculinity in the Hebrew Bible*, Hebrew Bible Monographs (Sheffield: Sheffield Phoenix Press, 2020), 184.

50. A classic example is the Priest Eli in 1 Samuel.

51. Kirova, *Performing Masculinity in the Hebrew Bible*, 186.

52. Clines, "David the Man: The Construction of Masculinity in the Hebrew Bible," 219.

53. Wilson, *Making Men: The Male Coming-of-Age Theme in the Hebrew Bible*, 33.

54. Haddox, "Is There a 'Biblical Masculinity'? Masculinities in the Hebrew Bible," 2.

55. Ibid., 3.

56. Theodore W. Burgh, "Music," in *The Interpreter's Dictionary of the Bible*, ed. Katherine Doob Sakenfeld (Nashville: Abingdon, 2009), 166.

57. Ibid., 172.

58. "Sons of Israel" is generally understood to be a collective term that includes women and children.

59. Clines notes that it seems to be David's skill on the lyre which receives special attention. Clines, "David the Man: The Construction of Masculinity in the Hebrew Bible," 228.

60. It is worth noting here that Hannah's "song" in 1 Samuel 2 is introduced as "And she said. . ."

61. Duane L. Christensen, *Deuteronomy 21:10–34:12*, Word Biblical Commentary (Nashville: Thomas Nelson, 2002), 777.

62. Ibid.

Chapter Two

Moses and Aaron

A common theme of the bible, and in particular the Old Testament, is brothers at odds with one another. It is a pattern established by the first brothers, Cain and Abel, and is a theme that recurs throughout the Genesis narrative. So pervasive is the theme, that a midrash on Exodus goes so far as to state that all brothers hate one another.[1] The relationship between Moses and Aaron is quite clearly the most significant human relationship in Moses' life, and one which, despite some challenges, transcends the expectations of brotherhood established in the Genesis narrative. However, the circumstances of Moses' life in Egypt present particular difficulties in thinking through concepts of familial relationships, separated as he was from the kinship unit in which these relationships develop and have meaning. Relationships within family units occur between gendered individuals and form a significant context for the development of gender identity.[2] Homosocial relationality begins in the family unit. Alongside the matters of characterization and masculinity, then, this chapter will also explore issues concerning the expectations surrounding familial relationships, and how they find expression in the relationship between Moses and Aaron.

Despite Aaron's significant place in the life of Moses, and the important role that he appears to play in the events narrated in Exodus and Numbers, the reality is that, typically, the text gives us very little information about Aaron. Aaron is a character who has very little agency in the story. Almost uniformly, he is told what to do and what to say by his brother, Moses. On only two occasions does Aaron speak in his own voice, and in both those instances, Aaron is presented in a poor light. These two passages, Exodus 32 and Numbers 12, are crucial in understanding Aaron and his relationship with Moses. These passages will be considered, alongside other significant episodes in which Aaron's character is developed in more indirect fashion.

INTRODUCING AARON—EXODUS 4

The first mention of Aaron comes in Exodus 4, as Moses tries to evade the commission being issued to him. Seeking to have someone else sent to speak to the Israelites on account of his slow tongue (Exod. 4:10), Yahweh responds in anger, that Moses' brother, Aaron the Levite, will serve as Moses' mouthpiece. This introduction is significant. To this point in Moses' story, we have not known of Moses having a brother. We know that an older sister plays an important role in his survival as a baby (Exod. 2:4–8), though she is unnamed in that episode. There is no mention of any other siblings at that point. The introduction of Aaron as Moses' brother is immediately supplemented with another piece of information: that he is a Levite. This is a strange qualification. We know already that Moses is a Levite: his birth story in chapter 2 has already made this clear. This identification has the effect of weakening the identification of Aaron as Moses' brother in the familial sense. While at other points there is evidence to suggest that Moses and Aaron are siblings, such as the report in Exod. 6:20 and the challenge of Aaron and Miriam in Num. 12, it seems that there are at least two traditions operating within the broader narrative, and that here, the narrator may well be using "brother" in a more generic sense.[3]

This generic use of 'brother' language occurs throughout the story, as Moses goes out to his 'brothers' and sees one being beaten by an Egyptian (Exod. 2:11), and following the encounter with Yahweh in chapters three and four, when he asks leave of his father-in-law to return to his "brothers in Egypt." In these instances, and in others, the sense is not the visiting of siblings, but this more universal sense of the word "brother." Given that one tradition clearly does seem to identify Aaron as Moses' brother, and the other does not disqualify its possibility, this reading will understand this to be a relationship of siblings. But it will do so bearing in mind not only this variance in tradition, but also the reality that Moses and Aaron do not meet until they are men, and so do not have the emotional connection one might expect from brotherhood. Further, we recognize that any familial relationship needs to be understood against cultural expectations which differ from ours, as has been outlined already.

It is worth noting also that the language of brotherhood complements the language of fatherhood which commenced Moses' dialogue with Yahweh. We read Yahweh self-identify as the "god of your father, the god of Abraham, the god of Isaac, the god of Jacob" (Exod. 3:6). Who Moses understands his father to be is a significant question, but the point here has to do with shared identity, and this forms the context in which Aaron is referred to as brother. It may well be a term of kinship, but is not necessarily so. That said, the double identification of Aaron as brother and Levite is significant. The relationship of brotherhood brings certain sets of expectations, and the designation of Levite is also telling. Across the Torah, the Levites have a particular teaching function, and so Aaron is being identified within that office, though, as Dozeman points out, it is also being made clear that Aaron's role is subordinate to that of Moses.[4] Aaron's role, or more broadly, the role of the Levites is authoritative only in so far as it conveys Mosaic authority.

The following phrase about Aaron also has significance for his trajectory trough the narrative, and that is that is he a fluent speaker. In terms of the immediate context, it satisfies the lack that Moses has identified in regards to his own heavy tongue. Aaron, the more fluent brother, will relay the things that Moses instructs him through Yahweh. But there is more to it than this simple solution. Moses and Aaron are being differentiated here, from the very moment of Aaron's arrival into the story.[5] While their fates are being drawn together, and Aaron's capacity for speech is being celebrated, this ability in no way sees him usurp his brother. As Meyers suggests, Aaron's fluency with speech is always in service to Moses' own role of prophetic domination.[6] At the same time, the trajectory of Aaron as the genesis of the High Priestly office is established here, and so we can see a narrative ploy being exercised within the broader frame.

However, there is another aspect to this report which bears examination. The description of Aaron as a fluent speaker creates an expectation in the reader. It activates the reader to anticipate something from him.[7] Aaron's fluency in speech is reduced to the repetition of what Moses says. This reduction is further demonstrated in the way in which Aaron's speaking role is represented. More accurately, it is demonstrated in the way that Aaron's speaking role is not represented. The way speech is represented in the narrative is a crucial way of understanding the nature of the characters, and signals who is important by way of speaking, and in the nature in which they are spoken to.[8] Very early in the ensuing plague narrative, Moses has Aaron performing signs, while he takes responsibility for speaking to Pharaoh. Pharaoh responds to Moses, further sidelining Aaron from the narrative structure. In the instances that Aaron may speak, what is reported is not what Aaron says, but what he is told to say. That is, Aaron, the fluent speaker, is essentially without voice in the narrative. Somewhat ironically, when Aaron does speak of his own accord, the results are less than satisfactory for him. And so this initial characterization[9] of Aaron as the fine orator is disrupted in the instances when his own voice is used.

The final thing that we learn about Aaron in this scene is that he is one the way to meet Moses, and that on seeing him, his "heart will be glad." This is an unusual expression in the biblical materials. Most commonly, biblical references to the heart are related to maters of rationality and understanding,[10] not this type of emotional experience. The heart goes beyond what we might otherwise think of as "mind" in that the heart is often linked to the concept of striving for good in our lives.[11] This clearly does engage matters of the emotions. Aaron, a leading figure in the Israelite community would no doubt be gladdened by any suggestion that the plight of the people in Egypt was to be overthrown. That sense of striving for good, for happiness or gladness, is satisfied by this understanding of the heart. But the heart often is presented negatively in the bible, where the hearts of humanity are quickly characterized as intractably evil. The prophetic testimony, in Jeremiah and Ezekiel most famously, is that humanity needs a new heart given the maladies of the old. This mention of Aaron's heart, then, seems to say something quite significant about this meeting of brothers, in a way that appears to go beyond normal ways of thinking about the heart. This meeting of brothers springs something within him; a response that overwhelms both mind and heart. And that might give us an insight into the character of Aaron: that he is a figure moved by emotion.

This brief introduction to Aaron, a passage from which he is absent, presents us with quite a lot of information about him. All of it, in one way or another, informs the subsequent development of his character across the rest of the narrative.

AARON'S CALF—EXODUS 32

The story of the golden calf in Exodus 32 is one in which has fascinated readers for centuries. With the miracles of the Exodus behind them, and with Moses meeting with God on the mountain following a terrifying display of divine presence (Exod. 19:16–19), the people are quickly dismayed by Moses' slow return. Presumably feeling quite anxious as they camp around a seemingly unsound mountain, and without the figure who had led them thus far, the people agitate for the creation of gods that may "go before us." That is to say, the Israelites want to leave the mountain and desire some physical symbol of divine power to comfort them as they embark of the dangerous task of travel. The object of their agitation is Aaron, the assistant of Moses, who has been left in charge in Moses' absence (Exod. 24:14).[12] Quickly, Aaron's accedes to their request, insisting that they bring to him all the gold rings they have available to them. There is no sense that Aaron seeks to delay them, nor defend his brother. Instead, perhaps out of fear of an angry mob, he moves to placate them, forming a golden calf, and after seeing the satisfaction of the people with his handiwork, an altar, proclaiming that the next day would be a festival to Yahweh. The people are pleased with this, and early the following morning, the celebrations begin.

In this, we learn quite a deal about Aaron. Clearly, the people seek him out, which indicates their acknowledgment that he is a leader amongst them. Given his reputation for fine speech and the dramatic role he has played alongside Moses in the escape from Egypt, this is perhaps no great surprise. Such a reading is confirmed by the people's quick responses to Aaron's suggestions: firstly to hand over their gold, and secondly, their quick embrace of the festival which Aaron announces. But we may also read this differently. Why is it Aaron and not Hur that is approached by the people? Perhaps this is a pragmatic choice made on the assumption that Aaron is not likely to resist their demands. Given Aaron's quick agreement to the plan, there is certainly grounds for this reading as well. So rather than looking to Aaron for leadership, perhaps what is being sought is legitimation for their plans. Their agreement to hand over their gold demonstrates their happiness with them at accepting their request, at once making him a type of leader to them, while also being a soft target. The narrator's lack of judgement in the telling of this part of the story enables all of these options to be possible to this point.

Aaron's announcement that the following day would be a festival to Yahweh brings an ambiguous response. Aaron's intention here seems positive, attempting to ensure that the people are reminded that the golden calf is intended to point towards Yahweh, their deliverer. Confronted with what seems to be a difficult situation, partly of his own making, Aaron attempts to direct the people in a way that honors what has happened amongst them. The people certainly embrace the festival, and the text reports that a great deal of sacrificial activity takes place, and is followed up with what is described as "revelry." This revelry is described by Durham as "an orgy of the desertion of responsibility,"[13] an indication of the way in which the behavior of the people deteriorated across the course of the festival![14]

This revelry attracts the attention of Yahweh who sends Moses and Joshua back down in order to deal with the situation as it has escalated. Moses understands what has happened, and on seeing the calf, destroys the handiwork of his brother, and serves the burnt dust of the calf with water as a punishment to the Israelites (vss. 19–20). Immediately he turns his attention to Aaron, asking a question which lays blame for the situation on Aaron and the people. The first part of his question assumes the culpability of the people: "what did they do to you?" while the second part of his statement makes Aaron responsible: "that you have brought such a great sin upon them" (vs. 21).

Aaron's response, his first recorded conversation with Moses, provides great insight into their relationship, and Aaron's experience of the earlier events. His immediate response is to plead for understanding and a lessening of Moses' response to him (Don't let the anger of my lord burn hot), which, incidentally, includes an attempt at flattery by referring to Moses as "my lord" before turning the blame squarely on the people, claiming that they are "bent on evil." There is some narrative skill here, in as much as Aaron's words about anger running hot echo the words Moses has used just moments before in his discussions with Yahweh, a conversation that Aaron was not privy to. Moses himself has urged Yahweh not to let the divine anger burn hot and managed to secure the safety of the people whom Yahweh had determined to destroy (vss. 11–14). Confronted with the magnitude of the disaster, Moses' own anger burns hot, and while he hears from Aaron his own words, he is less willing than Yahweh, it seems, to have it doused with anything that may cause it to cool.

As it turns out, Aaron provides nothing which may have a cooling effect. He recounts to Moses the approach made to him by the people, and his response of gathering from them all their gold. It appears that his earlier comment about them being "bent on evil" is in some way related to this report, though it is not made clear and so we are left to piece this together ourselves. Perhaps the suggestion is that there was implied aggression in the approach which Aaron felt incapable of resisting, though, again, there is nothing explicitly mentioned here. Alternatively, perhaps Aaron is suggesting that there was no point trying to stop them, given their tendency to evil, and so he became involved as a way of trying to control the excesses of what was happening.

The following two verses provide the greatest insight into Aaron's involvement. In verse 24, he claims that the calf mysteriously appears from the fire, a direct contradiction of the earlier report in verse 4 which said quite plainly that Aaron had made the calf using tools. The expression "molten calf" suggests an involved manufacturing process, including the melting of the metals, and the pouring into a particular shape.[15] This is the very way the actions of Aaron are reported. The effect of telling the truth to this point, and then attempting to avoid responsibility has the effect of making Aaron appear absurd, and lacking the strength to take responsibility for his own involvement in the debacle.

In verse 25, the narrator inserts a comment which delivers a crushing blow to Aaron's credibility. Moses sees that the people are running wild, which is supplemented by a parenthetical comment that this state is a result not of their own evil intent, but on account of Aaron's shortcoming as their leader. It is worth noting that the narrator stretches this too far by suggesting that the actions of the people had earned the derision of their enemies, a state which is at best highly unlikely given the placement of the people in the mountain of god.[16] That flourish aside, the effect is to condemn the role of Aaron in this affair, and causes us to reconsider Aaron's responsibility concerning these events. Aaron disappears from the narrative immediately at this point, and Moses takes charge, ordering the execution of guilty parties by those who would stand on "Yahweh's side."[17] The effect is to make a dramatic contrast between Aaron, the ineffectual and weak leader, and Moses, the man who takes charge and leads.

Following the execution by the Levites, Moses confronts the people and tells them of his hope to atone for their sins. Alas for them, Yahweh declares that because of their deeds a great plague will come and punish them for their iniquities. In all this, there is no mention of Aaron: from Moses, the people, or Yahweh. Blame for the sin is laid squarely on the shoulders of the people who have made for themselves "gods of gold." The narrator is not so keen that Aaron's fault be overlooked. The chapter ends by damning Aaron for his role: "The Lord sent a plague on the people because of the calf they made—that Aaron made." The production of the calf—that Aaron made, is responsible for the death of thousands of people. The narrator makes it clear: Aaron made it.

Across the course of this chapter, it becomes clear that the narrator is presenting a very negative picture of Aaron. He is easily manipulated by the crowd and panders to their desires; he attempts to influence the people for good but in the end lacks the capacity to control them; he (unknowingly) uses the words of Moses, but without any positive effect; he lies and attempts to misdirect blame for his actions. The man presented in chapter 4 as being a good speaker is revealed as ineffectual and misguided in chapter 32, and in the first instance of having his own voice present in the text, he is seen to lack any power of persuasion whatsoever.

MIRIAM (AND AARON) VS. MOSES—NUMBERS 12

In Numbers 12, Moses' siblings, Miriam and Aaron, raise a two-fold complaint. Firstly, they complain about their Cushite sister-in-law for reasons which are left unspoken, and secondly they complain that their relationship with Yahweh is not as highly regarded as that of Moses. Where this complaint takes place, aside from a report that the people are camped at Hazeroth, and to whom the complaint is directed, remains unclear. Given that they speak about Moses (Has God spoken only through Moses?), and against him on account of his wife, presumably this is a complaint they are spreading amongst the camp. Pressler notes that from the earliest *midrashim*, this has been understood as gossip of slander.[18] This is the way Milgrom speaks of it as well.[19]

We assume that Miriam is Moses' sister, though this is not explicit. The family listing in Exodus 6:20 mentions only Aaron and Moses, though it is no surprise given that only sons are mentioned in that segment. In Exodus 15:20 when Miriam bursts into song, she is referred to as the sister of Aaron, with no mention of Moses. In Micah 6:4, Moses, Aaron and Miriam are listed as leaders provided by God, though there is no marking to indicate kinship. Tradition holds that this Miriam is the unnamed sister who watches over her little brother as he drifts along the waters of the Nile in Exodus 2. In this chapter, the relationship between Aaron and Miriam is more important than Moses and Miriam, but here I will assume that the three are siblings. 1 Chronicles 6:3 lists the three of them as children of Amram,[20] so following that tradition, we will assume a connection between them through a connection to at least one parent, which helps to make sense of the grievances they put forward.

The first thing to notice here is that Miriam is listed before Aaron, perhaps suggesting that she is the chief instigator of these complaints. This, as Milgrom suggests, also may explain the reason that she alone is punished in the aftermath of the incident, especially given that the speaking verbs are all presented as feminine singular conjugations.[21] More likely, as Sakenfeld suggests, that this is simply an example of the way in which the challenging of authority inevitably has graver consequences for women rather than men, and serves to inscribe the authority of both Moses and Aaron.[22] Similarly, Davies notes that the text demonstrates the swift and devastating punishment that awaits women attempting to upset the established patriarchal order.[23]

The first complaint regards the marriage between Moses and his Cushite wife. No consensus stands regarding much of this seemingly simple statement. There is no agreement about whether or not this wife is the same wife, Zipporah, who is identified as Midianite elsewhere (Exod. 2:21), or whether Cush should be identified as being in Africa, possibly giving the text racist overtones given that would make this unnamed wife a black woman. An emblematic example of this type of reading is that of Davies,[24] who follows the Septuagint's reading of Cush as meaning Ethiopian. The reasoning follows that the objection of Miriam and Aaron to Moses' wife is ethnically motivated, and that the siblings make their claim to prophetic office with recourse to the proverbial "race card." This reading makes assumptions about skin tone which are unknown in the biblical world and play to more modern concerns about racialization.[25]

So why do the siblings make this objection? Perhaps the issue is one of endogamy. That is, given that Aaron and Miriam are closely related to Moses, his marriages have a bearing on the community in which they live, relying on each other for matters of protection, provision of food and so on.[26] Boer points out that the clan was primarily endogamous, and that at least by understanding, it was difficult for outsiders to enter the social collective unit.[27] However, such practices were constantly under negotiation, and the social boundaries were far more malleable than the laws around them. Endogamy creates a framework for what Boer describes as a practice of constant and creative adaptation.[28] Indeed, information about the institution of marriage, laws governing it, vocabulary related to it and so on are largely absent from Old Testament materials,[29] which may explain the spectrum of marital practices found within its pages.

Despite these flexible frameworks, the concept of endogamy appears as an answer to the motivation of the siblings, particularly given the double emphasis of Moses' wife being a Cushite, thereby highlighting her outsider status. Endogamy may not have been practiced strictly, but it clearly seems to be a preferred model.[30] If we assume that this Cushite wife is a different woman to Zipporah, we might explain their protests on the grounds that Moses was separated from his family when he and Zipporah were married. Rather than the usual practices of negotiation between fathers, Zipporah's father offers her as a wife to Moses (Exod. 2:21). Now, though, Moses is reunited with his kinship group, and so the circumstances have changed. Miriam and Aaron, as insiders, appear to exercise their right to protest this new marriage, even if only as an accessory to their larger issue: jealousy regarding Moses' exalted position.

There is no suggestion here that Moses is aware of the slander his siblings are spreading about him. Nor is any information offered as to how the slander is being received by those who hear it. We are unaware whether or not their campaign is taking traction. However, the narrator reports that Yahweh hears it, and promptly intervenes (vs. 2,4). Between Yahweh's hearing and intervention, the narrator gives a character reference for the maligned brother Moses, calling him the most humble man to ever walk the face of the earth. Presumably, this description of Moses is to differentiate him from Miriam and Aaron, who by their claims are being judged as lacking humility.[31] Quickly the three siblings are summoned to the tent of meeting. The order of summoning is Moses, Aaron and Miriam (vs. 5), reversing the initial introduction of Miriam and Aaron. The two older siblings are called forward, and Yahweh speaks to them from a cloud, the message being quite clear: speaking against Moses is unacceptable. He is above all the other prophets on account of the special relationship between them, characterized by their meeting "mouth to mouth." The speaking which brought rise to this episode is contrasted with the siblings' inability to speak. The cloud ascends, and Miriam is left with snow-white scaly skin,[32] which Sakenfeld calls "poetic justice."[33]

To this point, Aaron has seemingly been an accessory to the proceedings. He appears to be an accomplice to Miriam's campaign against their younger brother, and he is spared the punishment so quickly administered to his sister. Miriam and Aaron are described as speaking against Moses. We know that Aaron has been described as a good and fluent speaker. He has been, after all, the mouth of Moses. But it appears that in this instance, his skills are being put to use in a fashion which is destructive.

His voice is finally heard as he sees his snow-white sister, and unlike the episode of the golden calf, what we have here is acknowledgment of wrongdoing. As in Exodus 32, Aaron refers to Moses as "my lord" and asks for a lessening, or removal of punishment. Crucial here, is Aaron's words which confirm his involvement: "a sin *we* have so foolishly committed" (vs. 11). He describes Miriam's appearance as one like a stillborn, with half consumed flesh and so on. Pressler notes the irony that Aaron, who had earlier been attempting to claim the authority of prophet, now implores Moses to act as one in petitioning Yahweh for mercy.[34] Whether Aaron speaks with a hope of having Miriam restored, or simply in order to evade a similar fate is unclear, though Moses' response to cry out for Miriam's healing may suggest the former, even while the latter is almost certainly also possible. Moses is clearly moved, perhaps by Aaron's words spoken in such horror, urgency, and what appears to be sincere contrition. It is also possible to imagine Moses being motivated by the reality that it was his sister who had been afflicted with such a horrible condition.[35] In the end, Yahweh relents and Miriam is healed, though she spends seven days ostracized from the community.

The character of Aaron is ambiguous throughout this chapter. He appears to be complicit in an attempt to undermine his brother, Moses, with whom he has worked successfully in the past. His skills in speech are being used to cut down his brother's authority, both in terms of his marriage, and in regards to his social leadership. There are hints that he is led by his sister in this matter, which provides an echo of his lack of moral fibre in the golden calf incident. We appear to have a building up of data taking place.[36] Aaron's relationships with other characters—named, related or otherwise—appear to always place him in the position of subordinate. Yet even amongst that, Aaron demonstrates a certain growth in this episode in so far as he acknowledges his wrong doing in a fashion that he has not done previously. It would have been easy to simply blame Miriam in the same way that blamed the people in Exodus 32. And yet he takes a higher road here, acknowledging the foolishness of his own ways, even if only to avoid the same grisly fate of his sister.

AARON THE HERO—NUMBERS 16

In the aftermath of the Korahite rebellion in Numbers 16, Aaron has what is certainly his finest moment. The day following earth's dramatic swallowing of Korah and his family, the subsequent fire-lashing that killed 250 men, and the terror which understandably shook those who witnessed it causing them to run in fear of their lives (Num. 16:33–35), the people of Israel reconvene against Moses and Aaron, accusing them of killing people of the Lord. Yahweh appears in response to the people's cry, and issues a plague with the express intention of consuming them. Moses and Aaron are warned to stay away from them in order to avert danger (vs. 45). Typically, it is Moses who responds to the crisis, instructing Aaron to take is censer are incense and to walk to the middle of the congregation in order to make atonement for them. Aaron doesn't hesitate. Indeed, he runs to the middle of the gathered assembly, surrounded there by those dead and others already dying. The text says he stood between the living and the dead, and that on account of his actions, the plague ceases, but not before the death of some 14700 people.

This story, and the one which follows in chapter 17 regarding the sprouting of Aaron's rod are typically understood to be vindications of the Aaronide priesthood, and clearly that is a function they play. On a narrative level, however, the Aaron presented here is a heroic figure. While he is again portrayed as the assistant of Moses, he shows no hesitation in rushing into harm's way. The divine warning to separate from the people (vs. 45) indicates that what was unleashed had the capacity to kill Moses and Aaron, and yet Aaron rushes to the middle of the congregation, endangering his life in order to try and save others. This is a far cry from the Aaron of Exodus 32 who shirked all sense of responsibility, or the Aaron of Numbers 12 whose admission of guilt may be read as an attempt to evade his own punishment. This Aaron is an altogether different figure: a heroic, salvific figure who places himself at great risk in order to save those who have wished him harm.

AARON AND MOSES: MEN. BROTHERS

The narrative analysis of these four scenes has ultimately revealed a quite uneven characterization of Aaron. In this section we will examine notions of masculinity within the texts we have considered, and also think through the way these things engage with ideas around brotherhood, given the nature of Aaron and Moses' sibling relationship.

As we have noted, one of the challenges facing an analysis of Moses and Aaron as siblings is the reality that they spend the first decades of their lives separated. They do not share any of the normal experiences of growing up, positively or negatively. Much modern psychology, from Freud onwards, comes close to the phenomenon we have considered in relation to hegemonic masculinity. The competitive aspects of homosociality begin in the context of the family unit: brothers compete against each other for their parents' love, for success in their work, for inheritance and so on. The family unit becomes the context for the mastering of one's aggression and the establishment of personal identity within that particular hierarchical framework.[37] Moses and Aaron don't share these formative experiences together and so the emotional bonds which are forged through those experiences of kinship are not a part of their story. Perhaps this explains something of the differentiation that exists between Moses and Aaron and other presentations of brotherhood in the biblical material. The notion that brotherhood should be a site of reliability and solidarity is quite at odds with the presentation of brothers in the biblical text, who are more likely to fight, cheat, hate and kill each other![38] Instead, Moses and Aaron tend towards the more idealized picture of brotherhood, present in principle in the scriptures—the book of Proverbs, for example, contains many exhortations to brotherly solidarity[39]—but commonly missing from amongst the primary narratives. It appears, then, that Moses and Aaron demonstrate something closer to the ideal image, unencumbered as they are from the competitive history of brotherhood, and removal from questions of inheritance and so on that punctuate other brotherly stories throughout the biblical materials. And indeed, the notion of friendship categories extends from these brotherly ideals.[40] Moses and Aaron are brothers, but brothers without a shared history. Thrust together as adults, their relationship is established across those lines, at times demonstrating the types of competitiveness that characterizes male-male homosociality, but more commonly tending towards something slightly different.

In describing his category of "the bonding male," Clines asserts that the bond is one of friendship rather than kinship.[41] Clines mentions three aspects which form the ideology of such relationships: a dyadic relationship with exclusive tendencies, a commitment to a common cause, and a valuing of the relationship ahead of all others.[42] These things come together for Clines because he is considering the relationship of David and Jonathan, who largely fit into the proposed scheme. However, as Wilson has recently recognized, the importance of male-male friendships so described need not stand outside kinship groups.[43] Wilson goes so far as to use kinship solidarity as a defining characteristic of masculinity, recognizing commitments to clan and tribe as an essential part of the male role, but also extending outwards towards solidarity with all Israelite men.[44] Clines himself says a similar thing in a different article when he refers to Israelite men as something approaching a "band of brothers."[45] That is, Clines notes that the responsibilities of the man extend outwards from the immediate family environment, to the broader levels of engagement in much the same way that Wilson suggests. As Perdue notes in language close to that of Clines, the "ethics of solidarity" (analogous to Clines' "band of brothers") moves beyond the family to include clan, tribe, and all the children of Israel.[46]

I think it is reasonably clear that Clines' three-part scheme fits Aaron's relationship with Moses. Moses and Aaron present as a dyad. Aaron is called into service to counter Moses' own shortcomings. The common cause is in the first instance, the execution of the plan to have the people of Israel removed from Egypt, which develops into leadership of the mass of people as they move through the various experiences in the wilderness and the establishment of worship apparatus. And the exclusivity of the relationship appears in the way in which Moses and Aaron are commonly attacked together, and the way in which Moses responds to protect his brother.

And so Aaron and Moses demonstrate this characteristic of the bonding male with each other and do so in a fashion that also demonstrates kinship solidarity. However, it must be noted that Moses is portrayed as doing this more successfully than Aaron. It is Aaron who from time to time fails Moses on this front, by simply acquiescing to the crowd in the golden calf incident, and in his role in plotting against Moses with their sister Miriam in Numbers 12. There is little solidarity demonstrated in those episodes. Moses, however, defends Aaron against Korah and his insurgents in Numbers 16 and so on.

As we have noted earlier, this relationship is the most intimate of human relationships Moses develops in his story. Zornberg suggests that Moses' life can be imagined as a type of quest for brotherhood, perhaps a response to his liminal existence: a child of two cultures, a man without fixed identity.[47] The expression "Aaron your brother" then is a loaded one in this story. Perhaps it is this experience of being brother-less, of lacking all solidarity, which drives Moses to overcome Aaron's failings. After all, apart from Moses' relationship with Zipporah's father, we see no other meaningful human relationship in Moses' life. His relationship with Aaron is as exclusive as one could imagine!

AARON THE ELOQUENT

A key characteristic of Aaron's character is his status as a good speaker. His introduction to the narrative is marked by divine recognition of this skill, and his role in the narrative is defined by his position as Moses' speaker. As Clines' explains, to have a way with words, or to have the power of persuasion is an important part of the masculine ideal: it is a complement to physical prowess, part of the repertory of the powerful male.[48] Aaron's introduction suggests that this is the way his character will function, especially gives Moses' lack of persuasion skills. The reality is that Aaron's performance of this aspect is uneven. It seems that when he functions as Moses' mouth, things go reasonably well. But the times in which Aaron speaks with his own voice are presented as episodes of personal failure in which the things he says give evidence of his shortcomings. And, incidentally, it appears that in each of these episodes he has been persuaded to act in a particular way. In Exodus 32, the idea of the calf belongs to the crowd, not to Aaron, and while the idea of the festival to Yahweh appears to be his, he certainly lacks the persuasive capacity to prevent the people from a touch too much revelry and is condemned for it. He the proceeds to lie about his role in the manufacture of the calf, a lie which either Moses believes, or, more likely, dismisses as completely ridiculous. To be fair to Aaron, there is no indication given in the text. In Numbers 12, it seems possible that the instigation of the complaints against Moses comes from Miriam, and that Aaron has been persuaded by her to use his gifts in this cause. On the punishment of Miriam, Aaron admits to the foolishness of their actions, including, we assume, the foolishness of using his gift in a destructive way. He implores Moses to speak to Yahweh in his stead; that is, he recognizes the inherent power of Moses' words, an ironic twist indeed.

Moses' words do prove to be powerful, and persuasive. Moses is able to convince Yahweh not to destroy the people for their indiscretions, indiscretions of which Aaron is intimately involved. He chastises the people for their failures and is able to speak to them in a way that has them commit to change their ways (even if only momentarily), and in response to Aaron's plea, he is able to have Yahweh move regarding the punishment of Miriam. In short, it appears that Moses' self-proclaimed lack of power with words and the provision of Aaron to play that role is a device to simply magnify Moses' skill. In the end, it is Moses' words delivered from his own mouth which prove to be truly effective.

WISDOM

In light of the previous discussion, it is perhaps no surprise that one of Aaron's great failings is the demonstration of wisdom. In Exodus 32 he lacks the wisdom to stand against the crowd's urges for the production of molten gods. Having melted in the heat of their demands, he attempts to salvage the situation by proclaiming a feast day for Yahweh, which quickly escalates into an orgy of human excess and depravity. With the evidence of his failing lying dead or drunk all around him, Aaron cooks up a story of a miraculously emerging calf in order to deflect attention from his own role. At every turn, it is a failure of wisdom.

Miriam begins to speak ill of Moses and his foreign wife. In doing so, she brings family tensions into the public sphere, undermining Moses' leadership in the broader community. Aaron doesn't resist, indeed it appears that he joins Miriam in this public condemnation of his brother. Further, Miriam is upset at the role Moses plays in the community and wanting recognition for her own gifts and graces. Rather than point to the things Moses has accomplished and recognizing the role he has played alongside Moses, Aaron too turns against Moses, the one whom he had been so glad to greet in the wilderness. Aaron, it appears, confuses his words with Miriam's words, his words with Moses' words. It is a failure of wisdom at every turn. Haddox's definition of wisdom: showing good judgement and acting appropriately in different circumstances[49] appears lacking in all Aaron's actions.

By contrast, Moses always acts in a way that makes sense of his circumstances. To modern readers, the bloody response to the golden calf incident is unlikely to find many supporters, but is presented in the text as an appropriate response to an extreme event. The following day he demonstrates his care for the people by seeking atonement for their waywardness. Here, however, he is unable to win a concession from Yahweh, but Moses never suggests that he will be able to avert the divine judgment, only that he will endeavor to do so.

Confronted by a revolt from within his own family, Moses does nothing rashly, allowing Yahweh to act on is behalf. When his sister is struck in punishment, rather than celebrate her misfortune, Moses acts with compassion and seeks her restoration, not only to physical well-being, but presumably also to familial relations. In this, he is revealed as a man of patience and prudence, acting in ways that will not jeopardize his own reputation, maintaining or restoring good relationships with his family, and representing the best interests of those that he leads. In these matters, Moses is a model of wise living.

CONCLUSION

The relationship between Moses and Aaron is the most important human relationship in Moses' life. While they may be biological brothers, their relationship lacks the formative aspects born of time spent together as children, competing with and against each other in the family group. Such experiences tend to be dangerous in the biblical materials, and so unlike many biblical brothers who do hate each other—as the Rabbis suggested—Moses and Aaron demonstrate a healthier, more idealized (though not yet ideal) version of brotherhood.

Introduced to us as Moses' brother, assistant and prophet Aaron is consistently cast in a way that serves to further elevate Moses' character. Ironically, it is the gift with which he is announced—that he is a good speaker—that most often marks this differentiation. Aaron may have good skills of presentation and charisma, but he lacks wisdom and prudence. Left to his own devices, Aaron consistently fails, speaking and acting rashly to his hurt and others', and leaving a situation for Moses to repair. In regard to homosociality there is a complexity here. In some respects the relationship between Moses and Aaron transcends the type of competitive animosity that characterizes male-male relationships, even at the fraternal level. The rabbinic comment here points to that homosocial, familial reality. Aaron's failure, most notably in Numbers 12, points to that underlying sense of competition by which he seeks to gain parity or perhaps usurp his brother. He doesn't *hate* Moses, though perhaps he hates being subordinate to him. Between men, even brothers, homosocial competition runs deep.

NOTES

1. Tanchuma Shemot, 27, cited in Avivah Gottlieb Zornberg, *Moses: A Human Life*, Jewish Lives (New Haven: Yale University Press, 2016), 111.

2. David H. Morgan, "Family, Gender and Masculinities," in *The Masculinities Reader*, ed. Stephen M. Whitehead and Frank J. Barrett (Cambridge: Polity Press, 2001), 223.

3. See Dozeman's discussion of this phenomenon, which he separates along the lines of the P-history and Non-P history. Thomas B. Dozeman, *Exodus*, The Eerdmans Critical Commentary (Grand Rapids: W.B. Eerdmans, 2009), 143–45.

4. Ibid., 145.

5. Uri Margolin, "Character," in *The Cambridge Companion to Narrative*, ed. David Herman (Cambridge: Cambridge University Press, 2007), 72.

6. Carol L. Meyers, *Exodus*, New Cambridge Bible Commentary (Cambridge: Cambridge University Press, 2005), 62.

7. Mieke Bal, *Narratology: Introduction to the Theory of Narrative*, 3rd ed. (Toronto: University of Toronto Press, 2009), 125.

8. Bronwen Thomas, "Dialogue," in *The Cambridge Companion to Narrative*, ed. David Herman (Cambridge: Cambridge University Press, 2007), 82.

9. Alan Palmer, *Fictional Minds*, Frontiers of Narrative (Lincoln: University of Nebraska Press, 2004), 40.

10. Andreas Schuele, "Heart," in *The New Interpreter's Dictionary of the Bible*, ed. Katherine Doob Sakenfeld (Nashville: Abingdon, 2007), 764.

11. Ibid., 765.

12. Note that Aaron is left in charge with Hur, who had also acted as an assistant in the battle with the Amalekites in Exod. 17. However, there is no mention of Hur beyond these two reports.

13. John I. Durham, *Exodus*, Word Biblical Commentary (Waco: Word, 1987), 422.

14. It is this orgy, brought to life so vividly in Schonberg's opera, which accounts for the infrequency of its staged performance. The music to which the actions are set, however, remain the most-performed of his works in concert-form for Orchestra. See, Malcolm MacDonald, *Schoenberg*, Rev ed., The Master Musicians (New York: Oxford University Press, 2008), 280–8.

15. Dozeman, *Exodus*, 703.

16. Ibid., 711.

17. Interestingly, it is the "sons of Levi" who take responsibility for this action, given that as we have seen, Aaron is identified as a Levite in his first introduction to the story.

18. Carolyn Pressler, *Numbers*, Abingdon Old Testament Commentaries (Nashville: Abingdon, 2017), 100.

19. Jacob Milgrom, *Numbers: The JPSTorah Commentary*, ed. Nahum M. Sarna, JPS Torah Commentary (Philadelphia: Jewish Publication Society, 1990), 93.

20. The order there is Aaron, Moses and Miriam. Given that Aaron is only three years older than Moses, we are left to assume that Miriam must be the oldest of the three and that the arrangement in Chronicles lists sons and then daughters, rather than a chronological ordering irrespective of gender.

21. Milgrom, *Numbers: The JPS Torah Commentary*.

22. Katharine Doob Sakenfeld, *Journeying with God: A Commentary on the Book of Numbers*, International Theological Commentary (Grand Rapids: Wm. B. Eerdmans, 1995), 84.

23. Eryl W. Davies, *Numbers: The Road to Freedom*, Phoenix Guides to the Old Testament (Sheffield: Sheffield Phoenix, 2015), 24.

24. Ibid., 27.

25. Sakenfeld, *Journeying with God : A Commentary on the Book of Numbers*, 80. While Sakenfeld's understanding does damage to the thrust of Davies' assertions in this instance, it is undeniable that Davies' comments about the significance of racially sensitive readings rings true, and that such readings undermine and transform white readings of the text in a way which is enriching of our understanding of these texts and their reception histories. Sakenfeld, I feel sure, would have no hesitation in agreeing with that!

26. Timothy M. Willis, "Clan," in *The New Interpreter's Dictionary of the Bible*, ed. Katherine Doob Sakenfeld (Nashville: Abingdon, 2006).

27. Roland Boer, *The Sacred Economy of Ancient Israel*, ed. Douglas A. Knight, Library of Ancient Israel (Louisville: Westminster John Knox, 2015), 90.

28. Ibid., 103.

29. Mary E. Shields, "Marriage, Ot," in *The New Interpreter's Dictionary of the Bible*, ed. Katherine Doob Sakenfeld (Nashville: Abingdon, 2008), 818.

30. Ibid., 819.

31. The Hebrew here may also mean "devout" rather than humble, which slightly alters the allegation made against Moses' older siblings.

32. Traditionally this has been rendered as "leprosy" or what is better described as Hansen's disease. However, this is not an accurate description of the affliction described. See, John J. Pilch, "Leprosy," in *The New Interpreter's Dictionary of the Bible*, ed. Katherine Doob Sakenfeld (Nashville: Abingdon, 2008).

33. Sakenfeld, *Journeying with God: A Commentary on the Book of Numbers*, 83.

34. Pressler, *Numbers*, 105.

35. Pekka Pitkanen, *A Commentary on Numbers: Narrative, Ritual, and Colonialism*, Routledge Studies in the Biblical World (London: Routledge, 2018), 112.

36. Bal, *Narratology: Introduction to the Theory of Narrative*, 126.

37. Rainer Albertz, "Ambivalent Relations between Brothers in the Hebrew Bible," in *With the Loyal You Show Yourself Loyal*, ed. T. M. Lemos, et al., Ancient Israel and Its Literature (Atlanta: SBl Press, 2021), 31.

38. Ibid.

39. Ibid., 33.

40. Ibid., 30.

41. David J.A. Clines, "David the Man: The Construction of Masculinity in the Hebrew Bible," in *Interested Parties: The Ideology of Writers and Readers of the Hebrew Bible* (Sheffield: Sheffield Academic Press, 1995), 224–5.

42. Ibid.

43. Stephen M. Wilson, *Making Men: The Male Coming-of-Age Theme in the Hebrew Bible* (New York: Oxford University Press, 2015), 44.

44. Ibid., 45.

45. David J. A. Clines, "Being a Man in the Book of the Covenant," in *Read the Law: Essays in Honour of Gordon J. Wenham*, ed. J. G. McConville and Karl Möller (London: Bloomsbury, 2007), 6.

46. Leo G. Perdue et al., *Families in Ancient Israel*, 1st ed., Family, Religion, and Culture (Louisville: Westminster John Knox, 1997), 167.

47. Zornberg, *Moses: A Human Life*, 120.

48. Clines, "David the Man: The Construction of Masculinity in the Hebrew Bible," 220.

49. Susan E. Haddox, "Is There a 'Biblical Masculinity'? Masculinities in the Hebrew Bible," *Word & World* 36, no. 1 (2016): 7.

Chapter Three

Moses and His Father-in-Law

A constant challenge in any consideration of Moses' father-in-law is the reality that the biblical witness appears to give him three names: Jethro, Reuel and Hobab. Adding complexity to this assortment of names is that at one point, two of them are used to create a father-son relationship. That is, in Numbers 10:29, Moses is reported as speaking to an individual identified as "Hobab, son of Reuel the Midianite, Moses' father-in-law." The issue is that it is ambiguous who is to be identified as the father-in-law in this construction, with appeals to other mentions of these names doing nothing to clarify the situation. Both Hobab and Reuel are used elsewhere as names for Moses' father-in-law. Milgrom gives a detailed summary of the various explanations given to explain this riddle,[1] but for the sake of this reading, Reuel, Jethro and Hobab will be dealt with as a single individual, even while each of the attributed names of this character will be considered. This position has strong historical warrant. As Levine points out, Rashi, fascinated by this phenomenon, solved the problem by assuming this was a single character with a variety of names, a real possibility given the Ancient West Asian context.[2] While this does not respond to all of the textual problems, most notably that Hobab is identified as a Kenite rather than a Midianite in Jdg. 1:16 (an issue which we will deal with in turn), there appears to be enough consistency in the characterization of this individual to proceed in this particular fashion. All three names share common ground: at some point, each is used to name a figure identified as Moses' father-in-law.

INITIAL IMPRESSIONS

The first mention of Moses' father-in-law is indirect. He is introduced by the narrator, though he would play no role in the immediate scene. In this first mention, no name is given either. He is introduced by the narrator with three pieces of information. He is a Priest, a Midianite, and the father of seven daughters (Exod. 2:16). Immediately after this information is given the attention turns to Moses' protection of these daughters in the face of seemingly hostile shepherds.[3] But Moses is unaware of who these women he meets are, nor the significance of their father, who is he soon to meet. However, each these pieces of information provide crucial clues for the way in which the narrative will develop, and in particular, the role that this Midianite Priest will play in Moses' life.

THE PRIEST

To this point in the narrative, very little has been learnt about Moses' character aside from his tendency towards violence, though notably, in each case Moses appears to be acting out of some type of moral response to oppression. Born as a foreign slave, adopted into the royal court, and now exiled on account of his murder of an Egyptian man, we have no sense of who Moses actually is. Given the experiences of his life, and the recent trauma attached to his exile, the emergence of a Priestly figure is of no small significance.

While Priesthood almost certainly had particular traits and practices within the different, defined ethnic groups of the Old Testament, it is also true that there are significant overlaps in the status and role that these figures played in their community. As Kugler notes, their main function was to serve as intermediaries between the divine and human realms, maintaining that equilibrium through their ritual acts. Their role was not solely contained within the cultic realm. Often, it was the Priestly class that took responsibility for the judgement of disputes within the community, so that their mediation was not solely human-divine, but also human-human. These skills were taught, a tradition developed and passed on from senior figures to those training within the developing professional priesthood. Such systems were a cross-cultural phenomenon across Ancient West Asia.[4] These two functions—cultic and judicial—become a significant part of the characterization of Moses' father-in-law, as we will see in the subsequent analysis. It is significant, then, that in this first moment of characterization, Priestly office is attached to this new figure. As Durham observes,[5] the priestly vocation of Moses' father-in-law seems more readily remembered than his name(s). At this moment in the narrative, of course, he is not yet Moses' relation, but this introductory comment establishes a trajectory for his ongoing development.

THE MIDIANITE

As well as identifying the vocation of the father of these seven sisters Moses encounters, he is further identified as a Midianite. This is less shocking, given that Moses has already been reported as settling in the land of Midian. Genesis 25 identifies the Midianites as descendants of Abraham through his son, Keturah. Midianites appear as traders in the story of Joseph, used interchangeably there with the term Ishmaelites. It appears that "Ishmaelite" may function as a generic term for the desert dwellers, a group including the more tightly defined Midianites.[6]

Throughout the ensuing story of Moses, the Midianites are portrayed in a fashion which is notoriously difficult to explain. Dozeman comments that they are allies of Yahweh, able to discern divine instruction, and play a role in the deliverance of the Israelites from Egypt. In support of this view, Dozeman notes the hospitality of this figure, the would-be father-in-law of Moses and the effective actions of Zipporah in saving Moses' life in Exod. 4. In summary, he suggests that they are neither the people of, nor the enemies of Yahweh, but instead divine allies.[7] Carol Meyers notes the close genealogical link between Midian and Israel, and with the positive view of Zipporah and her father, suggests that it is possible that at some point, Midian has played a formative role in Israel's development.[8] In light of the previous section, it is noteworthy that this formative role is characterized through the actions of a priest and his daughter: that is, through religious means. Moses, no doubt motivated by his familial connections, but also recognizing the valuable role the Midianite people have played in his life offers them a share of the promised land in Num. 10:29, an offer which is initially rebuffed, but which seems to be taken up at a second offer. Moses notes the contribution Hobab has made in navigating the Israelites through the wilderness, which cuts against the tradition that establishes that the people are led by a pillar of cloud. It seems that human engagement, and in this case, specifically Midianite engagement, is still held in high regard.

And yet, it is hardly the case that Midianites are uniformly positive characters in Moses' story. In Numbers 22, elders of Midian, in league with Moabites, attempt to engage the prophet Balaam in order to curse the advancing Israelites. In chapter 25, a Midianite Princess, Cozbi, is murdered (by a Priest, no less) as she consummates her marriage to an Israelite prince in the aftermath of the apostasy of Baal Peor.[9] Immediately, Yahweh orders a battle with Midian, and this battle takes place in chapter 31. Moses seems unmoved by is connection to the Midianites, expressing his dismay at the mercy demonstrated to the women and children of Midian by his troops. In response, he order that all the women who have "known a man" be put to death along with all the young boys, while the virgin girls are spared "for yourselves" (Num. 31:15–19). In the period of the Judges, the Midianites are remembered as the enemies of Israel before being routed by Gideon (Jdg. 6–8). This victory over the Midianites becomes a significant event in the memory of Israel, commemorated in Psalm 83. With contemporary enemies in mind, the congregation sings "Do to them as you did to Midian," which is set in parallel with remembrances of Sisera and Jabin, enemies chastened by Yahweh in Judges 4, suggesting that the mention of Midian's defeat here is that of Gideon, rather than the war on Midian in Numbers 31.

So we can see that even in the telling of Moses' story, Midian is a slippery term. In the early part of Moses' life it is clear that he enjoys peaceful relations with the Midianites, who allow him a place to be home. At some point though, these relations take a bitter turn for reasons which are left unexplained. In terms of Moses' relations with the Midianites, and in particularly his family, it is difficult to make a clear statement about what the insistence of his father-in-law's ethnicity amounts to. All we can say is that throughout the narrative, Moses appear to retain amicable if not particularly close relations with him, and that the escalation of enmity between the two groups appears to be prompted by something external to his familial affairs.

THE FATHER OF SEVEN DAUGHTERS

The final piece of information we glean from this initial mention of this character is that he is the father of seven daughters. There is no mention of wives nor sons, just these seven daughters who are out to water their father's flock. This piece of information is all the more telling because of the setting in which they encounter Moses, namely, the well where he has sat down to rest (Exod. 2:15).. Wells are places where men first encounter women who will become their wives. This happens two times in Genesis, when Isaac meets Rebekah (Gen. 24) and his son Jacob meets Rachel (Gen. 29).. Dozeman notes that this meeting at the well is intended to announce an imminent marriage,[10] though unlike the Genesis examples, the bride-to-be is yet unclear.[11]

In the biblical world, the negotiation of marriage contracts was an important fatherly role. While it is difficult to ascertain the types of rites and practices that were involved in the marriage of two individuals, what is clear is that typically, marriages were normally negotiated agreements between the fathers of the couple.[12] Matthews and Benjamin point out that marriage was regarded as more than the joining of individuals. Rather, a marriage wasa union of families, forming a political and economic relationship. In simple terms, it is a matter more of business than pleasure.[13] A father of seven daughters, then, was likely a man with his eyes open, looking for appropriate matches for his daughters. And yet, there is a sense that Moses' story is resisting the type of set up the narrator is suggesting. Some of the essential elements are absent. Moses is alone. He has no one to broker such a marriage for him. All he owns he carries on his person. Politically and economically, he appears to have little if anything to offer. Despite this great lack, Moses appears to win over the sisters' father on account of his character demonstrated in his protection of them.

These three descriptors: Priest, Midianite, and father all serve to build a sense of anticipation regarding the roles this character may play in Moses' life. While nothing can be said to be certain, and while there are clearly a range of obstacles to be overcome, the narrator has clearly crafted this introduction in a fashion which enables the reader to sense that something significant is likely to come from this relationship.

FIRST APPEARANCES

Following the events at the well, the daughter's rush home, evidently reaching their home ahead of schedule. The narrator tells us their father's name: Reuel. The name means "friend of God"[14] so it appears that the narrator is indicating that this is a positive character, the name being a way of describing his nature.[15] His response to their early return is immediate, and distinctly parental: "Why have you come so early today?" (Exod. 2:18). His question demonstrates that he knows the patterns of life in his house, and closely monitors the coming and going of his daughters. The response of the daughters to his question shows how abnormal this encounter with Moses was. They excitedly claim that they have received assistance from an Egyptian man. While their father is ignorant to the error of this report, the reader is not. There are two clear options to explain this error in the sisters' report. The first is that the narrator has omitted an episode of dialogue between Moses and the women, in which Moses has identified himself as an Egyptian, or at least from Egypt. This option has a number of dimensions regarding Moses' self-identity. There is certainly a sense in which Moses is indeed Egyptian, having been raised in the heart of Egyptian society. All the while the narrator has made it clear that Moses is an Israelite, born into the tribe of Levi, nursed by his mother, and the brother of those who are oppressed by the Pharaoh. However, whether or not Moses understands that remains unclear. The second explanation for the sisters reporting this is that Moses appears to be an Egyptian, whether by accent, appearance or both. Durham disputes this, claiming that there is no reason to believe that the sisters assume Moses to be Egyptian on account of his clothing when in 2:14, a Hebrew man does appear to understand Moses to be a Hebrew, even while excluding Moses from them with his question "Who made you a ruler over *us*?" He suggests that this is a way of bringing the two contexts of Moses life together, contrasting what Moses appears to be with what he is.[16] But the effect of the Hebrew man's question is to exclude Moses, and so what Moses is appears to be neither Hebrew nor Egyptian.

This matter aside, Durham understates the importance of this identification, given the nature of the characterization of Moses, and the way in which this report is being made. It appears that in their rush to get home and tell their father about this Egyptian man, they have forgotten to deal appropriately with him given his acts of valour. This haste has included an assumption regarding his ethnicity, and a host of other matters which are revealed in his next brace of questions: "Where is he? Why did you leave the man?" These questions are accompanied by an instruction: "Call him, and he can eat bread." Reuel seems incredulous that his daughters have returned without their Egyptian hero, particularly given their report that he had "rescued"[17] them from the obnoxious actions of the shepherds. Such actions require adequate recognition, particularly given Reuel's significant social position as a Priest. Reuel's response then is entirely appropriate, and his urgency in demanding his daughter's go and call Moses indicates a high level of commitment to these social protocols. That is to say, the narrator is continuing to portray Reuel in a positive fashion.

The narrative lurches forward. The sisters' evidently locate Moses and extend an invitation to him on behalf of their father. As the head of the house, such invitations were his responsibility, which he fulfils here.[18] But immediately it becomes apparent that Moses does a lot more than "eat bread." In what seems to be a response to Moses' actions in rescuing his daughters, Moses is invited to stay with Reuel, who gives one of them, Zipporah, to Moses. As we have noted, marriages were traditionally brokered by fathers for economic and political purposes, but Moses is alone. Unattached, Moses is free to accept Reuel's offer. Without means to support a family, Moses settles within house of his father-in-law, and is set to work as a shepherd (Exod. 3:1). So it appears that in response to Reuel's generosity, Moses offers his labor. Such arrangements were common, constituting an exchange of goods, or in this case service, over an extended period of time.[19] Reuel then, is revealed as a shrewd negotiator. It is certainly true that Moses gains a good deal from this arrangement: a wife, security, and a means of livelihood. But so too does Reuel. From his perspective, Moses has revealed himself as a man of courage and principle. Further, he gains a house member with what appear to be highly developed skills in violence, the sort of skills that are of great service to a shepherd. In terms of character and worth, Reuel acquires a suitable partner for one of his daughters, even while the arrangement may appear to be a little out of the ordinary.

The ending of this report regarding Moses' joining of a Midianite family comes with a birth announcement. Zipporah conceives and gives birth to a son named Gershom (Exod. 2:22). The text narrates that this name means something along the lines of "I have been a stranger in a foreign land." This explanation plays with the two components of the name, *ger*, meaning stranger or alien, and *shom*, an inexact spelling of the word meaning "there." This leads to a question of specificity. That is, is Moses a stranger in Egypt, or in Midian? Or another way, is Moses at home in Egypt, or in Midian? Dozeman considers just one option: that the name refers to Moses' experience as an outsider in Midian.[20] Durham contends, convincingly, that in retrospect, it is in Egypt that Moses is the stranger, no matter how familiar the places, people and practices, whereas in Midian, he is home, no matter how unfamiliar those things are.[21] In Midian, Moses is welcomed, embraced, and allowed to discover who he is. And as Meyers notes, this language of stranger links the birth of Moses' son to the ancestral narrative of Abraham[22] which talks of descendants described as strangers in a land not theirs: Egypt. If this interpretation is correct, then the naming of Gershom is a tribute to Moses' Midianite family, and in particular, we might say, to Reuel, who welcomed an unknown, unattached stranger into his home and made him family. This being the case, Reuel's first entry into the story serves to surpass the already lofty expectations set up in his introduction.

The explanation offered by the narrator regarding the meaning of this name, overlooks a significant point, being that the name Gershom is built on a different tri-consonantal root, *grš*, a word meaning "drive out." The same root is used to describe the bandit shepherd's actions towards the sisters earlier in the chapter ahead of Moses' rescuing of them, and is used in Chapter 6, anticipating the urgency with which Pharaoh will drive the Israelites from Egypt on account of his dread at the divine actions (Exod. 6:1). In Exod. 23:29 it is the word used to describe the way in which the Canaanites will be expelled from the land in order that Israel may inhabit it. So the name Gershom is a play on words. In one respect, the narrator's explanation can be taken on face value, in so far as the sounds of the words make such a reading possible. Greenberg is less forgiving, describing this reading as inept.[23] The written text allows another possibility: that the name points backwards to a key moment in the narrative, but also points forward to Yhwh's actions in aid of Israel.

FAREWELLS AND ARRIVALS

Immediately following the announcement of Gershom's birth, the narrator indicates a long passage of time passing: "In those many days, the King of Egypt died." A report that God heard the cry of the Israelites, remembered the covenant with the ancestors, and somewhat cryptically "knew" (2:23–25). This forms the context for Moses' epiphany on the mountain which commences in chapter 3, in which we learn that he is working as a shepherd for his father-in-law, now named as Jethro, who is again identified as the Midianite Priest. The news that Moses is working as a shepherd confirms what appeared to be the case in the previous section, namely, that Moses is fully engrained within the family unit, in so far as the flock represents the capital of the family.[24] Durham suggests that the emphasis of Jethro's vocation as Priest may be a way of preparing the reader for the religious experience that will soon follow, suggesting that the many days Moses has now spent with a priestly figure may well have prepared Moses for the intensity of what lays before him.[25] On this reading, Jethro stands as a crucial mentor in Moses' religious development, which also appears to be the case in subsequent episodes.

The events on Horeb need not concern us here, but having spoken with Yahweh and being convinced to return to Egypt, Moses goes first to his father-in-law to request leave to depart. This action demonstrates the respect that Moses has developed for his father-in-law, but also that Moses understands his own position within the context of Jethro's family, or using terminology Boer has recently stressed, household.[26] Moses may well be developing into the hero of the story, but within the family unit he inhabits, he is very much aware of the authority of his father-in-law. Jethro, for his part, responds with the type of grace and goodwill that we have come to expect. He sends Moses off with a blessing of peace. Despite this shared good will, it is noteworthy that Moses is not a forthcoming with Jethro as he may be. Having accepted a commission to confront Yawheh and deliver the Israelites from oppression, Moses reduces the reason for his visit to inquire after the well-being of his family in Egypt. Propp sees an act of deception here on Moses' part,[27] which, given the danger that Moses potentially takes Jethro's daughter and grandchildren into, is understandable. Perhaps Moses, assured by the divine promises, sees no need to unnecessarily burden his father-in-law with thoughts of danger and confrontation. The men take their leave of each other, Moses taking with him a wife, two sons, and a donkey, none of which were in his possession on his first encounter with Jethro.

A great deal takes place between this farewell and their reunion which takes place in chapter 18. In regards to their individual circumstances, much needs to be pieced together by the reader. In chapter 4 it seemed as though Moses was travelling to Egypt with his family, having secured Jethro's blessing. But the beginning of chapter 18 suggests something quite different. Exod. 18:2 says that Moses had sent his wife and children back to Jethro, who had taken them back. As Dozeman suggests, while the text allows a reading that sees this as divorce, it hardly makes sense of the events in which Jethro announces his return.[28] We learn here also the name of the second son, Eliezer. The departing family in chapter 4 included Moses' sons, though the narrative had only detailed the birth of Gershom. The name Eliezer means "my God is help," and the explanation in Exod. 18:4, seemingly from the perspective of Moses, indicates that this is a reference to God's help of Moses in his dealings with Pharaoh, presumably, his flight from Egypt in chapter 2.

We are left to guess then, that at some point after their departure in chapter 4, Moses decides that it is better for his wife and children to be with Jethro, rather than him. Moses most likely returns to Egypt with some sense of trepidation, even given the long span of time that has elapsed since his departure. He is also aware that his commission is likely to make him an enemy of Pharaoh and so place his family in harm's way. Whether Zipporah, Gershom and Eliezer make it to Egypt at all is unknown. Perhaps it was not until they reached the imperial centre that Moses understood what danger he was in. Perhaps Moses found that his focus was best placed on the new responsibilities he was taking up, or rather, he was consumed by them. None of this is stated. However, what is clear is that at some point, this family was separated, and that Moses was relieved of his familial responsibilities, such as they were for an indeterminate amount of time.

Jethro announces his visit to Moses, and arrives as the Israelites are camped in the wilderness, close to his home. His visit is prompted, it seems, by the positive reports that he has heard regarding Yhwh's deliverance of the people from Egypt, and all that had been done for his son-in-law, Moses (Exod. 18:1). Perhaps Jethro wants to see things for himself, or, perhaps, getting on in age, he is looking to return responsibility for his daughter and grandchildren back to their husband and father. His arrival is a significant event and demonstrates the regard in which he is held by Moses. Moses "went out to meet his father-in-law" (Exod. 18:7), and on finding him, bows reverently before him and greets him with a kiss. This act of bowing suggests that Moses is greeting Jethro as his superior,[29] or as Pixley vividly notes, their meeting seems to solemnly bring together two great chiefs, of which Jethro is the greater.[30]

Dozeman notes the similarity here with a previous meeting: that between Aaron and Moses in chapter 4.[31] This is a telling comparison. It is clear that the relationships with Aaron and Jethro are far and away the most significant in Moses' life. Following this public greeting,[32] which also includes inquiry into each other's welfare (Exod. 18:7), they retire to a tent, where Moses proceeds to tell Jethro about Yhwh's deliverance of the people from Egypt, including the range of difficulties they had faced thus far (Exod. 18:8). Jethro's response is one of great elation, and he rejoices in response to what Yhwh has done for Israel (though notably, no mention is made of what has been done for Moses). His rejoicing is coupled with words of blessing and confession. Jethro claims that "god is greater than all other gods" on account of this deliverance from the arrogant Egyptians. "Now I know," he says. Childs notes that this exclamation need not be understood as a conversion, for to do so serves to detract from Jethro's understanding of Yhwh prior to this utterance. Throughout, Jethro has been a faithful witness to Yhwh, rejoicing at Yhwh's gracious acts, and here, blessing the god of Israel in its own vocabulary.[33] For the narrator, and for Moses, Jethro has never been an outsider to Israel, a reality made all of the more obvious in the events which follow.

Jethro moves from confession to worship, presiding over sacrifices to which Moses, Aaron and the elders also attend. The text makes it quite clear that Jethro initiates this sacrificial meal, and that Moses, Aaron and the elders come to eat in the presence of God in response to Jethro's action (Exod. 18:12). The significance of this cultic event can hardly be over stated. Dozeman points out that this is the first Israelite sacrifice, and alongside Zipporah's circumcising act of chapter 4, sees this as completing a transfer of ritual acts from Midian to Israel.[34] Meyers notes that Israel had persistently asked for leave to sacrifice to their god in the wilderness, and yet here, when the sacrifice takes place it is both initiated by and presided over by a priest from outside Israel![35] Clearly, the narrator is presenting Jethro as a model Yahwist. His influence extends now far beyond his relationship with Moses, extending into the heart of Israelite religious practice through the sacrificial system.

But the role of Jethro does not come to an end in his initiation of Israelite sacrificial rites. Immediately following the sacrifice and communal meal, the narrator opens a new scene with a temporal marker: "The next day" (Exod.. 18:13), a day in which Jethro's influence will extend from the cultic to the judicial aspect of Israelite society. He observes Moses at work, surrounded by people looking to him for judgement related to various issues. The task is consuming, with Moses surrounded from morning to evening (Exod. 18:13). Jethro speaks candidly to Moses, pointing out the unsustainable nature of what he is doing. He does not wait for Moses to approach him, or to complain about the burden he is carrying. Instead, Jethro initiates the conversation, asking why things take place in such a fashion, and concluding that the system is bound to break Moses and those waiting for him (Exod. 18:14–18).

By this stage, we should hardly be shocked by Jethro's willingness to engage Moses in this type of discussion. Throughout the narrative Jethro has consistently taken the lead in his relationship with Moses: by insisting his daughters go and call him to eat; by offering his daughter as a wife and providing a means by which Moses could find a home in Midian; by alerting Moses to the fact that he was on his way, accompanied by Zipporah and Moses' sons; and in the initiation of the celebration which had taken place the evening before. At each point, it has been Jethro pushing the narrative forward, demonstrating an agency not seen amongst other characters in Moses' story. Jethro has proven himself to be trustworthy, and engaged in actions which are to Moses' benefit,[36] so it is of no surprise when Jethro offers advice, nor that Moses acts upon it. The advice is straight forward and two-fold. Jethro commends Moses' role as the mediator between God and the people, and that he should continue to bring their cases to god and instruct the people in the ways and laws of god (Exod. 18:19–20). However, alongside that responsibility, Jethro suggests Moses establish a judicial bureaucracy with "men of valour, God-fearers, men of trust that hate extortion" (Exod. 18:21). These men are to be appointed over various levels of authority, making judgements within their scope, and escalating only the most serious cases to Moses. Jethro buttresses his advice with the assurance that this is god's intention, acting in some sense as a prophet to Israel's great prophetic figure.

Moses takes Jethro's advice, "doing all he said." In doing so he demonstrates his respect for Jethro, and tacitly acknowledges that this advice is indeed of divine origin. As Moses had once requested Jethro for leave to return to Egypt, he now grants Jethro leave to return to his homeland (Exod. 18:27), but not before the Midianite Priest had left an indelible mark on Israelite society. Unlike his foreign prophetic counterpart, Balaam, there appears to be no attempt to vilify Jethro. Yes, Midian soon come to be enemies of Israel, in an episode in which Balaam is cast as a villain. Yet at no point is there any condemnation, nor any sense of awkwardness regarding the seminal role the Midianite Priest Jethro plays in the development of Israel's religious and civic institutions.

A FINAL FAREWELL?

The final appearance of Moses' father-in-law comes much later in Numbers 10, and creates a conundrum with the end of Exodus 18. As we have seen, Moses' father-in-law departs for his homeland at the end of that scene. But at the conclusion of Numbers 10, a man related to Moses by birth, identified by the name Hobab, enters the story. We have already noted the difficulty this character creates by means of the narrator's categorization of him. For the sake of this reading, I am using the description in Judges 4:11, in which Hobab is named as Moses' father-in-law to guide me. In this reading, it appears that Moses' father-in-law has returned to Moses, Zipporah and his grandsons. The text is silent on this, but so too has it been silent on many other things, and so reconstruction of any sort requires a degree of speculation.

It seems that the circumstances of Hobab's entry into the text can support the reading of Hobab as Moses' father-in-law. Moses goes to Hobab in the hope that he will help him. Moses values the local knowledge of his father-in-law in regards to safe places to camp (Num. 10:31). His father-in-law has offered strong advice in the past, and Moses seeks it out again here. In exchange for his assistance, Moses offers him a share of the land to which they are travelling. Hobab declines the invitation, opting instead to return to his land and family, which, given his priestly vocation, is an understandable response. Having seemingly helped establish sacrificial rites in Israel, he is likely aware that members of the local priestly family will take ownership of them. Moses presses him, offering a share of the Lord's goodness, but the story abruptly ends without confirming one way or the other the final decision made by Hobab. The reference to Hobab in Judges 4:11 seems to suggest that Hobab ultimately does travel to Canaan, as he and his descendants to appear to live together with the Israelites in that place,[37] though here, it remains ambiguous.

It is interesting to note that the guidance through the wilderness is usually attributed to the pillar of cloud. Here, though, that divine guidance is partnered with human knowledge. Or rather, an attempt is made to join human knowledge to the divine sign, suggesting some anxiety regarding the reliability of the divine leading. This divine-human partnership has already been established in the character, Jethro, who is presented as offering divine guidance to Moses previously, and it is exactly this thing which Moses seeks out here. Moses' leadership is exemplified by his embrace of the wisdom of an outsider,[38] and a coupling of both human and divine guidance.[39] The narrator relays all this with no sense of anxiety regarding the father-in-law's alien status within Israelite society. Instead, what is displayed is an openness to difference, and a recognition of the presence of god beyond what might be considered normal bounds.

ON MASCULINITY AND HOMOSOCIAL RELATIONS

As we have seen throughout Moses' story, the sinister aspect of male-male homosocial relationships demonstrated in the sexual abuse of women is absent. And yet some other crucial components remain. We saw in our examination of Moses' relationship with Aaron a sense in which Moses' life was a quest for brotherhood. Something similar appears to be operating in respect to his father-in-law. Jethro becomes an affirmer of Moses' masculinity. On Jethro's arrival with Zipporah and their sons (Exod. 18:6–8), it is Jethro that Moses takes into his tent, quick to report the wonders that had been done. The following day it is under Jethro's gaze that Moses sits as judge (Exod. 18:13), exercising his power and demonstrating his status. As he tells his father-in-law, ". . . they come to me and I decide. . ." (Exod. 18:16). As Kimmel notes, "Manhood is demonstrated for other men's approval. . . because we want other men to grant us our manhood."[40] Moses, it would appear, craves Jethro's approval. The text also suggests the significance of Jethro in relation to Moses, five times introducing him as Moses' father-in-law (Exod. 18:1, 2, 5, 6 and 7).[41]

It should be clear that the relationship between Moses and his father-in-law is the closest thing he has to a meeting of equals. Indeed, it appears that in some ways we might even see Jethro as a figure of authority in Moses' life. Moses comes to rely on Zipporah's father in ways that he is unlikely to have imagined at their first meeting and the influence of his father-in-law profoundly shapes Moses' life, and in turn, the life of Israel more broadly. Here, then, we will consider some of the categories of masculinity by which Jethro leaves his mark on Moses, and in turn, the ways in which those marks demonstrate themselves in Moses' own development.

HONOR

As we have seen, Susan Haddox has developed an understanding of honor that takes in a number of facets. The first she notes is the protection of and provision for one's family. Jethro is revealed as a family man, and with seven daughters, he has a large responsibility! We might raise some questions here about Jethro's success in this arena. It seems that Jethro is in the habit of having his daughters take his flocks to the well for watering, which we see in his surprise at their early return (Exod. 2:18). Such a statement suggests a familiarity with routine, a routine which appears disrupted in this case. It also seems that the daughters are used to encountering these shepherds, as they speak of them to their father in a matter-of-fact fashion. Perhaps we may argue that in their going together, there is a sort of solidarity that serves as a type of protection, but even so, their numerical value did not deter the shepherds from harassing them on this particular occasion. It does not require too much imagination to conjure up a more traumatic experience for one or all of these daughters of the Midianite Priest. We might also see that the advent of Moses presents an opportunity to Jethro to remove his daughters from this dangerous work, an opportunity he takes. No sooner than Gershom is born, Moses is reported as tending to the flocks of his father-in-law. We might say then, that Jethro grows in this aspect of honor as the narrative progresses. At his first entry, he is seemingly a man struggling to maintain various aspects of his life, and perhaps by necessity, placing his daughters in harm's way. But by acquiring a husband for one of his daughters, a very manly thing to do, he is able to overcome this deficiency in a socially desirable fashion.

A second aspect of honor is hospitality, and care for those beyond one's own house.[42] We have seen Jethro's apparent dismay at his daughters' failure to practice customary patterns of hospitality when they return without their hero. He quickly sends them back out to gather him in. The eating of bread (Exod. 2:20), a very private activity, demonstrates Jethro's regard for Moses, showing himself as a man of honor even as he bestows honor upon Moses for his deeds. The offer of shelter, and the subsequent partnering of their lives through marriage demonstrates a thorough commitment to the type of hospitality practices common in Ancient West Asia. And in this arrangement, as we have seen, the honor of both men increases. Jethro gains a functional member of his household who contributes to the flourishing of the family. Moses, in turn, receives a wife and family, and a means by which to provide for them.

Haddox's final aspect in relation to honor is honesty and forthright speech. In relation to his daughters we see this demonstrated by Jethro, but perhaps within such close familial relations such a virtue is not so appropriately measured. We have no report of dialogue regarding his negotiations with Moses regarding Moses joining his household, only the result, being that Moses does indeed join the house and is reported as being glad to do so.

The key speaking event of Jethro is his instruction of Moses in Exodus 18, an event which has much to say regarding aspects of Jethro's performance of masculinity. After observation of Moses' practices, he asks a series of questions. They are, of course, questions he already knows the answers to. By asking for a response, he invites Moses into an act of self-reflection. Having allowed Moses to explain, Jethro makes his mind clear: the thing is not good! He outlines a three-fold analysis: "you will wear yourself out. . . the task is too heavy. . . you cannot do it alone" (Exod. 18:18). This is honest and forthright speech! Additionally, it comes with a familial concern, as the sage advice of a father-in-law is imparted to his overworked son-in-law.[43] As we have seen, Jethro goes on to outline an alternative way of organising the judicial system, or more pointedly, becomes the architect of the judicial system, which allows an examination of another significant category: Wisdom.

WISDOM

Haddox defines wisdom as demonstrating good judgement and acting appropriately in a range of situations.[44] Jethro moves through a variety of settings through this story. In his first engagement in the story he is in his home, urging his daughters to bring Moses home for purposes of hospitality. This is quickly followed by a determination that Moses is an appropriate husband for one of his daughters, which he is able to negotiate. There may be some discussion as to the qualities Moses displays as a husband and father, but it seems clear that for his part, Zipporah's father is pleased with the situation he has engineered. This is demonstrated in the joy that is evident on their reunion in chapter 18. His joy at hearing of Moses' success is genuine, and his care for his son-in-law is evident in his anxieties about Moses' workload. Additionally, Jethro is able to extend his range of contacts through Israel by means of his cultic practice, engaging Aaron and the elders in a fashion which creates significant bonds across ethnic boundaries.

In all these things, we see a wisdom in Jethro, and his wisdom is recognized by those with whom he shares it. Moses hears Jethro's words and joins his family. Moses, Aaron and the elders of Israel join Jethro in worship of God in response to his enthusiastic response to Moses' telling of the events which have transpired in their midst. Moses hears his father-in-law's words regarding the toll his work is taking on him and implements in full the suggestions made to him. This aspect lends itself to a consideration of Haddox's third category, potency.

POTENCY

Potency, like honor, has a number of aspects. Warfare or skill in violence is often among those things considered in this category, though there is no record of such activity with Jethro. Sexual potency, or the ability to procreate is clearly evident in Jethro's life, given the report that he has seven daughters. The common preference was for sons to be born, and while there being no mention of them does not exclude the possibility of Jethro having sons, the immediate engagement of Moses as a shepherd suggests that sons were not a part of Jethro's progeny. Here too, we note the absence of any mention of a wife.

But it is in other aspects of Jethro's characterization that we see him as a character of unusual potency. He is able to make all of his plans come to pass: he convinces Moses to join his family; he alerts Moses that he is coming and Moses responds by greeting him and treating him with honor; he initiates cultic activity to which the leaders of the community attend; he outlines a structure for a significant civic institution and it is accepted and implemented. In all this, Jethro is presented as a man of unhindered agency, able to achieve all that he sets out to do, and exerting influence is a range of spheres.

CONCLUSION

It appears difficult to overstate the importance of Reuel-Jethro-Hobab in Moses' life. This character provides a home for Moses, and while Moses lives with him, he is prepared for the commission which lies before him. As Durham notes, in this home Moses dwells with a family familiar with the God of the fathers,[45] preparing Moses for the encounter which takes place in Exodus 3. Moses is clearly taken by his father-in-law's wisdom, quickly embracing his cultic leadership and implementing various structures in regard to the administration of disputes. Moses' own leadership, and by extension his performance of masculinity, is indelibly shaped by his observation of Jethro. Further, it seems that it is Jethro's approval that motivates Moses' growth in masculinity. Jethro becomes the authority figure that affirms Moses' status as a man. He is not Moses' father, but he welcomes Moses into his family[46] and provides the context in which Moses develops his own. This is a gendered relationship, but one in which competition gives ways to respect and gentle approval. Despite the fact that Moses usurps the other men in his story, it is the elderly authority of Jethro that Moses craves, and which Jethro in turn, gives.

NOTES

1. Jacob Milgrom, *Numbers: The JPS Torah Commentary*, ed. Nahum M. Sarna, JPS Torah Commentary (Philadelphia: Jewish Publication Society, 1990), 78–9.

2. Baruch A. Levine, *Numbers 1-20 : A New Translation with Introduction and Commentary*, 1st ed. (New York: Doubleday, 1993), 335.

3. See Chapter 1, 23ff.

4. Robert Kugler, "Priests and Levites," in *The New Interpreter's Dictionary of the Bible*, ed. Katherine Doob Sakenfeld (Nashville: Abingdon, 2009).

5. John I. Durham, *Exodus*, Word Biblical Commentary (Waco: Word, 1987), 22.

6. Michael G. Vanzant, "Midian, Midianites," in *The New Interpreter's Dictionary of the Bible*, ed. Katharine Doob Sakenfeld (Nashville: Abingdon, 2009), 80.

7. Thomas B. Dozeman, *Exodus*, The Eerdmans Critical Commentary (Grand Rapids: W.B. Eerdmans, 2009), 96.

8. Carol L. Meyers, *Exodus*, New Cambridge Bible Commentary (Cambridge: Cambridge University Press, 2005), 12.

9. On Numbers 25, see Anthony Rees, "[Re]Naming Cozbi: In Memoriam, Cozbi, Daughter of Zur," *Biblical Interpretation* 20, no. 1–2 (2012); *[Re]Reading Again: A Mosaic Reading of Numbers 25*, Playing the Texts (London: Bloomsbury, 2015).

10. Dozeman, *Exodus*, 90.

11. Bearing in mind that in the example of Jacob and Rachel, Jacob is at first duped by his father-in-law into marrying his other daughter! So while the well is a place that Jacob meets his future wife, it is not quite as straight-forward as he may have hoped.

12. Mary E. Shields, "Marriage, OT," in *The New Interpreter's Dictionary of the Bible*, ed. Katherine Doob Sakenfeld (Nashville: Abingdon, 2008), 819. This is not uniformly the case, as the examples of Ishmael (Gen. 21) and Samson (Jdg. 14) demonstrate. None the less, the paucity of examples otherwise serves to highlight the general rule.

13. Victor Harold Matthews and Don C. Benjamin, *Social World of Ancient Israel, 1250-587 Bce* (Peabody: Hendrickson, 1993), 13.

14. Kevin A. Wilson, "Reue," in *The New Interpreter's Dictionary of the Bible*, ed. Katherine Doob Sakenfeld (Nashville: Abingdon, 2009), 785.

15. Timothy M. Willis, "Name, Naming," ibid., 218.

16. Durham, *Exodus*, 23.

17. NRSV rather inadequately renders this as "helpe," ignoring the reality that such language is used later in *Exodus* to describe the divine action of liberating Israel.

18. Matthews and Benjamin, *Social World of Ancient Israel, 1250-587 Bce*, 83.

19. Ibid., 13.

20. Dozeman, *Exodus*, 91.

21. Durham, *Exodus*, 24.

22. Meyers, *Exodus*, 46.

23. Moshe Greenberg, *Understanding Exodus: A Holistic Commentary on Exodus 1-11*, Second edition ed. (Eugene: Cascade Books, 2013), 41.

24. Durham, *Exodus*, 30.

25. Ibid.

26. Roland Boer, *The Sacred Economy of Ancient Israel*, ed. Douglas A. Knight, Library of Ancient Israel (Louisville: Westminster John Knox, 2015), 95. Using broad base anthropological studies, Boer suggests that households is preferable to home or family, allowing as it does a more flexible understanding of the way humans live together irrespective of biological linkages, as well as respecting the place of animals within human groups. Given that Moses is identified as a shepherd, and that previously the seven daughters of Jethro have been seen caring for animals, the point is well taken.

27. William Henry Propp, *Exodus 1-18: A New Translation with Introduction and Commentary*, 1st ed., 2 vols., The Anchor Bible (New York: Doubleday, 1999), 215.

28. Dozeman, *Exodus*, 399.

29. Brevard S. Childs, *The Book of Exodus: A Critical, Theological Commentary*, Old Testament Library (Louisville: Westminster John Knox, 2004), 327.

30. Jorge Pixley, "Exodus," in *Global Bible Commentary*, ed. Daniel Patte (Nashville: Abingdon, 2004), 25.

31. Dozeman, *Exodus*, 402.

32. Powery points out that kissing as a greeting gesture is most commonly an action performed in public. Emerson B. Powery, "Kiss," in *The New Interpreter's Dictionary of the Bible*, ed. Katherine Doob Sakenfeld (Nashville: Abingdon, 2008), 536. Presumably, the demonstration of respect or affection is intended as a sign of solidarity for those who are witness to it.

33. Childs, *The Book of Exodus: A Critical, Theological Commentary*, 329.

34. Dozeman, *Exodus*, 405.

35. Meyers, *Exodus*, 405.

36. Mieke Bal, *Narratology: Introduction to the Theory of Narrative*, 3rd ed. (Toronto: University of Toronto Press, 2009), 126.

37. Carolyn Pressler, *Numbers*, Abingdon Old Testament Commentaries (Nashville: Abingdon, 2017), 86.

38. Ibid., 87.

39. Katharine Doob Sakenfeld, *Journeying with God: A Commentary on the Book of Numbers*, International Theological Commentary (Grand Rapids: Wm. B. Eerdmans, 1995), 66.

40. Michael S. Kimmel, "Masculinity as Homophobia: Fear, Shame and Silence in the Construction of Gender Identity," in *The Masculinities Reader*, ed. Frank J. Barrett and Stephen M. Whitehead (Cambridge: Polity Press, 2001), 275.

41. Ursula Rapp, "Zipporah: The Vanishing of a Wife," in *Torah*, ed. Imtraud Fischer, Mercedes Navarro Puerto, and Andrea Taschel-Erber, Bible and Women (Atlanta: SBL Press, 2011), 323.

42. Susan E. Haddox, "Is There a 'Biblical Masculinity'? Masculinities in the Hebrew Bible," *Word & World* 36, no. 1 (2016): 6.

43. Meyers, *Exodus*, 138.

44. Haddox, "Is There a 'Biblical Masculinity'? Masculinities in the Hebrew Bible," 7.

45. Durham, *Exodus*, 22.

46. David H. Morgan, "Family, Gender and Masculinities," in *The Masculinities Reader*, ed. Stephen M. Whitehead and Frank J. Barrett (Cambridge: Polity Press, 2001).

Chapter Four

Moses and Pharaoh (and Yahweh)

The relationship between Moses and Pharaoh differs from Moses' relationships with other human figures in one crucial aspect. Namely, Pharaoh is not entirely human, or more accurately, Egyptian understanding of the Pharaoh elevates him to a quasi-divine status. While this godlike quality may not be immediately evident in the textual representation of the various Pharaohs that punctuate the biblical narrative, nonetheless, this attribution of divine status is a significant historical reality, one that was certainly known to the writers of the Hebrew bible. Any attempt to examine the characterization of the Pharaoh of Exodus, then, requires a preliminary examination of the various beliefs that were held around this office, not because we anticipate them being worked out through the text, but to raise our awareness as to how the writers may use those traditions, particularly in subversive ways.

The homosocial aspects of this triangulated relationship are equally complex. Ultimately, the battle that plays out in Exodus is between Yahweh and the Pharaohs. Here, the destructive, competitive nature of homosocial relationships is laid bare, with countless innocent victims left in the wake of this hyper-masculine battle for supremacy. Yahweh may emerge as the victor, and assert himself as the supreme exemplar of hegemonic masculinity, but the nature of his victory is morally questionable. Moses likewise engages in a confrontation with Pharaoh, though perhaps the stakes are not so high, devoid as they are of the battle for divinity played out between Yahweh and the self understood god-man Pharaoh. That said, it is in his dealings with Pharaoh that much of Moses' own masculinity is demonstrated, even while, as DiPalma notes, those understandings of masculinity are simultaneously called into question.[1]

THE ROLE (AND THEOLOGY) OF PHARAOH

The Pharaoh was the king of Egypt. In a similar fashion to other cultures of Ancient West Asia, the king was the centre of political life in Egypt. He was charged with responsibilities centred around the maintenance of order and justice as a defense against the threat of chaos, a significant belief in ancient cosmology.[2] That is to say, Pharaoh's social role in the upholding of social order and well-being was believed to have cosmogonic effect. The maintenance of justice was tied to matters commonly referred to in our times as "social justice," which is to say, the protection of the weak from the powerful, the poor from the rich and so on. However, this role of the maintenance of civic order was derivative. The primary work of the Pharaoh was the establishment and maintenance of relations with the divine world, a role that only Pharaoh could fulfil, given his status as a god on earth.[3]

The maintenance of relationship with the gods draws us into the world of the Egyptian cult, at which the Pharaoh stood as head. The day-to-day practice of the cult was delegated to an established priestly cast who administered the appropriate rites in temples across Egypt. In relation to the official cult, Pharaoh seems only to have been directly involved in major festivals,[4] even while the theology supports the idea that it is through the figure of Pharaoh that divine and human worlds are joined. It appears then, that by reason of the theology of Pharaoh as an incarnate god, he had the authority to delegate aspects of his divinity to cultic officiants in this fashion.[5]

The nature of Pharaoh's divinity demands further comment. As an intermediary between earthly and divine realms, Pharaoh is both man and god. Assman notes that the emphasis on the divinity of the ruler, whereby Pharaoh becomes not only god on earth but also the son of the highest god, namely the sun god Re, is the most extreme practice of sacred kingship in the ancient world.[6] This does not have the effect of placing him in the realm of the "great gods" of the Egyptian pantheon, but regarded as a lesser "good" god, dependant on the great gods for life, success and power.[7] And yet while Pharaoh was accorded this elevated status, this only extended to the execution of his office. That is, as a human being he remained fallible.

To these two realms, social and cultic, a final is significant: the battlefield. Pharaoh was, like many ancient kings, the leader of the Egyptian military, though often in an honorary capacity. As imperial aspiration grew, Pharaoh was expected to push Egypt's borders in order to grow her own wealth. Egypt's enemies were to be subdued by force. Higginbotham notes that skill in violence was so crucial for the Pharaoh that in times of peace, hunting expeditions were organized so that the Pharaoh's skills could still be demonstrated.[8]

These three key areas comprised the Pharaoh's role: administration of cult, society, and military. Each were a part of the overarching responsibility Pharaoh which was to maintain order in the physical world as a way of demonstrating the ongoing positive relations between the divine and earthly realms. By resisting the advance of the forces of chaos, demonstrated by the oppression of the poor, or the breaching of Egypt's boundaries by enemy forces, or the corruption of the cult, Pharaoh fulfilled his sacred role. In doing so, he was understood not as a human, but as a god on earth.

PHARAOH(S) IN MOSES' STORY

There are two different Pharaohs in the story of Moses. The first is the Pharaoh who famously "did not know Joseph" (Exod. 1:8), a phrase which has frustrated historically oriented[9] reading for the way in which it refuses to reveal the identity of this Pharaoh. Neither does the text explain why this new Pharaoh doesn't know Joseph. Durham suggests that this lack of knowledge refers to a radically changed set of circumstances, rather than the more stable process whereby a family member of the previous Pharaoh may ascend to the throne. Instead Durham reads this Pharaoh as the first of a new dynasty, one with no need to respect the mores of the past, including commitments to non-native inhabitants of the imperial centre.[10]

The words reach back to the final part of Genesis in which Joseph became established as the lead administrator of a previous Pharaoh's empire, and the famous story of the reconciliation of his family. That family had become a significant factor in Egypt, having "multiplied and gr[own] exceedingly strong" (Exod. 1:7). So while the Pharaoh did not know Joseph, he was more than aware of his descendants. The unfolding of the story in chapter 1 of Exodus is of the increasing fear and paranoia of the new Pharaoh, driven by a lack of knowledge regarding this group of people within his kingdom. In relation to the responsibilities of Pharaoh as we have examined them, we see a grave failure in Pharaoh's response. By setting the Israelites to forced labor with cruel conditions (Exod. 1:11–14), Pharaoh violates his role to protect the weak from the strong. In commanding the death of sons (Exod. 1:16), he violates all laws of decency. The oppressive work of the Israelites forces them to cry out, a cry which is heard by God (Exod. 2:23–25). Dozeman notes that the cry of the Israelites has no object. Typically, cries are directed towards someone, most commonly god. But in moments of great desperation, of anguish, it is impossible to use the language of lament properly.[11] So instead there is simply groaning. God hears their groan, and in opposition to the Pharaoh who did not know Joseph, the narrator reports that quite simply that after hearing their cry and remembering the covenant with Abraham, God looked upon the Israelites and God knew (Exod. 2:25). God's "knowing" sets in train a sequence of events—events which to those who would experience them could only be described as chaotic—that a new Pharaoh would be powerless to resist.

The new Pharaoh is introduced in chapter 5. Again, knowledge emerges as a crucial theme as he exclaims that he does not "know" Yhwh (Exod. 5:2), and so need not release the Israelites from their duties for three days in order to worship this unknown deity as Moses and Aaron request. Angered by their insistence, the new Pharaoh builds upon the error of the old, setting even more rigorous demands on the Israelites (Exod. 5:7–9). The new Pharaoh might not know Yhwh, nor like his predecessor does he know Joseph. But like the old Pharaoh, this new one knows about the burgeoning population of the Israelites and is keen to set them to work to build his empire. Through the work of his taskmasters, Pharaoh torments the Israelites, leading to their anguish and complaints to Moses regarding the circumstances he has brought upon them (Exod. 5:21). That sets the stage for the unleashing of the divine wonders which lead to the flight of the Israelites, and the destruction of Egypt in the face of Pharaoh, god on earth.

Having briefly examined the performance of the two Exodus Pharaohs in relation to the various responsibilities of that office and the notion of divinity, we now turn our attention to the characterization of these two individuals. While the shadow of the Pharaoh's divinity may be present, our attention is on the way in which the character is portrayed, remembering that the Pharaoh is like all other literary characters: a paper person.[12]

THE FIRST PHARAOH

The Pharaoh is introduced with a simple statement: "And a new King arose over Egypt, who did not know Joseph" (Exod. 1:8). There are two notable features to this introduction. The first is that at his first entry, the title Pharaoh is not used. Instead, this figure is referred to as the king of Egypt. Alter suggests that the failure to call this character Pharaoh at his first introduction is to have the effect of casting him as the archetypal evil king, the type of king who will kill babies.[13] The second is, as we have noted above, this king of Egypt is not only stripped of title here, but also of name. Meyers notes that the stripping of the name is most likely an intentional move, making the untitled, un-named king a representative of all tyrants who would oppress Israel.[14] That is, it too has the effect of creating an archetype, one which will have its first successor even within the development of this same story. Telling too, is the contrast the un-named Pharaoh makes with the sons of Jacob, including Joseph, whose names are rehearsed in the opening verses. They are known, remembered, their names giving them dignity in this story. This new king is not afforded any such dignity: the absence of a name serving as an act of diminution.[15]

Despite this diminution, the king still wields power. He may lack a name but is still able to speak. His first words, and the way that they are presented to us, demonstrate that the new king harbours anxiety about the strength of his rule. The narrator reports that the Pharaoh speaks to "his people" regarding the numbers of "the people of the sons of Israel" (Exod. 1:9). The Israelites are immediately placed in the position of outsider, not a part of the group of people that Pharaoh identifies as his own. As the one responsible for the stability of social life, this distinction between "us" and "them" represents a failure on his part. This "Othering" becomes the justification for the oppressive treatment that follows and is a frequent technique amongst tyrannical regimes.[16] He suggests to his people that they must deal "shrewdly" with the Israelites, a hithpael form of the word commonly translated as "wise." Dozeman notes that the way the word is used perverts something good, namely, acting wisely, into something negative,[17] a sentiment echoed by Durham who reads the Pharaoh as suggesting something along the lines of "outsmarting" the people of Israel.[18] Pharaoh's anxiety is driven by the fear of war, or this is the reason he gives in any case. Again, Pharaoh uses divisive language when he speaks of the possibility of "our" enemies coming against Egypt in war, and the possibility that "they," being the Israelites, may join them in fighting against Egypt (Exod. 1:9–10) and so escape from the land.[19] To mitigate against this possibility, the Israelites are forced into labor, building the cities of Pith and Rameses. The word to describe their labor, *sebel*, is most commonly understood as corvée labor, the least restrictive type of forced servitude in the Old Testament materials,[20] and commonly used in Ancient West Asia to expedite state sponsored projects.[21]

The forced labor is a form of oppression, highlighted by the use of the root ענה in verses 11 and 12. This root is also used to describe acts of sexual humiliation of women[22] and so suggests a particularly cruel intention. The oppression of hard labor, given as a response to the anxieties concerning the growth of the Israelite population, is clearly intended to serve as a means of physically and emotionally draining the Israelites in order to lessen their procreative energies. And yet the scheme is a failure. Against what might be normally anticipated, the increased workload only serves to bring a spike to the birth rate. The root פרץ, often translated as "spread,," can also suggest breaking out. The Egyptian program of containing the Israelite populationhas proven futile. Instead, the population grows in a fashion that breaks Egyptian attempts at control.

The Pharaoh's failed shrewdness gives way to a collective dread. קוץ can also carry a range of meanings, from fear suggested by the common translation "dread" through to hatred or loathing. The same form is used in describing the feelings of King Balak in the face of the advancing horde of Israelites in Numbers 22 and given that the number of the Israelites is common to these stories, a common translation is easily understood. But the increased severity of the Egyptians towards the Israelites may well suggest something more than fear. The presumed imperial superiority of the Egyptians had in some way been undermined by their subjects. The impotence of the Pharaoh, god on earth, had been subverted by the creative powers of imperial laborers, and the response is one of increased force and ruthlessness, the root פרך appearing in verses 13 and 14. This ruthlessness is escalated in the Pharaoh's next plan, in which he orders the murder of all Hebrew baby boys (Exod. 1:16). But a pair of midwives, Shiphrah and Puah, resist the Pharaonic decree due to their fear of god, choosing to let the boys live. Called to account for their apparent failing, the midwives explain that just as the Israelite servants demonstrate unusual procreative energies, so too, the Hebrew women are marked by their own liveliness in childbirth. God's response to the midwives actions is to continue to swell the Israelite population, and increase their strength, the very thing Pharaoh had feared in verse 9.

To this point, Pharaoh has twice acted in ways to quell the growth of the Israelite population. The first attempt was conducted in concert with a group referred to as "his people" (Exod. 1:9). Given the callous intention of Pharaoh, and the anxiety regarding war which undergirds his intention,[23] it seems unlikely that "his people" refers to the Egyptian population at large, but rather, an inner council of advisors. The second attempt seems even more covert, given that the Pharaoh approaches just two midwives. There is no sense that Pharaoh is acting as a result of a collective decision. Rather, it seems that given his attempts to oppress Israelite adults has failed, he has turned his attention to babies. Perhaps such a drastic action was too awful to seek some form of support, and so Pharaoh goes directly to two women who he imagines will offer no resistance. In this instance, the Pharaoh's desire to kill is revealed very much in secret.

Pharaoh's ineffectual strategy for dealing with the surging Israelite population, indeed, creating the very thing he had attempted to avoid, is to issue a blanket command to all his people that every boy is to be thrown into the Nile (Exod. 1:22). The terror moves from the private sphere to an overtly public one. Translations of this verse usually stipulate that it is Hebrew boys that are to be drowned, but this detail is absent from the MT, suggesting a scribal omission, but allowing an interpretation that demonstrates an unravelling of an increasingly desperate monarch. Unable to contain his frustration, the Pharaoh issues a command of senseless cruelty, which, like his previous attempts, comes to nought. His callous command is immediately followed by the story of Moses' birth and salvation, in which Pharaoh's own daughter demonstrates an indifference to the royal decree.

Having been at the centre of the story in Chapter 1, the Pharaoh disappears at the beginning of chapter 2 as the story moves between his daughter, the sister and mother of Moses, and the little boy Moses. Quickly, Moses becomes a man and a story is told of him killing a man (Exod. 2:11–12). News spreads, reaching the Pharaoh, who re-enters the story with an intention to kill. But as we have now come to expect, the Pharaoh's ambition is thwarted by Moses' flight to Midian, and "after a long time," the Pharaoh dies (Exod. 2:23).

PHARAOH (I) AS GOD-MAN

In relation to masculinity, the first Pharaoh in the Moses story is an unusual case. Clearly the Pharaoh has a positional power: he is able to institute a plan of increased hardship upon the Israelites, a plan which seems to be embraced by those charged with carrying it out. While the intended result may not have been reached, the process still had a negative impact upon the Israelites, making their lives bitter. In this sense, Pharaoh is demonstrating a type of potency related to his social position. But the embittering of lives was not the intention. The intention was to render the Israelites impotent on account of their exhaustion, and on this count, the Pharaoh is a categorical failure.[24] Rather than controlling the population, instead the population spikes to the point of inducing dread within the Egyptians. Rather than displaying wisdom as he had hoped, his plan is revealed as foolish. So in this first aspect of the story, his words have the desired effect, but his plan is unsuccessful.

Pharaoh attempts to use his positional power in his second move by coercing the midwives, but in this instance, his plan fails because of their lack of willingness to be involved. Tellingly, their motivation is reported as being "fear of God" (Exod. 1:17), a simple expression which subverts the theological claim of the divinity of the Pharaoh. DiPalma sees in this arrangement with the midwives and his reliance on them as a failure in the category of "womanlessness."[25] However, this encounter does not fit within the boundary of the womanless male, in that the category refers to emotional relationships and entanglements. The Pharaoh engages the midwives precisely in an exercise of his power, and his command demonstrates that the women have a purely instrumental value to him. He is not attached to them in any meaningful fashion. Their resistance demonstrates a waning power in relation to his persuasiveness, and as we have seen, undercuts his status as a divine being and as a male.

In the final phase of his attempt to quell the Israelite population, the Pharaoh acts with a rashness that is beyond the sort of self-control that Wilson highlights as a masculine virtue.[26] The express command to cast all Hebrew baby boys into the Nile is exactly the type of excessive violence Exodus itself rails against in chapter 21. No report is given as to the uptake of this command, but the story of Moses in the river—not thrown but carried in a pitted basket, and saved by the Pharaoh's own daughter—seems to suggest that "all his people" took a similar view of the Pharaoh's blood-thirsty plans as the midwives.

The three attempts to deal with the Israelite population serve then as an indication of the Pharaoh's inadequacies. Even his positional power, by which he was able to commence the oppression of the Israelites seems to be failing by the time Moses enters the story. Two midwives and his own daughter defy his command to kill Israelite infants, seemingly indicative of a broader indifference to the infanticide desired by the erratic god-man.

The final failure of the Pharaoh is the failure to kill Moses. There is an irony here. He wishes Moses to die because Moses has killed someone. The word used to describe Moses' killing of the Egyptian (Exod. 2:12) is נכה, a word which is commonly translated as "strike." It can carry a fatal element, as it does here, but is not necessarily so. By contrast, the Pharaoh seeks to "kill" Moses, the verb being הרג, a form which requires an intent to kill. As opposed to his earlier plans to kill people which involved other actors, in this case the Pharaoh is the subject of the verb: *he sought to kill Moses* (Exod. 2:15). But in this, Pharaoh is again unsuccessful. Three times the Pharaoh has tried to kill Moses, and on each attempt he failed. In contrast, the only thing Moses has done as an adult in the story to this point is kill someone. So in a scheme in which skill in violence is held as a primary marker, Moses has in a single act differentiated himself from Pharaoh.

The Pharaoh dies (Exod. 2:23) after a long reign. His reign, as far as the biblical story goes, is one of failure. The people he tried to eliminate have grown. And yet they have also suffered, a point well made by the narrator here at the death of their oppressor. Their suffering, and the groan and cry which accompanies it (Exod. 2:23) reaches God and animates divine knowledge. This divine knowledge is set against the Pharaoh's own lack of knowledge (Exod. 1:8). The Pharonic ignorance led to a flurry of unsuccessful actions and failure. As he dies, the report that "God knew" sounds as an ominous signal to the reader that the coming flurry of action may not be quite so impotent.

THE SECOND PHARAOH

The second Pharaoh in the story has no introduction at all. Instead, his appearance comes with an instruction from Yhwh to Moses that he will be sent to Pharaoh in order to bring the Israelites out of Egypt (Exod. 3:10). A similar idea follows later in chapter 3, when he is told that he will go to the King of Egypt with the elders in order to request a release from work for the purpose of offering sacrifices to Yhwh (Exod. 3:18). The first information about the character of this new Pharaoh immediately follows as Yhwh declares "I know, however, that the king of Egypt will not let you go unless compelled by a mighty hand" (Exod. 3:19). This statement foreshadows the plague narrative, but also gives an insight into the confrontation which will soon ensue, alerting us to the reality that Moses' task, even from God's perspective, will not be straight forward, requiring adjustment and strategy.[27]

It should hardly be a surprise that Pharaoh, a figure understood as a god-man, might resist the type of suggestion being made by Moses and the Israelite elders. The theophany at the burning bush in chapter 3 revealed that the oppression of the Israelites had not ended with the death of the first Pharaoh, and so the idea that a tyrant king might release an oppressed people for religious observance seems far-fetched. With this resistance comes an important motif which is presented here for the first time: the hardening of Pharaoh's heart. Twenty times in the ensuing narrative the heart of the Pharaoh is hardened, ten times by his own volition, and ten times by Yhwh, as is the announced intention here: "I will harden his heart, so that he will not let the people go" (Exod. 4:21). The personal resistance of Pharaoh is seemingly exacerbated by divine aggravation and perhaps even cruelty. As Wafula notes, the urgency of the deliverance of Israel which permeates chapter 3 seems to subside quickly. The use of the mighty hand—which manifests itself in the sequence of plagues—is said to have the intention of softening Pharaoh's heart, while God simultaneously works against that softening. The only consequence of this can be the elongation of suffering for the Egyptians and the delayed deliverance of the people of Israel.[28] So while the self-hardening of Pharaoh's heart is a narrative device to turn readers against him, such a simple understanding fails to recognize Yhwh's culpability in this regard. The report of Yhwh hardening the Pharaoh's heart is a part of the characterization of Pharaoh, demonstrating his relative impotence in relation to Yhwh. But in doing so, it also relieves Pharaoh of some of the responsibility surrounding the hardening of his heart, and the suffering of the Israelites. Indeed, the attitude of Yhwh to Pharaoh and Egypt more broadly is best characterized as cruelty. The hithpael עלל is used in 10:2. NRSV translates it as "made fools" of the Egyptians. JPS follows in a similar fashion with "made a mockery."

But neither of these capture the sinister tone the Hebrew implies. Alter[29] suggests "how I toyed," again, coming some way short of the aggression implied. This is the same word used in Judges 19:25 to describe the treatment of the Levite's concubine. It is far darker than toying, or making sport.[30] Goldingay comes closest in his recent translation[31] by rendering "how I acted abusively." This captures the essence of the Hebrew and demonstrates the harmful intent inherent in Yhwh's actions against Pharaoh as representative of his people.[32]

Woven through this narrative of hardening are episodes in which Pharaoh seems willing to accommodate Moses' requests. In chapter 8 during the plague of flies Pharaoh relents and tells Moses is free to worship within the land of Egypt (8:25). Even as Moses insisted the sacrifices take place far beyond the border given the danger the people of Israel would face at the hands of the aggrieved Egyptian citizens Pharaoh seemed amenable, going so far as to request prayer for himself (8:28). And yet even as the flies subsided, Pharaoh changed his mind and determined not to let the Israelites leave. Prior to the locust plague in Exod. 10 Pharaoh's advisers suggest that he should allow the Israelites leave to worship their god (10:7). Indeed, this seems more desperation rather than advice, given that the officials seem to understand that Egypt is lost. It appears that all but the Pharaoh understand that Egypt is ruined. In the face of the advice of his officials, he seems convinced and allows Moses to go with the proviso that only the men are to go. Moses refuses, and so the locusts swarm amongst Egypt. Pharaoh is moved to repentance, but on the removal of the locusts is again hardened. The plague of darkness sees him appear to relent again, but only so far as to allow people to leave with animals left behind. Again, this falls short of Moses' request, and leads to a threat from Pharaoh that Moses will die the next time they see each other (10:28).

Immediately following this threat, Pharaoh's ambivalence is presented. Confronted again by Moses, this time with the announcement of the final plague—the Passover—Pharaoh does not kill Moses. However, on this occasion Pharaoh is struck dumb by the severity of the pronouncement. He says nothing, Moses leaves, and the preparations for the Passover commence amongst the Israelite community. Pharaoh reappears after midnight, awakened by the loud cry that had rung out across Egypt. As predicted, he urges the people of Israel out to worship. Again, the characterization of Pharaoh is mixed. He speaks seemingly in fear rather than anger or rage, requesting again that they pray a blessing for him (12:32). The urgency of the Pharaoh is intensified by the people. Pharaoh's words do not seem to have a sense of expulsion, rather a ceding to the request to worship Yhwh. But the people of Egypt seem to have other ideas, hastening the departure of the Israelites and freely giving their jewellery and clothing, presumably with the wish of providing the Israelites enough resources in order to eliminate any possibility of their return.

The final sequence regarding the Pharaoh again casts him as a pawn of Yhwh. Yhwh says he will harden Pharaoh's heart in order to agitate him to pursue the Israelites, the effect being to lead the army to their watery demise at the sea of reeds. Pharaoh is told that the people of Israel have fled, and immediately recognises his folly: "What have we done!" (Exod. 14:5). He immediately raises his army and proceeds out of Egypt to find them, only to drive his army into the trap. Yhwh performs his final sign, and the might of the Egyptian army is swallowed by the waters of the sea returning to place after the people of Israel had passed on dry ground (Exod 14:26–29). All this so that Yhwh might "gain glory for myself over Pharaoh and all his army, his chariots, and his chariot drivers" (Exod. 13:18).

PHARAOH II AS GOD-MAN

While the two Pharaohs in the Exodus story are presented as distinct characters, there is certainly a good deal of similarity between them. This is particularly true in relation to their performance of masculinity. A significant category for second Pharaoh is potency. In relation to the people of Israel, like his predecessor, the new Pharaoh treats them with great cruelty. The Pharaoh is very concerned with the productivity of his workforce, demanding that Moses and Aaron stop pestering him and to return to their work (Exod. 5:4–5). In these verses we also see a reference to the growth of Israel, linking it to the opening chapter. Like the previous Pharaoh, the new Pharaoh makes changes, but for altogether different reasons. While the Pharaoh of Exodus 1 aims to stop the procreative capacities of the Israelites, the Exodus 5 Pharaoh wants only to exhaust them to the point that they no longer listen to Moses and Aaron's words of "deception" (Exod. 5:9). In this regard Pharaoh's plan is a success. The people are made to work harder, crying out against the Pharaoh for the unjust conditions placed upon them. But as well as crying against the Pharaoh, the Israelites also direct their animosity towards Moses and Aaron (Exod. 5:21), to which Moses has no response but to question God as to the purpose in calling him. This too is a mark of the success of Pharaoh's plan: not only are the people no longer listening to the deceptive words of Moses and Aaron, they are rejecting their authority amongst the community. At this point, there is a direct contrast between Moses and Pharaoh. Moses' power of persuasion seems to have been lost, a point he makes in a complaint to Yhwh in Exod. 6:12: "The Israelites have not listened to me; how then shall Pharaoh listen to me, poor speaker that I am?" This same anxiety is repeated at the conclusion of chapter 6. Pharaoh on the other hand has been able to progress his own agenda with little more than a spoken directive.

The ensuing plague narrative (chapters 7–11) continue to demonstrate Pharaoh's power in relation to the movement of the people of Israel. He repeatedly refuses to let them depart, and his decrees are observed each time. In this way, his potency remains a visible part of his outward persona. However, across this set of chapters the Pharaoh is revealed as unsure and prone to significant changes in judgement: in his inner-life, the Pharaoh suffers greatly. At times, the Pharaoh hardens his own heart, which is a way of saying that he controls his own actions and responses. However, the reports that his heart is hardened by Ywhw suggest that there are times that Pharaoh is no longer in control of his own person, being acted upon by an outside agent. In not being in control of himself, Pharaoh becomes a toy-thing, akin to a slave.[33] This loss of agency and loss of masculinity is highlighted by the ways in which is blind to the reality that his Kingdom is slipping away from him, a fact all too easily seen by his advisors. That is to say, the loss of the Kingdom is a stripping away of his potency and his honor[34] and is reflected in his double-mindedness which also corresponds to the category of wisdom. In sum, the demise of Pharaoh's agency through the course of the plague narrative is a demonstration of his failings in the matter of masculinity.

THE DEATH OF PHARAOH?

The death of the first Pharaoh of the Exodus story is noted in Exod. 2:23, with no explanation given other than that a long time had passed. The death of the second Pharaoh receives even less attention. It is unclear whether or not he is amongst "the Egyptians" tossed into the sea in Exod. 14:28, or amongst the dead in 14:30. That Pharaoh leads the charge of the Egyptians is made obvious at two points. The chase begins in 14:6–8 with the final hardening of his heart by Yhwh. Pharaoh has *his* chariot prepared, as well as six hundred other chariots and all the other chariots of Egypt. The clear sense of urgency here in the pursuit of the Israelites stems from the hardening of Pharaoh's heart, which we have seen previously leads him to impulsive, reckless behaviour. In verse 10, it is the approach of Pharaoh that alerts the Israelites to the imminent threat posed by the advancing Egyptians. As the Israelites enter the sea on dry land with the Egyptians in pursuit, the singling out of the Pharaoh disappears and instead, the actors become "the Egyptians . . . all of Pharaoh's horses, chariots and chariot drivers" (Exod. 14:23 and 26) or the "Egyptian Army (Exod. 14:24 and 28). There is ambiguity here in so far as the Pharaoh is not explicitly mentioned amongst those who are killed. But neither is there a report of him being an observer, not any mention of him returning to Egypt in defeat. This disappearance is even more mysterious given that this destruction of the Egyptian forces is intended by Yhwh to be a way to "gain glory for myself over Pharaoh" (Exod. 14:4,17,18). It is clear that the victory over Yhwh is "personal," and so the absence of Pharaoh in the reporting of the destruction is peculiar.

Perhaps we might understand it in the same fashion as we understand the broader anonymity of the Pharaoh throughout the story. That anonymity appears to be a device to a-historicise the story, and also serves as a way of dishonoring the Pharaoh within the story. By failing to acknowledge his death explicitly and so understanding him as one of "all the Egyptians" this ideological play is strengthened. A way of Yhwh gaining glory over Pharaoh is to remove Pharaoh from the story, leaving him as one dead on the seashore amongst many, a mass of death symbolising the great work Yhwh had done against the Egyptians (Exod. 14:31).

Dozeman refers to this section as "Destruction of Pharaoh and the Egyptian Army in the Red Sea,"[35] seemingly agreeing that Pharaoh perishes in the waters of the sea surrounded by his army. This view is strengthened by his subsequent analysis of the confrontation at the sea as being fought not between Israel and Egypt, but rather, Yhwh and Pharaoh.[36] I think Dozeman is correct in his reading and that Pharaoh is imagined by the narrator as perishing in the confrontation with Yhwh. This is driven by Yhwh's hardening of Pharaoh's heart, the repeated desire for Yhwh to gain glory of Pharaoh, and Pharaoh's own desire for retribution at the loss of his slaves. His lack of wisdom in pursuing the Israelites through a seabed in wheeled chariots is demonstrative of a leader operating in a way which is not governed by rational thought but by more vengeful desires. This conflation of ideas makes it difficult to imagine a scenario whereby Pharaoh does not enter the sea amongst "all the Egyptians" and so fall victim to Yhwh's destructive plan.

If we assume the death of Pharaoh in this scene, there are two related aspects which require attention. The first concerns Egyptian conceptions of death, particularly concerning the Pharaoh, and the second circles back to the issue of masculinity.

A key aspect of Egyptian thinking concerns the passage from life to death. The discovery of the *Book of the Dead*[37] and other funerary writings[38] have allowed an understanding of the way in which Egyptians conceived of the afterlife and the processes through which the deceased were prepared for this journey. Successful navigation of these post-death experiences allowed Pharaoh the opportunity to become an *akh*, or a glorified body.[39] Before taking this journey though, the body was prepared through embalmment and mummification processes. Those processes were a part of the purification processes necessary for the trial that lay ahead,[40] trials which include the weighing of the heart against *ma'at*, which is to say truth and order and the so-named "negative confession." Preparations for this journey took some seventy days and included the removal of vital organs and a forty day period of dehydration before the mummification process took place.[41] The elaborate nature of this ritual points to the reality that preservation of the body—particularly though not exclusively the body of a deceased Pharaoh—was of crucial significance. While the trial which was imagined was a spiritual trial, it was inconceivable to the Egyptian mind that the spirit and body could be separated. The un-named Pharaoh's death at the sea becomes immensely significant in so far as it robs him of the possibility of undertaking this journey towards immortality. Rather than having his body preserved and prepared for the afterlife, he is instead left to rot, food for animals of the sea, land or air. The one charged with the responsibility for holding back the forces of chaos through military prowess falls victim to them.

The second issue comes to the masculine category of the fighting male. The end of the un-named Pharaoh is military defeat and his own death. That death is hastened by his own folly and lack of self-control making this a terrible failure in masculinity. And yet in relation to masculinity, the consequences of Pharaoh's death reach much further. Throughout the narrative Yhwh has repeated the refrain that the fall of the Pharaoh was a means of self-glorification. That is, the Pharaoh is dishonored in order that Yhwh may be glorified. Throughout these chapters Pharaoh's masculinity and honor have been stripped away. From the beginning he is nameless, both a literary device, but also a means of diminution. He is outsmarted by female slaves. He loses his first-born son. His empire is flattened by a series of divinely orchestrated plagues. He drives his military into oblivion and senselessly dies amongst them. In death, his name is forgotten forever. In short, Pharaoh is revealed as an immense failure in every aspect of his life, the quintessential image of the failed man.

CONCLUSION

While there are two Pharaohs in the book of Exodus, the narrator employs a shared strategy in his characterization of each. Both remain un-named. Both unravel in the face of pressure and trouble. The first is presented as unusually paranoid and engages in a series of ever-increasingly violent acts to suppress a potential uprising. In the process he is out-witted by a pair of quick-thinking midwives whose mental acuity forms a sharp contrast with the god-man Pharaoh. The second is revealed as indecisive and ineffective. At times he is little more than Yhwh's play-thing, and Yhwh humiliates him and his empire in a drawn out series of actions that lead to his dishonorable death in the sea.

Together, they fail in every category of masculinity, even while they enjoy a level of power unimaginable to the average man.

The relation of the Pharaohs with Moses is more complicated. It is Moses' fear of the first Pharaoh which drives him into exile. This is not the fear that might play against ones' masculinity by rendering one paralyzed, but rather the fear of dying. Moses' action in killing the Egyptian proves he is not afraid to kill, nor is he rendered idle by fear.[42] Paradoxically, it seems to be this experience which prepares Moses for his return to Egypt and his confrontation with the new Pharaoh. In the face of Pharaoh's indecision and cruelty, Moses retains a steady composure and emerges as a leader within the people of Israel. When they leave Egypt, it is Moses who leads. Moses' words (both to Pharaoh and the people of Israel) and Moses' actions prove to be reliable and so in this way Moses is characterized as a more successful man than Pharaoh. His active resistance of the Pharaoh's homosocial competitiveness asserts that it is he, the man Moses, that comes closest to the hegemonic ideal.

But in the case of Pharaoh it is not the human comparison to Moses which is most damning. Rather, it is the hubris of the god-man in the face of Yhwh which is his most powerful condemnation. While Moses speaks for Yhwh, it is clear that it is the potency of Yhwh that prevails and which relegates him to the position of the un-named, un-remembered, un-manned.

NOTES

1. Brian DiPalma, "De/Constructing Masculinity in Exodus 1-4," in *Men and Masculinity in the Hebrew Bible and Beyond*, ed. Ovidiu Creangă (Sheffield: Sheffield Phoenix Press, 2010).

2. Carolyn Higginbotham, "Pharaoh," in *The New Interpreter's Dictionary of the Bible*, ed. Katherine Doob Sakenfeld (Nashville: Abingdon, 2009), 484.

3. Jan Assmann, *From Akhenaten to Moses: Ancient Egypt and Religious Change* (Cairo: American University in Cairo Press, 2014), 9.

4. Higginbotham, "Pharaoh," 484.

5. Assmann, *From Akhenaten to Moses: Ancient Egypt and Religious Change*, 9.

6. Ibid.

7. Higginbotham, "Pharaoh," 483.

8. Ibid., 484.

9. For a brief survey of the historical problems related to the interpretation of Exodus, see Thomas B. Dozeman, *Exodus*, The Eerdmans Critical Commentary (Grand Rapids: W.B. Eerdmans, 2009), 26–30.

10. John I. Durham, *Exodus*, Word Biblical Commentary (Waco: Word, 1987), 7.

11. Dozeman, *Exodus*, 92–3.

12. Mieke Bal, *Narratology: Introduction to the Theory of Narrative*, 3rd ed. (Toronto: University of Toronto Press, 2009), 113.

13. Robert Alter, *The Five Books of Moses: A Translation with Commentary* (New York: W.W. Norton & Co., 2004), 300.

14. Carol L. Meyers, *Exodus*, New Cambridge Bible Commentary (Cambridge: Cambridge University Press, 2005), 34.

15. See further, Timothy M. Willis, "Name, Naming," in *The New Interpreter's Dictionary of the Bible*, ed. Katherine Doob Sakenfeld (Nashville: Abingdon, 2009).

16. Bill Ashcroft, Gareth Griffiths, and Helen Tiffin, *Post-Colonial Studies: The Key Concepts*, 2nd ed. (New York: Routledge, 2007), 156–8.

17. Dozeman, *Exodus*, 71.

18. Durham, *Exodus*, 7.

19. Dozeman notes the irony that the Pharaoh is anxious of the Israelites in the land, and the possibility that they might soon be out of the land. Dozeman, *Exodus*, 71.

20. T. M. Lemos, *Violence and Personhood in Ancient Israel and Comparative Contexts* (Oxford: Oxford University Press, 2017), 110.

21. A biblical example is the use of labor by Solomon in his own building projects.

22. David J.A. Clines, *The Concise Dictionary of Classical Hebrew* (Sheffield: Sheffield Phoenix Press, 2009), 334.

23. Dozeman, *Exodus*, 71.

24. On Pharaoh as a failed man, see DiPalma, "De/Constructing Masculinity in Exodus 1-4."

25. Ibid., 40.

26. Stephen M. Wilson, *Making Men: The Male Coming-of-Age Theme in the Hebrew Bible* (New York: Oxford University Press, 2015), 39.

27. Meyers, *Exodus*, 60.

28. R.S. Wafula, "The Exodus Story as a Foundation of the God of the 'Fathers,'" in *Postcolonial Commentary and the Old Testament*, ed. Hemchand Gossai (London: Bloomsbury, 2019), 15.

29. Alter, *The Five Books of Moses: A Translation with Commentary*.

30. Clines, *The Concise Dictionary of Classical Hebrew*, 328.

31. John Goldingay, *The First Testament: A New Translation* (Downers Grove: IVP, 2018).

32. While not a part of the biblical tradition, Ridley Scott picks this up in his depiction of Exodus: Ridley Scott, *Exodus: Gods and Kings* (Melbourne: Informit, 2014). Ahead of the final plague, Moses cries out against the figure of Yhwh (played by an eleven old boy) saying he wants nothing to do with the destruction of life about to be meted out. Yhwh response is tonally awkward: an eleven-year old boy screaming that he won't be satisfied until Egypt is on its knees begging for the punishment to stop. Despite the awkwardness, it is clear that Scott recognises this sequence of plagues is more than sport or tomfoolery.

33. F. Gerald Downing, "Honor," in *The New Interpreter's Dictionary of the Bible*, ed. Katherine Doob Sakenfeld (Nashville: Abingdon, 2007).

34. Susan E. Haddox, "Is There a 'Biblical Masculinity'? Masculinities in the Hebrew Bible," *Word & World* 36, no. 1 (2016).

35. Dozeman, *Exodus*, 314.

36. Ibid., 317. It is worth noting here that Dozeman makes no mention of the disappearance of Pharaoh from the narrative, presumably following suit with the narrator and folding Pharaoh into the broader category of "the Egyptians."

37. *The Ancient Egyptian Book of the Dead*, trans. Andrews Carol and R.O. Faulkner (New York: MacMillan, 1985).

38. Darnell John Coleman and Darnell Colleen Manassa, *The Ancient Egyptian Netherworld Books*, Writings from the Ancient World (Atlanta: SBL Press, 2018).

39. Alan F. Segal, "Dead, Abode of The," in *The New Interpreter's Dictionary of the Bible*, ed. Katherine Doob Sakenfeld (Nashville: Abingdon, 2007), 64.

40. Assmann, *From Akhenaten to Moses: Ancient Egypt and Religious Change*, 21.

41. Carolyn Higginbotham, "Egypt," in *The New Interpreter's Dictionary of the Bible*, ed. Katherine Doob Sakenfeld (Nashville: Abingdon, 2007), 219–20.

42. Wilson, *Making Men: The Male Coming-of-Age Theme in the Hebrew Bible*, 83.

Chapter Five

Moses and Korah

Korah is introduced at the beginning of Numbers 16. A Levite, he is a descendant of Kohath, the second son of Levi (Num. 4:17), and a cousin to Aaron, Miriam, and Moses. As a Kohathite, Korah is amongst those who have responsibility for the transportation of the most holy things. Their clan camped on the south side of the tabernacle precinct, creating a barrier in order to prevent the camp violating the sacred space.[1] Their clan was significant in the vision of the community given by Numbers 4. Of the three tribes appointed, those of Kohath, Gershon and Merari, it is only of the Kohathites that it is said that their clan must never be destroyed (4:17), so that Levine calls the Kohathites the highest ranking of the three Levitical clans.[2] It seems clear that Korah and his kin occupy a significant place in the newly configured community. But not as significant as they would like, so it seems.

Korah comes leading a rebellion. With some prominent Reubenites, and 250 other well-known leaders of the congregation, Korah confronts his cousins with accusations of arrogance and holding too tightly to cultic leadership. Moses' response to Korah and his followers, and the events which transpire represent in some sense the very pinnacle of Moses' demonstrations of masculinity through his story. Korah comes at Moses as a powerful figure; a leading member of a significant clan, and with the capacity to rally other leading figures to his cause. And yet his challenge falters nearly as quickly as it begins in the face of Moses' response.

WHAT'S IN A NAME?

The first thing we learn about Korah is his name. Korah is the Hebrew word for baldness (the root being קרח), most commonly, the type of intentional baldness that accompanies rites of mourning.[3] According to Hebrew law, this type of intentional baldness is prohibited for both Priests and regular men of Israel (Deut. 14:1). This naming has a bearing on the ideology of the story but is also significant in a discussion framed by masculinity. In regards to the first, it appears that Korah's complaint has to do with the Priestly roles being held exclusively by the Amramite clan. Amram was a son of Kohath, which is to say, Korah is a close relative of Moses and Aaron, and so his actions carry a significance beyond those of a member of a different tribe. Korah is family, and so his rebellion is familial and social.

And yet, in his name, the narrator hints that Korah is unworthy for the office to which he aspires. The text does not say that Korah is bald, but the choice of name creates an allusion. In the same way that Jacob's and Cozbi's name are designed to draw attention to their deceptive qualities, [4] so too, Korah's name suggests something about him. The narrator hints that Korah is bald, or balding, implicitly linking him with the prohibited Canaanite mourning rituals. A possible implication is that Korah has willfully engaged in these practices, practices which threaten the holiness of the community which he claims for it: "All the congregation are holy, every one of them" (Num. 16:3) he says, while his name hints at something altogether different. The narrator subverts the entirety of Korah's challenge in the simple act of naming. This is important data: the building of character begins immediately from the first act of characterization,[5] creating inferences from which we begin to construct the character in our own minds.

The issue of hair is an interesting one in the context of the Old Testament materials, particularly as it relates to masculinity. As Pilch notes, hair—and baldness—is multivocal, and so carries a possible range of meanings.[6] Three brief examples will help illustrate the semiotic richness of hair. The first is perhaps the most famous hair in the bible, that of Samson (Judg. 13–16). As a result of his mother's vow to raise Samson as a Nazirite, Samson's hair remains uncut (Num. 6:5). His hair comes to represent his super-human, hyper-masculine strength. When he reveals the secret of his strength to his lover (Judg. 16:17), Delilah, she engineers a situation whereby she can make financial gain from his capture, having his hair cut while he slept, thereby allowing Samson to be overcome by his Philistine enemies. Hairiness is a symbol of masculine strength. The hairy Esau is presented as more masculine than his smooth-skinned Jacob (Gen. 27:11), and as Hilary Lipka has noted, the shaving of beards of captured warriors was a means of humiliation given that beards are a masculine feature associated with the performance of hegemonic masculinity.[7] The change in appearance rendered by another person only serves to increase the shame, differentiating it in some way from natural patterns of hair loss. This same aspect is shared by Samson whose masculinity is undone both in the alteration to his physical appearance, in his case by a woman, but also in his lack of wisdom in revealing his secret in the first instance.

The second is that of the son of David, Absalom. Absalom is described as the most beautiful man in all Israel (2 Sam 14:25). While his entire body is said to be without blemish, it is his magnificent hair that the narrator seems most taken by. Bodner playfully notes that the description of Absalom suggests he is "a cut above"[8] the other hairy characters, most notably Esau and Samson. Rather than being bald, or even thinning, Absalom's annual hair cut provided two hundred shekels, or in excess of two kilograms of hair. By the end of the year, the narrator reminds us in something of an understatement, this weight of hair became heavy upon him. Absalom's hair is tied to his beauty and charisma, a combination which he uses to win the hearts of the people of Israel as he attempts a coup against his father. While that coup is ultimately unsuccessful, it is clear that Absalom's beauty, most clearly manifest in his luxurious hair, makes quite an impression on the narrator and Absalom's would-be subjects. Kirova notes that in Absalom's case, the hair is symbolic of a range of masculine ideals, seeing its abundance as a euphemism for sexual prowess and virility.[9] The combination of his physical perfection, his abundant hair, and sexual prowess serves as a strategy in building Absalom up as a rightful ruler in the fashion of Saul and David, both of whom are similarly praised for aspects of their physical appearance. Attractiveness serves as a marker of divine favor: Yahweh appears to have a preference for the beautiful.[10] In this case, it serves as a ruse. In the end, Absalom is revealed as a villain and his legendary hair proves to be his undoing.[11] During his attempted *coup d'état* his hair becomes tangled, leaving him defenseless against the pitiless Joab (2 Sam. 18:9–15). Macwilliam finds here an acknowledgment of Absalom's beauty symbolized in his hair, but alongside it an unease and jealousy.[12] While physical attractiveness may be important for masculine performance, it can also serve to make one vulnerable.

The third example is that of Elisha. In 2 Kings 2:23–25, Elisha has an encounter with some young boys near Bethel. The young boys see the prophet coming, but unaware of his identity call out to him: עלה קרח עלה קרח which translates as "Go up baldy, go up baldy!" Alter translates עלה as "Away with you,"[13] coming close to the NRSV which opts for "Go away." The word translated "baldy" is the same root which gives us the name Korah. The reason for the boys taunt is unclear, though the content of it may simply be enough. That is, baldness makes a stranger an easy target for boys looking to have fun. Olyan notes that baldness may also be understood to be considered "ugly."[14] In the same way that long hair is considered beautiful, loss of hair stands against it. We can hardly imagine someone saying, "Get out of here, you with the beautiful, flowing hair." Elisha's response—a curse which results in young boys being mauled by bears—suggests that perhaps this wasn't the first time that the prophet had been on the wrong side of this type of jeering.

These three examples illustrate something about perceptions of hair. It is important to note that these are not rules or to be uniformly applied in all circumstances. However, these examples do provide a context to think about the symbolic meaning of hair and how such attitudes might inform a reading of Korah. Hair can represent strength, beauty, and social acceptance. Lack of hair, then, potentially serves to bring the opposite of these things.

KORAH AND THE CROWD

A crucial aspect of the presentation of Korah is that is he is a leader. He bursts onto the scene leading a crowd of men, well-known men, to confront Moses and Aaron regarding their own leadership. This seems to suggest that Korah is an influential fellow, as we might have guessed from the genealogy provided earlier. Here, with this report, the inference is confirmed. Korah is a man who can lead and influence other prominent people and rally them behind a cause. An important way of understanding characters is to observe the way in which other figures in the story react to them.[15] While we don't have access to Korah's discussions with these men who make up his crowd, we can certainly hazard a guess that they have been stirred by his rhetoric, to the point of joining a march to confront Moses and Aaron, the leaders of the people.

The use of the word *laqah*, translated as "took" here, demonstrates the force of Korah's rhetorical skill. It is a word that implies strength and aggression, commonly used in reference to sexualized violence. So Korah "taking" these men to confront Moses suggests a certain menace on his part, so that we might imagine this crowd as a mob.

Korah's power with words is promptly on display. While the text allows a certain ambiguity, in so far as the speaker is not explicitly identified, the presentation of Korah in the first verse and Moses' response directed specifically to him in verse five seems to be clear enough evidence that Korah acts as the spokesperson for the mob. He immediately is on the attack: "You have gone too far! All the congregation, all of them are holy, and the LORD is among them. So why do you exalt yourselves above the assembly of the LORD?"

These are not words of reconciliation or gentle reason. The question which comes at the end does not present as an invitation to dialogue, but instead as an accusation. Korah looks to take control of the conversation,[16] and to force Moses into a defensive posture. They are the words of an aggressor, and they are also the only words that we hear from Korah. Given that communication is a key way that characters are developed,[17] the narrator gives us an important piece of data here: Korah is presented as a combative individual, a person interested in confrontation.

An interesting aspect of Korah's tactic is his rhetoric of totality. "All the congregation, all of them are holy." Zornberg describes his view as presenting an "oceanic holiness as the condition of the people."[18] That is, Korah presents himself not only in concert with the 250 men standing behind him, but rather on behalf of the entirety of the congregation. So not only does Korah present as combative, he also presents as a popular representative, his all-inclusive rhetoric seemingly designed to galvanize those that stand behind him, and those in the congregation who hear him.

MOSES' RESPONSE

In response to Korah's allegations, Moses falls on his face. There is no indication of how long he stayed prostrated before them, nor a reason given for this dramatic gesture. In normal circumstances, such prostration is a symbol of submission or grief.[19] Both possibilities are possible readings here. Moses could be grieving this mutiny against him, as it possibly represents a removal of God's blessing of him. We might simply read this as an act of despair from Moses.[20] If it is submission, the reading is a little more ambiguous. Is Moses submitting to Korah? And is that how Korah understands this action? Or is the act of prostration an act before the Lord? Later in the chapter (vs. 22) both Moses and Aaron lie prostrate before the Lord as they seek a reprieve for the congregation against the Lord's wrath. Milgrom suggests that Moses is seeking guidance from the Lord here, though he notes that that action would most commonly take place in the tabernacle, which does not appear to be the case.[21] So the intention of Moses' actions are unclear and allow a range of possible understandings.

At some point, he presumably rises to his feet and issues a test to Korah and the dissenters that will prove the legitimacy of Aaronic priesthood. Moses does this boldly, taunting Korah and the crowd, and bringing his own charges against them. Moses paints their rebellion as one against not he and Aaron, but rather, against the Lord (vs. 11). He combines rhetorical questions with statements regarding the Lord's great generosity to them (vs. 9) in order to ridicule this sense of ambition or entitlement. Moses' confidence is obvious. There is no evidence of the self-doubting of Exod. 3. Instead, we have a man of unusual strength and skill in matters of speech.

At the moment of decision, it seems that Moses persuades the congregation that his position is correct. In order to prevent innocent people being consumed in the punishment about to be meted out to the rebels, Moses calls on the congregation to separate themselves from the "wicked men" (vs. 26), which the people do. Their movement away from them suggests they have changed their minds about the legitimacy of Korah's claims. Korah and his men however, remain defiant, and as Moses suggests, are soon swallowed up by the ground, they and all their families, proving the special role held by Aaron and Moses, and that the rebels had despised the Lord.

MOSES AND KORAH

An interesting dynamic of this confrontation has to do with the matter of familial relations. Korah is a Kohathite. So too, Moses and Aaron, the objects of his rebellion. So the actions of Korah hit, literally, close to home. The clan, or *mishpaḥah*, is a "structural level between a tribe and ancestral houses" in Israelite society.[22] Clans are organizational units in regard to matters such as agricultural and military arrangement. As Boer has noted, the clan was the primary social horizon by which people understood their place in the world.[23] Clans were ideally endogamous in their practices, and so were heavily reliant upon each other in all matters of human life. It is important to note, though, that clan practices were often more fluid and flexible than the laws which codify behaviors. Nonetheless, clan identity was significant in regards to Israelite identity.

Korah's actions, then, bring internal clan tensions into public view. In some sense, the public disgrace of Moses and Aaron which Korah attempts also serves to dishonor his own family.[24] This action of confrontation is not unknown: men from within a particular lineage can confront each other, or other clans on the basis of dispute.[25] However, what differentiates Korah's actions from such normal practice is that he seeks to use a broader platform to address his own feelings of entitlement within his family unit, drawing on support from across the width of the congregation. Rabbis thought that Korah's mutiny was related to the leadership of the family, given that Moses and Aaron, sons of Amram had taken on national leadership roles. He, as the eldest son of the second son, Izhar, was the rightful leader of the family. However, that role had fallen to a younger cousin.[26]

Boer notes that in egalitarian societies, there is often a suspicion of those who become powerful, and an imagination of some secret society which allows this elevation.[27] The Moses-Korah relationship illustrates this point perfectly, and indeed goes beyond it is some respects, because it is not suspicion that animates Korah, but jealousy. And the secret society which elevates Moses and Aaron is not human, but divine.

DISAPPEARING KORAH

Extraordinarily, after the fervor of his initial complaints, Korah essentially disappears from the story. He remains the object of Moses' interest, but has no verbal response to Moses' reply. Thomas notes that who speaks most in a conversation can be an important interpretive clue,[28] and it seems that the narrator silences Korah as a way of indicating his defeat at the voice of Moses. While Korah stays silent, Moses speaks decisively, addressing Korah and the rebels and going so far as to taunt Korah by using his own words against him: "You Levites have gone too far!" Korah comes across as one-dimensional, lacking the mental agility to engage Moses in a debate. He remains in the narrative as an antagonist, but only acts in response to Moses' directives (vss. 16–19). He engages in no further dialogue, and is soon swallowed up by the ground in an act of divine judgement and Mosaic justification. His descent into Sheol along with the members of his family bring a shocking end to his attempted rebellion. Moses is confirmed as the undisputed leader of Israel, by the power of both his words and actions.

ON MASCULINITY

Persuasion

Skill with words is an integral part of being a successful male in Israel.[29] As our narrative analysis has demonstrated, both Moses and Korah give evidence of this ability in this particular passage. For Korah, some of his skill in persuasion is implied. That is, it appears that he is the driving figure of the rebellion, and so we can assume that it is he who has been able to inspire these other leading figures from the congregation to join with him in his stand against Moses and Aaron. By implication, these other men are also happy for Korah to speak on their behalf, suggesting that they recognize that Korah is equipped for this task. When Korah does speak, he does evince a certain style: combative, yes, but also effective, at least in the short term. He uses a mixture of rhetorical techniques which seem to make an impression upon Moses, to the point that he collapses on his face before him. It appears—at least in this moment—that Korah has won the day by the power of his words.

When Moses does speak, the dynamic of the scene shifts. No longer is he under attack, but instead, he seems to be the one controlling the events. It is he who announces the test to determine the legitimacy of the challenge, and this is accepted without a murmur. Having secured that detail, Moses goes on the attack, bitingly turning Korah's words against him in a manner which renders him mute. When the climactic moment arrives, Moses denounces

Korah and his followers as wicked men, rather than the holy ones they presented themselves as previously.

Honor

Related to this issue of speech is honor. Traditional honor/shame theories
suggest that honor is gained at the expense of another. In vying for soci-
etal respect, honor could be won, and conversely, shame bestowed in such
a contest.[30] The public confrontation that Korah initiates with Moses is an
example of such a contest. Korah seeks to publicly humiliate Moses, and
simultaneously boost his own social capital. As Haddox points out, displays
of honor require honesty and forthright speech.[31] Whether Korah is honest
is a matter of interpretation, but no one could argue against the forthright
nature of his speech, and so there is a degree of honor in the way in which
Korah approaches his actions. Mitigating this, however, is the reality that he
brings familial matters into a public domain, bringing shame to his clan, with
a particular blow to himself as the head of a household. Further, rather than
protecting his family (a crucial aspect of honor), Korah puts his family in a
position of grave danger.

Moses responds to the provocation by falling on his face, an act of submission which seems to suggest an acknowledgment of shame on his part.
However, his response, including the challenge of a definitive test, and his
own forthrightness certainly demonstrates that in this battle for honor, Moses
emerges victorious. By the end of the story, not only have the congregation
appeared to rally behind him, but his challenger comes to a violent end.

Potency

These two preceding categories tie into the notion of potency which Haddox
sees as crucial to masculine performance.[32] Potency most commonly refers to
success in violence and the capacity to procreate. The second of these is not
in view in this story, though we certainly see elements of violence in the smiting of Korah and his family. While the earthquake is noted as a divine act of
judgement, it is clear that it is Moses who benefits from it, and who appears
to know that it will happen.

Haddox also identifies skill in leadership as a component of potency. Both
men demonstrate capacity in this regard. Korah successfully convinces a
large group of men to support him, a work both of his persuasive skills, as
we have seen, and an indication of his abilities as a leader. But, as before,
Moses trumps Korah, being able to demonstrate his own superior leadership
abilities, which is highlighted by his submission to God. Korah's aggression

is met with an act of humility, and while this leads to Moses' own offensive, it seems that his demonstration of submission is regarded as evidence of his superior leadership.

On Hair

For all the material in the scriptures concerning Moses, we have no inference at all regarding his appearance, a common strategy in the building up of characters more broadly.[33] This is typical of biblical narrative, which is notably sparse in giving up this type of information. We know that Saul was unusually tall and handsome (1 Sam. 9), that Joseph is beautiful of form (Gen. 39:6), and, as we have seen already, that Absalom's hair was regarded as being particularly attractive. But even these definitions give little in the way of assisting a mental reconstruction. So Moses is more typical than atypical in this regard. It appears that his physical appearance is insignificant to the performance of his masculinity.

Korah also suffers an absence of physical description, but for one aspect: it is suggested that he is bald[ing]. We have noted already the significance of hair as a symbol of strength in the case of Samson and other warriors, or of male beauty in the case of Absalom. It seems reasonable to assume that hairiness—of head and face—was understood as being significant in assessments of masculinity (even when, as we have seen, masculine beauty serves to make a male vulnerable in the face of male jealousy).[34] The intent, then, appears to be a slight against him. In the same way that Saul distinguishes himself by his height, Korah is disqualified on account of his receding hairline. The handsome appearance, including a thick head of hair, which characterizes "real manhood" appears to be absent from the person of Korah.[35] It is important to note that baldness is not feminizing. As Graybill notes, baldness is a thoroughly male trait, one that indicates a departure from idealized embodiment.[36]

While the data regarding the physical appearance of Moses and Korah is limited, names often carry a metonymic function, and in this instance, Korah's name suggests something about his physical appearance, which, on the balance of other examples, appears to be pejorative. Graybill compares Elisha's baldness with his mentor Elijah, the so called "lord of the hair" The effect of the comparison is to highlight the relative masculinity of the two, a comparison which favors Elijah.. While we don't have such a colorful comparison between Moses and Korah—and certainly Moses is in no way a mentor to Korah—but we do have what appears to be a diminution of Korah. While Moses' appearance is not a matter of concern in the text here, and so we cannot explicitly claim that trumps Korah in this regard, it does appear that Korah's attempt at hegemonic masculinity is attacked, if only in a subtle way, through the choice of his name.

CONCLUSION

Numbers 16 is a story where passions run hot. It is a story of challenge, rebellion, even treachery. Homosocial dysfunction abounds! A family dispute is aired for public consumption. A man, who imagines himself entitled to more than he holds, wages a public showdown with his cousin. It is a battle of many things, but close to the surface of all them is a battle for manly superiority. Korah seeks a higher station, a station that is already solely reserved for men, but a group of men from which he is excluded. Here is the quintessential competitiveness at the heart of male-male homosociality and its buttressing of hegemonic masculinity. Drawing on his considerable personal resources and skills, Korah seeks a way to drag down Moses, and in doing so, drag himself up.

And yet in the face of this significant challenge, it is Moses who prevails. It is his skill with words, his gifts of leadership, his public actions of humility, which enable him to win the day. Korah is not only marginalized, he is destroyed, and his family with him. It is a horrific picture, no question. But it is a clear sign that the authority of Moses' leadership is beyond human dispute, and that any man who comes against him does so at great risk to themselves.

NOTES

1. Kevin A. Wilson, "Kohath, Kohathite," in *The New Interpreter's Dictionary of the Bible*, ed. Katherine Doob Sakenfeld (Nashville: Abingdon, 2008), 546.

2. Baruch A. Levine, "Korah, Korahites," ibid., 547.

3. John J. Pilch, "Baldness," ibid. (2006), 386.

4. See, Anthony Rees, "[Re]Naming Cozbi: In Memoriam, Cozbi, Daughter of Zur," *Biblical Interpretation* 20, no. 1–2 (2012).

5. Alan Palmer, *Fictional Minds*, Frontiers of Narrative (Lincoln: University of Nebraska Press, 2004), 40.

6. Pilch, "Baldness."

7. Hilary Lipka, "Shaved Beards and Bared Buttocks: Shame and the Undermining of Masculine Performance in Biblical Texts," in *Being a Man: Negotiating Ancient Constructs of Masculinity*, ed. Ilona Zsolnay, Studies in the History of the Ancient near East (London: Routledge, 2017), 182–3.

8. Keith Bodner, *The Rebellion of Absalom* (London: Routledge, 2014), 52.

9. Milena Kirova, *Performing Masculinity in the Hebrew Bible*, Hebrew Bible Monographs (Sheffield: Sheffield Phoenix Press, 2020), 20.

10. Saul M. Olyan, *Disability in the Hebrew Bible: Interpreting Mental and Physical Differences* (Cambridge: Cambridge University Press, 2008), 23.

11. Stuart Macwilliam, "Ideologies of Male Beauty and the Hebrew Bible," *Biblical Interpretation* 17 (2009): 280.

12. Ibid.

13. Robert Alter, *Ancient Israel: The Former Prophets: Joshua, Judges, Samuel, and Kings: A Translation with Commentary*, 1st ed. (New York: W. W. Norton & Co., 2013), 739.

14. Olyan, *Disability in the Hebrew Bible: Interpreting Mental and Physical Differences*, 20.

15. Mieke Bal, *Narratology: Introduction to the Theory of Narrative*, 3rd ed. (Toronto: University of Toronto Press, 2009), 127.

16. Bronwen Thomas, "Dialogue," in *The Cambridge Companion to Narrative*, ed. David Herman (Cambridge: Cambridge University Press, 2007), 84.

17. Uri Margolin, "Character," ibid., ed. David Herman, 72.

18. Avivah Gottlieb Zornberg, *Moses: A Human Life*, Jewish Lives (New Haven: Yale University Press, 2016), 129.

19. Baruch A. Levine, *Numbers 1-20 : A New Translation with Introduction and Commentary*, 1st ed. (New York: Doubleday, 1993), 363.

20. Jacob Milgrom, *Numbers: The JPS Torah Commentary*, ed. Nahum M. Sarna, JPS Torah Commentary (Philadelphia: Jewish Publication Society, 1990), 131.

21. Ibid.

22. Timothy M. Willis, "Clan," in *The New Interpreter's Dictionary of the Bible*, ed. Katherine Doob Sakenfeld (Nashville: Abingdon, 2006), 679.

23. Roland Boer, *The Sacred Economy of Ancient Israel*, ed. Douglas A. Knight, Library of Ancient Israel (Louisville: Westminster John Knox, 2015), 87.

24. Timothy M. Willis, "Family," in *The New Interpreter's Dictionary of Te Bible*, ed. Katherine Doob Sakenfeld (Nashville: Abingdon, 2007), 428.

25. Ibid.

26. Milgrom, *Numbers: The JPS Torah Commentary*, 129.

27. Boer, *The Sacred Economy of Ancient Israel*, 50.

28. Thomas, "Dialogue," 84.

29. David J.A. Clines, "David the Man: The Construction of Masculinity in the Hebrew Bible," in *Interested Parties: The Ideology of Writers and Readers of the Hebrew Bible* (Sheffield: Sheffield Academic Press, 1995), 219.

30. F. Gerald Downing, "Honor," in *The New Interpreter's Dictionary of the Bible*, ed. Katherine Doob Sakenfeld (Nashville: Abingdon, 2007), 884.

31. Susan E. Haddox, "Is There a 'Biblical Masculinity'? Masculinities in the Hebrew Bible," *Word & World* 36, no. 1 (2016): 6.

32. Ibid.

33. Margolin, "Character," 72.

34. Macwilliam, "Ideologies of Male Beauty and the Hebrew Bible."

35. Clines, "David the Man: The Construction of Masculinity in the Hebrew Bible," 223.

36. Rhiannon Graybill, "Elisha's Body and the Queer Touch of Prophecy," *Biblical Theology Bulletin* 49, no. 1 (2019): 32.

Chapter Six

Moses and Phinehas

The relationship between Phinehas and Moses is different to the others examined in this project. Indeed, there is a sense in which defining the link between Phinehas and Moses as a relationship may be stretching things too far. Together, they share only one scene, one which contains no dialogue between them. In fact, Phinehas says nothing at all. Everything we learn about him comes through the reporting of his actions by the narrator, and the commendation of those actions by Yhwh as he speaks to Moses in their aftermath. So rather than a relationship, we have a comparison; a comparison which brings great praise to Phinehas, and by nature of comparison, great shame to Moses.

We will examine the actions of Phinehas and of Moses, distinct as there are from each other and consider the contrast between them which is invited by Yhwh's interpretation of Phinehas' actions. Having done that, we will think through the scene with relation to relevant categories of masculinity. Given the nature of this story, in which women are both visible and victim, we will also consider the vulnerability of women inherent of displays of masculinity. This will include the daughters of Moab's victimization at the hands of their own men and of Israel, and the case of the Midianite woman whose life is taken at the centre of this story.

INTRODUCING PHINEHAS

Phinehas first appears in the scriptures in a genealogy. In Exod. 6:25 we learn that he is the son of Eleazer, the son of Aaron. This makes him the great-nephew of Moses, and more importantly, marks his priestly credentials as a direct descendant of Aaron. His name is of Egyptian origin, and appears to make reference to Phinehas' skin tone, suggesting he is a dark-skinned man.

As we have seen in the examination of Korah in Num. 16, these familial matters cause some deal of controversy for Moses, and while Phinehas does not directly oppose Moses in the fashion of a mutiny in the way his uncle does, nonetheless, the actions of Phinehas have an alternate set of consequences. While in the rebellion of Korah Moses emerges as a heroic figure, in this instance, the results are not so positive. As I have suggested elsewhere,[1] it is evident that it is Phinehas who is intended to emerge as the hero in this story, not Moses.

Phinehas' Priestly credentials are reinforced as he enters the scene in Numbers 25, with his father and grandfather again listed at his first mention (Num. 25:7). This repetition is not coincidental. It is an intentional act by the narrator to characterize Phinehas in a particular way, a way of building up expectation, even before Phinehas has even entered the story.[2] Phinehas' father Eleazer had been placed in charge of the sanctuary (Num. 3:32), guarding it against anything which might threaten the holiness of the precinct. Guarding the sacral precinct was a constant reality for the Levites, a pattern common to the surrounding nations' religious officials.[3] Intentionally, the narrator links Phinehas to this responsibility through his father, Eleazer.

NUMBERS 25:1–5—AN OVERVIEW

Numbers 25 has been the subject of significant scholarly work in recent times. The mix of gender issues, ethnic tensions and religious extremism with sex and violence mark it as a text with significant relevance in our own time.[4] These thematic matters emerge from a text which raises a number of questions quite apart from ones of masculinity which warrant some attention here.

The people of Israel are gathered at the tent of meeting, mourning the plague which had struck them on account of their apostasy at Baal Peor (Num. 25:1–5, 8). The context here is important. The people are gathered in a communal lament because of the events described in vss. 1–5, events which included acts of sexual congress with Moabite women as well as acts of worship to the Moabite gods. The location of their lament, Shittim, is the last stopping place of the Israelites before their crossing of the Jordan and destruction of Jericho (Num. 33: 50). This suggests that the story of Numbers 25 continues the narrative established in Numbers 22 where we read that the Israelites camp in the plains of Moab (Num 22:1). Some sort of engagement with Moabites, then, does not seem out of place, though the nature of the engagement—liturgical and sexual—has compromised the people of Israel who are now suffering a plague on account of their idolatry.

ON WOMEN (I): THE PEOPLE OF ISRAEL AND THE DAUGHTERS OF MOAB

Thus far, our reading of the biblical scenes has stuck close to the story as it is told to us. The story of Numbers 25, dangerous as it is for women, demands a slightly more expansive approach, particularly as it relates to the daughters of Moab (Num. 25:1). The narrator's version of the story suggests that "the people" (being Israel), whore themselves with the "daughters of Moab" through involvement in liturgical meals and actions, the result being a binding of Israel with Baal of Peor (Num. 25:3). It is worth noting here that throughout, the collective terms "the people" and "Israel" is used to describe the people of Israel, while feminine language is used to name Moabite involvement. Interestingly, the people of Israel are feminized, given that the form "whored" is grammatically feminine. This is an important point: the whores are not the daughters of Moab, but rather, the people of Israel.

A recent paper has demonstrated the ways in which the inclusive terms for Israel create a means of highlighting the possibility of reading this text in a way which de-centres a hetero-normative approach.[5] Eller rightly argues that amongst the Israelite congregation are women who may also find themselves drawn to the daughters of Moab. It is not my intention to dismiss this way of approaching the text precisely because it allows women agency over their own sexual expression in ways which, as we have seen, are often violently suppressed in patriarchal societies. Nonetheless, the presentation of the "daughters of Moab" is made problematic by early reception of this story.

At the end of Numbers 24, Balaam, having frustrated the Moabite King due to his lack of willingness to curse the Israelites, returns to his home (Num. 24:25). However, in the report of the war on Midian in Numbers 31, Balaam is listed as a casualty in a list which includes the five Midianite kings (Num. 31:8), suggesting he is a high-profile victim of the war. Balaam's role in the war and the events of Num. 25:1–3 have been imagined in the history of the story's reception.[6] Both Philo[7] and Josephus[8] imagine a scenario whereby Balaam is responsible for the setting of a trap for the Israelites. In both accounts Balaam is pictured as an advisor to the Moabite elders, suggesting they put their women near the Israelite camp with the instruction to lure the Israelite men, thereby angering Israel's god and ensuring the safety of Moab. This story enlarges a brief report in Revelation 2:14, that likewise presents Balaam as an advisor to Balak suggesting that the tradition was widespread by the 1st Century, even while it has no basis in the Hebrew Bible materials. The daughters of Moab are given an instrumental value: their sex. They do not offer themselves, they are offered. In an attempt to maintain power and political independence—a man's game—women's bodies are weaponized.

Reading this alongside the material on masculinity we have considered is instructive. A plan such as this only proceeds on the basis that feminine sexuality is controlled by men. The daughters of Moab are put at risk and their bodies used as a weapon by the Moabite leadership. In the biblical materials, the daughters of Moab are visible, the men who put them in harm's way lurking in the shadows. The daughters of Moab play their role and "invite" the people of Israel to them. The plan works: Yahweh is angered and orders the execution of the heads of the people in order to turn the divine wrath, and Moses orders the death of the men bound to Baal of Peor (Num. 25:1–5). This identification of men as the ones punished is significant because it corresponds to the suggestion in Philo and Josephus that men were responsible in the first place. Their punishment is not recorded, and their punishment in no way diminishes the trauma inflicted on the daughters of Moab by their own men, nor the Israelite men who used them. They are left to bear their damage, the Moabite men left untouched.

NUMBERS 25:6-18—AN OVERVIEW

At verse 6, the narrative shifts. The particle הנה introduces a new perspective as the view shifts from the breadth of the entire Israelite camp to a single couple.[9] Into that lamenting community comes the man and woman, seemingly disregarding the distress being felt by the community, and the cause of it.[10] Phinehas is introduced in verse 7 as a witness to the arrival of a couple to the congregation, identified as an Israelite man and a Midianite woman. The introduction of the woman as Midianite is significant because it marks her as "other" to the Moabite women who were part of the first five verses, even while Moabites and Midianites are often linked. In Num. 22:4 Moab laments the marauding Israelites to a group identified as the elders of Midian. When the Moabite King dispatches a delegation to engage the prophet Balaam in Num. 22:7, the delegation includes elders of both Moab and Midian. Balaam is later killed in the Midianite war which is commanded at the conclusion of this story, his reputation as a Yahwist tainted by the advice—an extra-biblical story—offered to the Moabites. Both groups have complicated receptions in the biblical materials. The Moabites prove to be a snare here, but the book of Ruth posits the Moabitess Ruth as an ancestor of the great King of memory, David. Midian has already given us Jethro and Zipporah—foundational figures in the life of Moses and so Israel—but as a result of this story become the victims of a significant war event.[11] It appears then that the text contains two traditions, collapsed here into a single story, yet showing evidence of differing provenance.

Immediately upon seeing them, Phinehas responds, leaving the congregation and taking a spear in his hand. When Phinehas, the son of Eleazer, a guard of the precinct takes a spear in hand and follows the couple, the reader is able to anticipate what is to come. Phinehas marches into the family tent and executes the offending couple. The only surprise is the brutality of the deed, the narrator reporting that the spear pierces the two of them through her belly, suggesting that these two were engaged in sexual activity, in parallel to the sexual activity reported in the first five verses. A textual note is in order here. The Hebrew is ambiguous in verse 8 due to the repeated use of the root הבק. The first time it is used is to refer to Phinehas' following of the couple into their "tent," the second referring to the point of his sword thrust. On the second use, the noun carries the third-person feminine possessive ending, translated here as "her belly," but as Reif and others have argued,[12] the use of "tent" could be justified on grammatical grounds, the word being the same as "shrine" in Arabic. In this way, the sin of idolatry in vss. −5 is linked to this new story. Such conclusions do not, though, fit with other aspects of the story, or its reception in other references to this event in the biblical, most notably Psalm 106.[13]

Having killed the couple, Phinehas disappears from the story, the narrator telling us that the action of the guard has served to put an end to a plague which has been afflicting the Israelites.

In regards to the characterization of Phinehas, then, we have not too much to say at this point. The narrator has been keen to stress his family linkages to Eleazer, Aaron, and by extension, Moses. By virtue of that link, in particular to Eleazer, he is presented as a guard of the sacral precinct. The encroachment of Zimri and Cozbi cause him to react with lethal force. He does so with no discussion nor warning. Instead, Phinehas is the quintessential man of action, immediately responding to a situation and acting to resolve it. Remembering the emphasis of his Priestly credentials, this act is understood in decidedly religious terms.

ON MOSES

The Moses of Numbers 25 is a curious individual. The people of Israel have involved themselves with the daughters of Moab in acts of worship of their gods, and as a part of those rituals, have engaged in sexual activity with them. Moses has had nothing to say about this. It seems unlikely that he would have been unaware of so serious a misdemeanor on what appears to be a large scale, and so we might detect a subtle critique of Moses in these early verses, particularly in light of how the scene develops. Yhwh is aware of what is unfolding, and orders Moses to impale the chiefs in the sun in order to turn away the fierce wrath of God from the congregation (Num. 25:4). Pressler notes that the reason the chiefs are singled out for punishment is not clear.[14] It is the "sons of Israel" that commit the offense, a group far larger than the "heads of the people" who are decreed to wear the punishment. It appears that the leaders are to suffer on account of their failure of vigilance,[15] their punishment being a type of substitutionary arrangement. What is curious is Moses' response to this divine decree. Rather than gathering the heads and erecting the poles for impalement, he calls the chiefs in and orders them to execute the offenders from within their own tribes (vs. 5). Having made the declaration as to how the punishment was to be meted out, the focus of the story shifts, with no indication given regarding the execution of his orders. It is precisely at that point that the scene shifts to the arrival of the Israelite man and Midianite woman (in the sight of all the congregation, with an explicit mention of Moses), and the intervention of Phinehas which we have already considered. Moses, then, is a witness to the entry of the couple, a spectator to Phinehas' direct response, and presumably, amongst those shocked by the brutality of what they see.

MOSES VS. PHINEHAS

Moses re-enters the events of the narrative when Yhwh speaks to him about what has transpired (vs. 10ff.) Rather than condemning Phinehas for taking matters into his own hands, Yhwh praises him for his actions. Again, Phinehas' genealogy is given: son of Eleazer, son of Aaron the priest, and the results of Phinehas' actions are explained, the execution of the couple turning back the wrath of God in a manner which had saved them from divine consumption. What is more, the actions of Phinehas are described as an enactment of Yhwh's own zeal, which is to say that Phinehas has demonstrated a unity with the divine in a way which has transcended Moses' own role in the community. It is difficult to read this and not see a condemnation of Moses' role throughout this drama. Moses has been unaware or unbothered by the events with the Moabite woman. Moses has taken it upon himself to alter the divine decree for reasons which are unclear, failing to execute those Yhwh has deemed responsible for the apostasy. Moses has seen the encroachment of an offending couple in the midst of the community and stood by while another man has responded in a way which has demonstrated the divine zeal.

As a reward for his exemplary zeal, Phinehas is granted a special covenant with Yhwh, the ironically named covenant of peace. The covenant extends to Phinehas and his descendants, making them perpetual priests.[16] Moses, the one who appears as a failure in this scene, is the one to make this proclamation on Yhwh's behalf, noting Phinehas' zeal for Yhwh, and the fact that his actions have made atonement for the people (vs. 13). This, no doubt, would have been a difficult thing for Moses to do, as he would have understood that such words were a stinging rebuke of his inaction. Perhaps this is why we have no report of Moses making this proclamation, the narrative quickly moving on to identify the people on Phinehas' spear, and the commissioning of Moses to lead an attack on the Midianites (vss. 14–18).

What we see in Yhwh's interpretation of events then, is a clear demotion of Moses. Moses is typically presented as Yhwh's man, but in this instance, it is Phinehas who emerges as the hero at the expense of Moses. The reasons for Phinehas' great success here cohere well with masculine categories.

POTENCY

The most striking difference between Moses and Phinehas in this story is around their ability to produce results. As we have seen, the story begins with what appears to be a critique of Mosaic leadership, the people easily led into idolatry by the daughters of Moab. As the spiritual leader of Israel, the one with the responsibility of teaching and maintaining the law of god within the community, it is easy to see this as a failure of Moses. That is, Moses' leadership has lacked potency; his teaching has lacked potency; his words have lacked potency. Given a divine instruction to avert the wrath of god, Moses fails to act accordingly and as a result, the people are engaged in lament while people die about them. In the midst of that distress, a new situation develops which threatens the community, and again, Moses is inert, seeing but failing to act. His standing in the community no longer commands the respect it once did. In the face of communal failures, he seems to have lost the passion which had previously driven him to anger.

Phinehas, on the other hand, is a model of pragmatism. No sooner is he introduced than he has a sword in hand and is rushing to act. His actions are commended by Yhwh as the quintessential demonstration of zeal, and they are uncommonly potent. His actions deliver atonement for Israel and serve to end the plague which had afflicted them. This is all we really know about Phinehas: that he acts, and his actions are efficacious in every way. The subsequent appearances of Phinehas in the biblical narrative buttress this characterization of him. In Numbers 31, the natural sequel to the events of Numbers 25, Phinehas is sent with the war troops to enact revenge on the Midianites. No other individual is named. Rather, a report is given that a thousand men from each tribe is sent, along with Phinehas who takes responsibility for the vessels and war trumpets (Num. 31: 6–7). The census lists of Numbers 1–4 and 26 make it clear that the Levites are not enrolled into military service, playing instead a cultic role in the life of the nation. Phinehas is not sent as a military man, but rather to exercise a priestly role to the armed men, what Milgrom describes as a type of "chaplain."[17] Given the way he had distinguished himself as a man of inspired zeal in the earlier episode involving Midianites, it is no surprise that he should reappear here.

In Joshua 22, Phinehas leads a delegation to visit the trans-Jordanian tribes, having heard that the tribes had erected a large altar there (Josh. 22:11). In confronting the tribes for the treachery, Phinehas uses the events of Numbers 25 to support his claim, reminding the tribes of the great plague and suffering that the congregation had endured on account of their failings. As it turned out, the construction of the altar was by no means an act of rebellion, but rather an act of witness between the trans-Jordanian tribes, and those that had settles in Canaan, an explanation that satisfied Phinehas and his delegation. Nonetheless, as Tatlock points out, it is no coincidence that the zealous priest was chosen to head the delegation investigation matters of cultic impropriety.[18] It is worth noting here that this is the only occasion that Phinehas speaks throughout his appearances in the scriptures and that his words are of great power and persuasion. With the use of rhetorical questions, his tone is reminiscent of Moses' speech to the Korahite rebels in Numbers 16, though on this occasion, the result is much different.

We see then, that Phinehas is a man of great potency, and that this initial characterization of him in Numbers 25 sets a trajectory for his subsequent appearances. When Phinehas is present, it is clear that a matter of cultic integrity is at stake and that he can be trusted to act accordingly. This is set against Moses, who in this instance shows nothing but apathy and indifference. The contrast is so stark that Moses himself recognizes it, or rather, is compelled to announce Phinehas' social elevation, casting him in a new role as a type of cultic overseer. He performs this duty in the ensuing war with Midian and takes on additional responsibilities after Moses' death.

THE (SEXUALLY) VIOLENT MALE

As we have seen, Phinehas' characterization is limited to the reporting of his actions. He is immediately roused into action at the sight of the transgressing couple, standing and taking a sword in his hand. The word used to describe his grabbing of the sword is the same word used by Yhwh when Moses is commanded to take all the heads of Israel for the purpose of their execution. That word, *laqaḥ*, often carries violent intent, as it does in both these instances. Phinehas does not take the sword to defend himself, but to inflict harm on the unsuspecting couple. Storming the tent, Phinehas spears the two of them, inflicting a lethal wound upon them in a display of something akin to superhuman strength. This strength is not so much a defining feature in itself, though it points to a physical wholeness which does define masculinity.[19] That is to say, it seems clear that Phinehas does not suffer from any physical impediment. Quite the opposite!

Discussion of Phinehas' strength cannot be divorced from a discussion of sexualized violence. As we have seen, violence is closely linked to masculine performance, and in this instance, Phinehas demonstrates the convergence of these two categories. Wilson has tempered Clines' early assertions about violence,[20] preferring to speak about "strength" as a key masculine category.[21] It is almost impossible to separate this category from the militarization of masculinity in Ancient West Asia, as Wilson demonstrates. Wilson expands this understanding of "strength" to include "courage."[22] And yet in Phinehas we have not a military man, but a cultic official. Nor, might we say, do we have evidence of an abundance of courage. His act is not one of battle, but of punishment, his victims un-armed and unsuspecting. The warrior-ideal of the hero skillfully dispatching enemies on the battlefield is not one that Phinehas fits. Even in Numbers 31, when Phinehas travels to the Midianite war he is armed not with weapons, but sacred vessels and trumpets. Wilson's addition of courage makes this point problematic: while strength does seem to be highly valued in Old Testament depictions of masculinity, it need not solely be through military means. But what of the act—military or otherwise—that is without courage? Acts of violence, or perhaps more broadly, violent demonstrations of strength, seem to have a particular place: unbridled aggression or bloodlust is condemned far too often for violence to be simply understood as a defining virtue.[23] But Phinehas' actions here are rewarded, divorced as they are from any of the definitions above.

This final point seems quite relevant to Phinehas' actions. There is a shocking brutality in his actions, spearing two humans on the one weapon. To modern sensibilities, this action is an obvious example of the sort of unbridled aggression that the scriptures often condemn. The Rabbis also thought this way, and were uncomfortable with the way in which Phinehas behaved, arguing that it was only the divine decree that would have prevented Moses and the elders ex-communicating him from the congregation for his impulsive acts beyond the reaches of the law.[24] Milgrom sees this critique present even within the biblical material, the psalmist refusing to describe the actions of Phinehas as zeal, but rather, a prayerful mediation (Ps. 106:30). That is, in the psalm, Phinehas doesn't slay the couple, but prays, and the plague ceases. This accords well with Wilson's comment that these type of impulsively violent actions are widely condemned. However, we are also left with the reality that Phinehas' deeds are not only endorsed by Yhwh, they are celebrated and rewarded, and presented as an example of Yhwh's own desires. So while such actions are normally not to be considered ideal, failing in the matter of what Wilson calls self-control,[25] the divine endorsement of them serves as a warrant in this instance. For our purposes, it is enough to say that Phinehas demonstrates a capacity for violence which is widely regarded as a significant masculine category, even while we may disagree around matters of the appropriateness of its execution. This, though, is hardly a unique case in that respect.

Phinehas' act of violence, prompted by nothing but divine zeal, is set in stark contrast to Moses' own actions throughout the episode. Moses is commanded to put the heads of the people to death by impalement, itself a gruesome means of execution. As it turns out, Moses resists the command to enact the punishment, deflecting responsibility to those he had been ordered to kill. That is, in this instance, Moses *resists* a divine command to violence. Later in the scene, while Phinehas responds and enacts violence in a way which gains divine approval, Moses has watched on, failing to take action, and then being forced to announce the divine praise of Phinehas. In this scene, then, we see a Moses unwilling to engage in acts of violence set in contrast to Phinehas who shows no such hesitation.

ON WOMEN (II): COZBI

In our earlier consideration of women in this passage we noted the ways in which the daughters of Moab were controlled by the invisible men of Moab. Unlike her "sisters" (Num. 25:18), Cozbi is named here,[26] but her naming does little to alter the outcome she suffers. Cozbi is "brought into his brothers" (Num. 25:6) by Zimri, suggesting a marriage but at the same time making Cozbi object rather than subject. Marriages in the ancient world are political and economic, a fact emphasized by the narrator who notes that both Zimri and Cozbi come from prominent families: Zimri the son of a Simeonite chief (Num. 25:14) and Cozi the daughter of the head of a Midianite tribe (Num. 25:15). Such high station means little for Cozbi. She is married to Zimri and comes to his family. Her body becomes a means of alliance between the two families.[27] While named, she remains without voice.

I noted above that this is an act of sexual violence. When Phinehas enters the tent Zimri and Cozbi are speared "into her stomach" (Num. 25:8), again marking her as object rather than subject. The spearing of the two—Zimri and Cozbi—on one sword suggests that they were locked in a sexual embrace, perhaps the consummation of the marriage hinted at in verse 6. This, though, is not the act of violence. Helena Sivan has described Phinehas' action as the rape of Cozbi,[28] realized through the penetration of her belly with Phinehas' sword, the most phallic of objects.[29] This interpretation is heightened by a tradition which understands the point of penetration as Cozbi's genitals.[30] More recently, Mark McEntire has examined the relationship between Cozbi's treatment and practices of lynching.[31] Phinehas demonstrates his potency, but in doing so, Cozbi becomes another female victim. Her body, pierced with his sword, becomes the means by which he establishes rank and places himself in a position of social dominance.[32] Her body, like those of her sisters, serve male ends.

Potency, as it relates to masculine performance, proves to be a troubling category throughout the chapter. The elders of Moab set a plan into action to save themselves: it is a success. They demonstrate potency. Phinehas storms a tent and executes a couple locked in sexual congress. They die, a plague stops, he receives divine approval. He demonstrates potency. Both demonstrations of potency come at a cost: the bodily integrity of women. Thiede puts it clearly: " Women's bodies are not their own in the Hebrew bible. . . they are foundational to the creation and sustenance of biblical hegemonic masculinity."[33]

HONOR

Honor is most commonly a commodity that is passed from one individual to another during a contest. It results in either a reduced or elevated place in society. As we have seen, Moses and Phinehas do not have a relationship in a strict sense in this story. They do not engage with each other in any direct way. And yet an obvious consequence of the events of Numbers 25 is the elevation of Phinehas—who emerges from the story with a great deal more than when the story began—and clear signs of the demise of Moses. This shift can be thought of in terms of honor.

Haddox reminds us that a crucial aspect of honor is honesty and forthright speech.[34] On this measure, Moses fails miserably in this story. Having been instructed to undertake a particular course of action, Moses deviates from his received instructions and involves other people in a task that is meant to be his own. In regards to his speaking, then, Moses shows (and gains) no honor. If we understand Israel as in some sense Moses' responsibility, we can also see in this episode a declining ability for Moses to protect the people. He is oblivious to or disinterested in the events of the opening verses which result in such great suffering. As the teacher of Israel, it seems clear that he has

Chapter Six

failed in this regard. In the latter part of the story, he sits idly by as the couple enter the congregation in disregard for the collective trauma being experienced, and flouting their relationship in the context of great suffering. Moses does nothing to prevent their actions, or the potential consequences for the rest of the congregation. That is, he fails in his masculine duties.

Phinehas, on the other hand, acts in a way to prevent further distress. His intervention signals to the rest of the community both that they are safe, but also that such brazen acts will be met with a swift response. Phinehas is in effect playing a parental role here, policing behavior which steps outside the accepted social norms while protecting the community from external threats (or in this case, an internal threat). This received the highest possible commendation, namely, the divine approval of verses 12–14, including the covenant of perpetual priesthood. That is, Phinehas is honored as a result of his actions in a way which increases his status in the society. So much so, that his descendants will also enjoy the fruit of his actions.

WISDOM

The final category to consider here is wisdom, and it relates primarily to Moses. Moses acts in a way which is contrary to the divine instruction, and then fails to act in a moment of urgency. If wisdom is conducting one's self in an appropriate way in various circumstances, then in this instance, Moses demonstrates a clear lack of wisdom. Phinehas acts impulsively, no doubt. His actions are not well-considered, but are instinctive. It would be difficult to ascribe wisdom to him here is any substantial way, a position strengthened by the traditional unease felt at his deeds. Nonetheless, the story makes clear that it is Phinehas who acts in an appropriate fashion while Moses watches on. We may be reluctant to call Phinehas wise, but we should have no hesitation in noting Moses' lack of wisdom throughout the story.

CONCLUDING THOUGHTS

As we have seen, the presentation of Phinehas and Moses in this chapter does not constitute a relationship in the traditional sense. The two characters exist separately from each other, bearing little influence over each other. There is no sense that Phinehas acts explicitly on account of Moses' inaction, but the comparison invited by Yhwh's interpretation of the events certainly allows the reader to make this connection. It also draws attention to the fact that masculinity is performed in the presence of other men. Yhwh, the ultimate male, gives his approval to Phinehas, expressly at the expense of Moses. In this homosocial contest, it is Phinehas who emerges on top.

In regards to presentations of masculinity, Phinehas certainly emerges in a positive light, even while his characterization is limited. While it would be wrong to say that Moses is feminized in this text, it would be true to say that his masculinity is diminished, given the bold presentation of Phinehas. Aspects of Moses' character which have been developed elsewhere are absent in this episode which follows quite soon after the waters of Meribah incident (Num. 20) which is held out as the reason that Moses will not enter the land of Canaan. It could be that in the shadow of that event, the presentation of Moses has shifted, and his vulnerability is now exposed. To that end, an energetic, zealous relative emerges and wins for himself a perpetual covenant and a crucial social role. In this troubling story, Phinehas is "the man."

NOTES

1 Anthony Rees, *[Re]Reading Again: A Mosaic Reading of Numbers 25*, Playing the Texts (London: Bloomsbury, 2015), 115.

2. Alan Palmer, *Fictional Minds*, Frontiers of Narrative (Lincoln: University of Nebraska Press, 2004), 40.

3. Jacob Milgrom, *Numbers: The JPS Torah Commentary*, ed. Nahum M. Sarna, JPS Torah Commentary (Philadelphia: Jewish Publication Society, 1990), 341.

4. Horst Seebass, "The Case of Phinehas at Baal Peor in Num 25," *Biblische Notizen*, no. 117 (2003); Max Sicherman, "The Political Side of the Zimri-Cozbi Affair," *Jewish Bible Quarterly* 36 (2008); Barbara E. Organ, "Pursuing Phinehas: A Synchronic Reading," *Catholic Biblical Quarterly* 63, no. 2 (2001); Wil Gafney, "A Queer Womanist Midrashic Reading of Numbers 25:–18," in *Leviticus-Numbers*, ed. Athalya Brenner and Archie C.C Lee, Texts@Contexts (Minneapolis: Fortress, 2013); Rees, *[Re]Reading Again: A Mosaic Reading of Numbers 25*; Brandon R. Grafius, *Reading Phinehas, Watching Slashers: Horror Theory and Numbers 25* (Lanham: Lexington Books / Fortress Academic, 2018); John J. Collins, "The Zeal of Phinehas: The Bible and the Legitimation of Violence," *Journal of Biblical Literature* 122, no. 1 (2003); Harriet C. Lutzky, "The Name "Cozbi" (Numbers XXV 15, 18)," *Vetus Testamentum* 47, no. 4 (1997); Helena Zlotnick Sivan, "The Rape of Cozbi (Numbers XXV)," ibid. 51, no. 1 (2001). This is by no means an exhaustive list. See also the two relevant papers in Monica Jyotsna Melanchthon and Robyn J. Whitaker, *Terror in the Bible: Rhetoric, Gender, and Violence*, International Voices in Biblical Studies (Atlanta: SBL Press, 2021).

5. Karen Eller, "Numbers 25: A Reading by a Queer Australian," in *Terror in the Bible*, ed. Monica Jyotsna Melanchthon and Robyn J. Whitaker (Atlanta: SBL, 2021).

6. For an overview of the reception history of Numbers 25 see, Rees, *[Re]Reading Again: A Mosaic Reading of Numbers 25*.

7. Philo, "On the Life of Moses, I," in *The Works of Philo: Complete and Unabridged* (Peabody: Hendrickson, 1993), 487.

8. Flavius Josephus, "The Antiquities of the Jews," in *Complete Works of Flavius Josephus* (Grand Rapids: Kregel, 1960), 91.

9. B. T. Arnold and John H. Choi, *A Guide to Biblical Hebrew Syntax* (Cambridge: Cambridge University Press, 2003), 158ff. Arnold and Choi describe the various ways in which this particle operates, including matters of perception and immediacy, both of which seem to be functioning here.

10. To be fair, any blame here is lain squarely on the shoulders of the Israelite man, later identified as Zimri. The woman, Cozbi, holds no responsibility to the people of Israel. For a fuller treatment of Cozbi, see Anthony Rees, "[Re]Naming Cozbi: In Memoriam, Cozbi, Daughter of Zur," *Biblical Interpretation* 20, no. 1–2 (2012).

11. See, Thomas B Dozeman, "The Midianites in the Formation of the Book of Numbers," in *The Books of Leviticus and Numbers*, ed. Thomas Römer (Leuven: Uitgeverij Peeters, 2008); Rees, *[Re]Reading Again: A Mosaic Reading of Numbers 25*, 91ff.

12. Stefan C. Reif, "What Enraged Phinehas : A Study of Numbers 25:8," *Journal of Biblical Literature* 90, no. 2 (1971); Baruch A. Levine, *Numbers 21–36: A New Translation with Introduction and Commentary*, 1st ed. (New York: Doubleday, 2000), 287; G.P. Hugenberger, "Phinehas," in *International Standard Bible Encyclopedia*, ed. Geoffrey W. Broimley (Grand Rapids: William B. Eerdmans, 1986).

13. See Rees, *[Re]Reading Again: A Mosaic Reading of Numbers 25*, 81.

14. Carolyn Pressler, *Numbers*, Abingdon Old Testament Commentaries (Nashville: Abingdon, 2017), 226.

15. Ibid., 227.

16. This is often understood to mean the High Priesthood, though this is not made clear in the text. As Milgrom notes, the idea that it I the High Priesthood comes later with the emergence of the Zadokite priests, who trace their lineage to Phinehas, rather than the Elids whose lineage comes through Ithamar, the uncle of Phinehas. See, Milgrom, *Numbers: The JPS Torah Commentary*, 61.

17. Ibid., 257.

18. Jason R. Tatlock, "Phinehas," in *The New Interpreter's Dictionary of the Bible*, ed. Katherine Doob Sakenfeld (Nashville: Abingdon, 2009).

19. Susan E. Haddox, "Is There a 'Biblical Masculinity'? Masculinities in the Hebrew Bible," *Word & World* 36, no. 1 (2016): 6.

20. David J.A. Clines, "David the Man: The Construction of Masculinity in the Hebrew Bible," in *Interested Parties: The Ideology of Writers and Readers of the Hebrew Bible* (Sheffield: Sheffield Academic Press, 1995).

21. Stephen M. Wilson, *Making Men: The Male Coming-of-Age Theme in the Hebrew Bible* (New York: Oxford University Press, 2015), 31.

22. Ibid.

23. Ibid., 33.

24. Milgrom, *Numbers: The JPS Torah Commentary*, 215.

25. Wilson, *Making Men: The Male Coming-of-Age Theme in the Hebrew Bible*, 32.

26. See Rees, "[Re]Naming Cozbi: In Memoriam, Cozbi, Daughter of Zur."

27. Barbara Thiede, *Male Friendship, Homosociality, and Women in the Hebrew Bible: Malignant Fraternities*, Routledge Studies in the Biblical World (London: Routledge, 2021), 8.

28. Sivan, "The Rape of Cozbi (Numbers XXV)," 80.

29. Claudia V. Camp, *Wise, Strange and Holy: The Strange Woman and the Making of the Bible*, Journal for the Study of the Old Testament. Supplement Series (Sheffield: Sheffield Academic Press, 2000), 266.

30. Reif, "What Enraged Phinehas : A Study of Numbers 25:8," 202.

31. Mark McEntire, "Cozbi, Achan, and Jezebel: Executions in the Hebrew Bible and Modern Lynching," *Review & Expositor* 118, no. 1 (2021): 24ff.

32. Thiede, *Male Friendship, Homosociality, and Women in the Hebrew Bible: Malignant Fraternities*, 9.

33. Ibid., 11.

34. Haddox, "Is There a 'Biblical Masculinity'? Masculinities in the Hebrew Bible," 6.

Chapter Seven

Moses and Yahweh

To this point we have examined relationships shared between Moses and other male characters. These have been, necessarily, of different types and with differing degrees of intimacy. Whatever intimacy we have discovered there, most notably in the relationships with Jethro and Aaron, pale into insignificance be comparison to the relationship Moses comes to share with Yahweh. Howard Eilberg-Schwartz describes this relationship as "the closest male-male relationship in Israelite religion."[1] But closeness does not mean smoothness. Tracing the relationship between Moses and Yahweh is far more involved than the other human characters given the enormous amount of ma-terial which is involved, and the complexity inherent in attempting to come to grips with the bible's most enigmatic character: Yahweh. In some respects, the story of Exodus-Deuteronomy is the story of Moses and Yahweh and so a thorough examination of the twists and turns of their relationship exceeds the more modest goals of this work, even while, as Gunn and Fewell note, understanding Yahweh remains one of the great challenges for readers of the Hebrew bible.[2] To that end, we will focus on some key scenes which are pivotal in the development of their relationship and which give insight to the ways in which categories related to masculinity might enable us to understand the developing dynamics of their relationship and of their characterization more broadly.

It is worth noting that this exploration of the character of Yahweh is limited to those interactions with Moses considered here. While Clines' observation that sustained analysis of Yahweh's masculinity has been lacking in bibli-cal studies continues to be true,[3] further work has continued to deepen this understanding of this enigmatic figure.[4]

INTRODUCING YAHWEH

Yahweh is first mentioned in Exodus 1:17. The midwives resist the demands of Pharaoh on account of their fear of God.[5] The response of God to this resistance is a blessing which extends from the midwives to the people (Exod. 1:20–21). The characterization is indirect but immediately has the effect of creating a contest between Yahweh and Pharaoh. Pharaoh is resisted and responds with malicious intent, while Yahweh is feared and responds with blessing.

Chapter 2 relays the birth narrative of Moses, from which Yahweh is completely removed. It is only after Moses' fleeing of Egypt (2:15) and his marriage to Zipporah that God is mentioned, and again, this has nothing to do with Moses. It is, rather, a report that God hears the cry of suffering that comes from the people of Israel, and a note that God then remembers the covenant made with the Patriarchs (2:24). This hearing and remembering is joined with seeing and knowing, an ominous sounding expression (2:25) somewhat softened in the NRSV. To this point Yahweh and Moses have had no engagement, but the gathering of knowledge by Yahweh forms the immediate context for their meeting in chapter 3 and signals the divine intent to act.

Chapter 3 commences with a report that Moses is out tending to his Father-in-law's flocks. The first verse contains two seemingly innocuous pieces of information which point to the significance of what is to come. The narrator reinforces the fact that Jethro is a priest, and secondly, the location of Moses is qualified: Mt Horeb, the mountain of God. These two pieces of information, both unnecessary, alert us that something significant may be about to take place. Why mention the Priestly function of Jethro if not to raise the issue of religion? And why reiterate the fact that Mt. Horeb is the mountain of God, if not to foreshadow the presence of God in the coming scene? Dozeman notes an awkwardness in the MT which he suggests might be an instance of fantastic geography, creating a mysterious location at which unusual events might occur.[6] That is, Moses has taken the flock beyond the wilderness, beyond his normal routes to a strange, distant place.[7] Quickly, this strategy reveals itself. An angel (or perhaps more usefully, messenger) of the Lord appears[8] in the midst of the burning bush, but after this solitary mention disappears from the story and it is Yahweh who calls to Moses.[9] This use of the divine voice and the super-natural burning of the bush marks this episode as a theophany which is here combined with a form of call-narrative or commission. The mixing of genre marks this episode as distinct from other call narratives or theophanies and serves to shift the point of focus from Moses to an establishment of the identity of Yahweh.[10]

Yahweh calls to Moses, using his name. That is, Moses is known to Yahweh, furthering the list if things Yahweh "knows." The significance of knowing someone's name is well known in ancient literature,[11] especially when set against the practice of refraining from sharing one's own name. Here, having got Moses' attention through the miraculous bush and the calling of his name, Yahweh instructs Moses to come no closer and remove his shoes on account of the holy ground upon which he unwittingly treads (Exod. 3:5). Immediately, a power imbalance is created within the relationship. One partner knows the other, and this knowledge is enough to compel action. Moses though remains ignorant to any detail regarding the character with whom he is dealing. Yahweh further establishes his identity in the following verse, sharing not his name, but his personal and historical significance as the god of "your father," and the god of Abraham, Isaac and Jacob. The sphere of Yahweh's knowledge grows: I know you, your father, and the patriarchs. As we have seen, Moses' own sense of self is a complicated issue, and who Moses understands his father to have been, plus any sense of connection to the patriarchal history is difficult if not impossible to ascertain. Nonetheless, in the face of this overwhelming demonstration of knowledge, Moses hides his face in fear of the God. As Hamilton notes, quite quickly Moses' curiosity (vs. 3) has turned to fear (vs. 6).[12]

Having established this aspect of his identity, Yahweh continues, informing Moses of his knowledge of the Israelite oppression. The report follows much the same pattern as the end of chapter 2: Yahweh has seen, heard and known. This is laid out in verse seven and repeated in verse 9, perhaps to underscore the severity of the violence committed against the Israelites.[13] And now, Yahweh has come down to deliver them from the Egyptian servitude and to bring them into the good land of Canaan, a land described in utopian terms,[14] though not without difficulty given the presence of inhabitants. In verse 10 the opening move of plan, and Moses' central role within it is revealed: I will send you to Pharaoh to bring my people, the Israelites, out of Egypt.

To this point Yahweh has dominated this first meeting with Moses. Moses' actions have been responses to Yahweh: seeing the bush and approaching, responding when his name was called, removing his shoes when bid to do so, and then hiding his face when confronted with a sense of whom he was talking to. This passivity is seemingly at odds with the more active Moses of chapter 2, the Moses who stood up to the shepherds at the well in defense of unknown women. Conversely, Yahweh has projected nothing but power, revealing an intimate knowledge of Moses, his family and the people of Israel; an awareness of the plight of Israel; and the announcement of a plan to release the people of Israel from captivity and place them in a land of inordinate natural riches. This plan of deliverance also serves to characterize Yahweh as compassionate and concerned with exacting justice for the suffering Israelites.[15]

Yahweh's confidence is without limit: "I have come down to do this," and it appears that Yahweh assumes Moses will simply bow to his plan: "And now, go, and I will send you." The construction suggests an immediate response is required, with the assumption that the preceding material is all that is needed to compel action. The masculine category of potency is immediately evident, as Yahweh asserts himself over Moses with the aim of conscripting him into the divine plan. Yahweh has also demonstrated considerable skills of persuasion, drawing on historical material and present days realities in a fashion designed to move Moses to action. And as we have seen, Yahweh is presenting himself as a defender of honor, the actions to be taken a way of delivering the Israelites from their oppression and gifting them a new home. By referring to the Israelites as "my people" in Exod. 3:7, Yahweh makes this a matter of personal concern.[16]

Given the responsive actions of Moses in the opening verses of the chapter, we are left to assume that Yahweh's plan will succeed. But this Moses is somewhat at odds with the Moses we had come to know in chapter 2: a man who was not afraid to kill, a man willing to stand up to defend strangers in the face of danger. The re-emergence of this Moses signals the beginning of the relationship between Moses and Yahweh and demonstrates that Moses will be a dynamic partner, willing to speak his own mind and express his own sense of agency. That agency first reveals itself as resistance. Rather than meekly yield to Yahweh's insistence or simply runaway, Moses questions Yahweh: "Who am I that I should go to Pharaoh and bring the Israelites out of Egypt?" The willingness of Moses to speak—uninvited—signals a major departure from the face covering of verse six. His question demands a response from Yahweh, but also reveals certain things about Moses' own self-awareness. Moses is a fugitive and has a history of violence in Egypt.[17] If Yahweh knows Moses' name, he must also surely know this and so realise that a return to Egypt, and specifically the Pharaoh, puts Moses' life at risk. Moses' life is now in Midian, with his Midianite family. His reference to "the Israelites" is indicative of the distance he imagines between himself and that group, and resists Yahweh's opening approach to him through the patriarchal lineage.

Yahweh's response serves to further demonstrate divine confidence. Rather than respond to Moses' question directly, Yahweh's response, "I will be with you" has the effect of minimising Moses' own role. As Meyers notes, the promise of divine protection is intended to function as an assurance that the mission will be successful precisely because of the divine intervention and not because of any skill or strength of the commissioned individual.[18] The sign pledged as the evidence that it is Yahweh who has sent Moses, the people of Israel worshipping together on the mountain, likewise betrays a misguided confidence, a point clearly seen by Moses. Moses recognises that between his own approach to the people of Israel and their worshipping on the mountain lies a large volume of work, none of which appears to be easily achieved. Even the very first step, acceptance into the people of Israel, seems to be a difficult proposition for Moses. He is able to anticipate the doubt in their minds,[19] and crucially, cites his ignorance to the divine name as a stumbling block to his mission. Yahweh's response is significant here in so far as the revelation of the divine name echoes Moses' own question of his ability to fulfill this task. Whereas Moses had asked "Who am I?," Yahweh's response comes "I am who I am" (Exod. 3:14).[20] Moses' self-questioning is trumped by Yahweh's bold self-assurance, an assurance that washes over inherent difficulties. Dozeman notes that Moses' two objections are answered in the same fashion. The question about his own sense of identity is answered with an assurance of divine presence. His anxiety about presenting this plan to Israel and demonstrating knowledge of God is answered with "I am who I am." The movement from Moses' person to the people of Israel is answered in the same way: I am.[21] Durham observes that Moses essentially asks two questions: "who am I?" and "who are you?"[22] This second question is more urgent, because it reveals a question that Moses anticipates from the people of Israel about the nature and identity of this god in the midst of their suffering. That is, what can he do?[23] What does this god have in his history or reputation that might matter here in the place of suffering?

The third response from Yahweh, in which the divine name is revealed forms a type of *inclusio* with Yahweh's initial interaction with Moses, with reference to the "God of your fathers." This also serves to answer the question suggested by Durham. That is, it is precisely this link with the ancestors that reveals Yahweh's credibility. As Yahweh had proven himself faithful to the ancestors, here he lays claim to Israel and vows to make good for them. While Moses attempts to differentiate himself from the people of Israel, Yahweh draws him into them. Moses and Israel have a common ancestry and so a common ancestral god, the god of your fathers, revealed now not so much with a name, but rather an assertion of authority and confession of an essential reality: I am what I am, I will be what I will be, This is my name forever.[24]

The final verses of Exodus 3 outline what Moses is to say to the people of Israel. The content of this speech develops the themes already established in this interaction with Moses. Firstly, Yahweh knows. He knows the ancestors (vs. 16), the things that have happened to Israel in Egypt (vs. 16), the place he intends to lead Israel (vs. 17), the reality that the elders will listen and respond to Moses (vs. 18), and likely resistance of Pharaoh (vs. 19). Further, Yahweh is able to enact this plan. His knowledge is coupled with potency, and we have here the image of the outstretched hand that will strike Egypt and work wonders (vs. 20).[25] Beyond that, Yahweh knows that the response of the Egyptians will be to raise the Israelites in favor (vs. 21) such that they will hand them silver, gold and clothing as they leave. The outstretched hand of Yahweh will fill the otherwise empty hands of the Israelites (vs. 21).

This section is an impressive display of masculinity! Knowledge, power, potency and provision all feature as a part of Yahweh's character. Clearly this pronouncement is an attempt to win over Moses into his role by persuading him of the ultimate triumph of his mission, first with Israel, then with Pharaoh, and ultimately, with all Egypt. Yahweh brushes over the challenges with no great concern: the people of Israel will listen; the Pharaoh will resist but ultimately come under Yahweh's hand; the people will leave with adequate resources to begin new lives. Also appearing here is the reality that the new home is already inhabited, a fact which is noted, but not explored in any substantive way. However, as chapter four commences, it is clear that Yahweh's words of persuasion are yet to convince Moses who is still concerned about the very first obstacle: acceptance from the people of Israel. His question, "who am I?" continues to haunt him.

Yahweh attempts to overcome these anxieties with further demonstrations of power. Moses is asked to perform a series of signs: he throws his staff to the ground and watches as it turns into a snake, which he then picks up (vss. 3–4); he places his hand in his cloak and it becomes leprous, only to be restored by placing it again in his cloak (vss. 6–8); and finally, is told of a further sign that he will perform, turning water from the Nile into blood (vs. 9). In having Moses perform these actions, Yahweh is demonstrating further aspects of his power, a power that transcends natural laws and what might be considered possible. In the first, the image of the snake may speak to power over royalty, the staff being a symbol of royalty and the snake being understood as a protector of Pharaoh.[26] The second sign points to a power over death and the ability to heal.[27] The third appears to foreshadow the plagues which will afflict Egypt in the coming narrative. While each of these signs are enacted by Moses, he knows that they are not the work of his own power but displays of Yahweh's powers.

But this scene also plays out a more subtle display of power. Moses submits to Yahweh's bidding such that he appears as a type of puppet, a man under the control of another. This posture of submission is given voice in verse 10, where Moses refers to Yahweh as "my lord" and to himself as "your servant." Clearly some of this is conventional speech, but it does mark a new way in which Moses identifies himself in relation to another. His has not been a way of submission, nor self-deprecation. Indeed, his willingness to raise objections to Yahweh's call suggests something of his sense of agency.

And yet here, that sense of agency is undermined in a fashion that creates a good deal of ambiguity around Moses' sense of self. Moses' words are part of a new strategy to avoid the commission of Yahweh. Having first claiming that he would not be accepted by Israel or Pharaoh, Moses' turns to a more personal defense: his own incapacity in the arena of speech. Durham refers to this strategy as a "trump card," [28] a last-ditch attempt to use his (claimed) inadequacy as a reason to have him excused. Yahweh's response is emphatic, drawing on the divine role as creator and author of human existence. The questions in verse 13: "Who gives speech to mortals? Who makes them blind or deaf, seeing or blind?" underscore these particular powers. This passage is reminiscent of the disputation between Yahweh and Job in Job 38, where a rhetorical ploy is utilized which accentuates the power of god as creator.[29] This assertion of divine power is intended to render the human complaint irrelevant, which seems to lie behind the reiteration of divine presence which immediately follows: I will be with your mouth. The use of the first-person verb mirrors the revelation of the divine name earlier but is made more emphatic here with the use of the singular pronoun: I, I am with your mouth. Despite these assurances, Moses next words, rendered in NRSV as "please send someone else" anger Yahweh. The Hebrew is confused, and read in one way, may indicate Moses yielding to the divine commission.[30] However, this makes no sense of Yahweh's response who clearly understands Moses' words as a plea for release. Yahweh's anger seems driven by the lack of ability to persuade Moses: the assurances should have been sufficient, the signs should have been sufficient, the divine word should have been sufficient. But instead, Moses resists, and Yahweh institutes a secondary plan through which Moses' brother, Aaron, will speak in his stead. Despite the anger, Moses retains his place in the divine plan, and carries a staff, a tool for the performance of signs, and a symbol of Yahweh's power.

EXODUS 4:24–26

In chapter 1 we considered the difficult passage from Exodus 4:24–26 where Yahweh attempts to murder Moses. At that point we were considering the story in relation to Moses' relationship with Zipporah, but here we might reconsider it from the perspective of the relationship shared by Moses and Yahweh. Having established a relationship with Yahweh and agreeing to travel back to Egypt, Moses is attacked in the night. Moses, the divine appointee comes under a potentially lethal attack from Yahweh, saved only by Zipporah's actions in circumcising their son and dashing the bloodied foreskin on the feet or genitals of Moses (or those of their son, or perhaps Yahweh's feet, the thematic difficulty of the text matched by its syntax). It is incomprehensible and scandalous.[31] Zipporah's words emphasise that masculinity is at stake in this encounter: "you are a bridegroom of blood to me" (Exod. 4:25). As Eilberg-Schwartz notes, ". . . Moses' manhood must already be exposed. God's attack on Moses is in part an attack on his masculinity."[32] Circumcision, here enacted by Zipporah on her son, symbolizes male submission to the ultimate male, Yahweh. Zipporah intervenes in order to keep Moses. A genital injury to her son secures her husband. As Eilberg-Schwartz recognises, Zipporah's actions are about danger she feels: "You are a bridegroom of blood *to me*."[33]

God's attack on Moses' masculinity demonstrates an element of darkness which resides within his character[34] and suggest that—at least in the mind of the narrator—Yahweh does not stand outside normal masculine behaviour. That is, Yahweh too, participates in the social system of masculine differentiation and asserts himself in ways designed to demonstrate the hegemonic nature of his gendered performance. Thiede is right when she notes that Yahweh exists in a hierarchical relationship with his chosen men,[35] a system in which he always takes the premier position. But what does it mean for a friend to attack another friend with the intent to kill? What does it mean to enter a partnership and then attack the partner? Eilberg-Schwartz notes that from Exodus 3 onwards, the relationship between Moses and Yahweh is one of deepening intimacy, becoming, as we have seen, the closest in Israelite religion.[36] As we have noted, that does not necessarily mean smoothness in all aspects. But this scene bursts beyond what we could possibly consider acceptable behaviour and signals that Yahweh's masculinity is of a piece with that of the rest of the masculine world and prepared to assert itself with (inexplicable) violence. Yahweh attacks Moses, and he is saved by a woman. The effect for Moses is feminizing,[37] and demonstrates early-on in this story that while Yahweh and Moses are partners—perhaps even friends—this is no meeting of equals.

EXODUS 11

In Exodus 11 the final plague to be inflicted upon the Egyptians is announced. In the introduction of this plague some curious information is offered. Firstly, the people of Israel have found favor in the eyes of the Egyptians. This will later manifest itself in the Egyptians giving their jewellery to the Israelites on their departure (Exod. 12:35) and is indicative of the ways in which Yahweh is controlling the situation. Previously despised, the Israelites now find favor. As Hamilton remarks, "And this after all the heartaches brought on Egypt in the earlier plagues!"[38] This is a statement of Yahweh's potency, and the effect of his presence,[39] as noted in chapters 3–4. Yahweh's promise of being who he is, and being with Israel, is coming to fruition. Yahweh had announced this coming favor in Exod. 3:21–22, and now, in spite of the calamity which has fallen upon Egypt, it is coming to be.

Significant also, are comments regarding Moses. Moses has become a figure of significant importance in Egypt, described as being a great man in the land of Egypt,[40] in the eyes of both the people, and the servants of Pharaoh (Exod. 11:3). The construction emphasises something about Moses: "The man Moses was very great in the land of Egypt." This use of "The man Moses," repeated in Numbers 12 appears to be a type of accolade. He is not just a male adult. This construction suggests something akin to an "aura of awe,"[41] which surrounds Moses' person as a man, *the* man of great importance. Von Rad notes that in spite of all the achievements attributed to him and the great office he holds in Israelite tradition; despite being a figure of incomparable greatness, this simple description—the man, Moses—has its own special significance.[42]

EXODUS 19

Some of the features reappear in Exodus 19. Having established camp in the shadows of Sinai (Exod. 19:2), Moses ascends the mountain to converse with Yahweh. The location of this conversation of the mountain is important for a number of reasons, most notably that mountains are traditionally the abode of the gods. Mountains have already featured through the story, notably the "mountain of God" which was the site of Moses' commission in Exodus 3, as well as Mount Horeb, where Moses draws water from a rock in Exodus 17. This mountain, though, is distinguished as "the mountain" (Exod. 19:2), a qualification that seems to speak to its significance. This makes sense given the paradigmatic experience which will unfold there over the following chapters, a process whereby the house of Jacob and Yahweh are bound together in covenant, and through which Moses' position as law-giver is enshrined. All this happens at "the mountain," established in verse 3 as the residence of Yahweh.[43] That is to say, this location matters, and is fraught with significance. This is a sacred place,[44] a place where Yahweh's power and presence is most clearly manifest, and where Moses is most clearly Yahweh's guest. The power differential between them seems most acute here, in Yahweh's home.

This power imbalance is clearly established as the story proceeds. Yahweh instructs Moses on what he is to do and what he is to say. The message Moses is to give amounts to a summary of covenant theology[45] (Exod. 19:4–6) which will later be expanded through the formal statement of covenant obligation.

Crucial here though is that Moses returns to the elders and reports what he has been told to say. The people agree to the offer and Moses returns to Yahweh (Exod. 4:7).

Within these verses we see that the power dynamic between Moses and Yahweh has become well-established. In this episode Moses has ceded his agency. He speaks nothing other than what he is told and in this demonstrates himself as an exemplary prophet. But it also indicates that his authority is derivative. As Yahweh has elevated Moses in Egypt, so too he is elevating Moses in Israel. And yet the story has shown that Israel have been less than hasty in their embrace of Moses, a point still at stake in the shadows of Sinai. Moses' complaint in Exodus 3 that the people will not listen to him has been proven correct. In Egypt the Israelites resented the harsh treatment that came as a result of Moses' provocations (Exod. 5). The drawing of water from the rock in Exodus 17 was itself a response to Israelite quarrelling with Moses. Moses may well be the leader in some respects, but not in a way that shielded him from dissent.[46] In response to this, Yahweh proposes an action in order to authenticate Moses' leadership. By providing a multi-sensory theophany, by which the people will hear (vs. 7) and see (vs. 11), and presumably feel, Yahweh intends to provide an experience that will ensure the peoples' enduring confidence in Moses. That is to say, Moses' authority is established not through his own person, but the action of Yahweh. And yet the theophany itself is to establish Moses' own authority, not that of Yahweh.

EXODUS 33

Exodus 32 relays what is the paradigmatic story of Israelite apostasy: the story of the golden calf. Not surprisingly, Yahweh is furious with the people and orders them away. The promise of the land remains intact through the provision of a warrior-angel, but Yahweh resolves to remove his presence from Israel. That presence, once protective, has turned lethal[47] given the extent of the divine rage. The people enter a period of mourning on hearing these words (Exod. 33:4), which only adds to what has been a period of significant trauma. Moses himself was enraged by the events of Exodus 32, commanding a purge of the camp that led to the execution of some 3000 people. With instruction to kill family members, it is certain that this fratricide had already devastated a large part of the population. A divinely sent plague is also sent in response to the apostasy, all of which comes before the events of Exodus 33. The Israelite response then needs to be read in this context: one in which personal failure and loss are already close to the surface.

Moses, putting aside his own sense of anger resolves to speak to Yahweh and convince him to change course, but before doing so, an interlude appears that provides information that is crucial to understanding the ensuing conversation. A series of verses appear which describe Moses' practice of entering the tent of meeting and the reverent response of the people to what would occur through these meetings (Exod. 33:7–11). A brief line appears in this description which signals a fundamental shift in how we may consider the relationship between Moses and Yahweh: "And Yahweh spoke to Moses face-to-face as a man speaks to a friend" (Exod. 33:11), a thing von Rad describes as being "something out of the ordinary."[48] Olyan notes that the NJPS rendering "as one speaks to another" misses something important by neglecting the language of friendship. It is precisely the singularity of Moses' relationship with Yahweh that this verse highlights with an emphasis on the intimacy born of friendship.[49] It is certainly some distance from the relationship in Exodus 19 in which Moses merely acts as a messenger with no involvement in the conversation at all. Greater still from the initial encounter in Exodus 3 and 4 in which Yahweh is frustrated by Moses' lack of willingness to yield to the divine command.

ON BEING A FRIEND AND BEING A MAN

Olyan provides a very useful survey concerning the nature of friendship in the Hebrew bible, much of it relevant to our consideration here. Friendship involves a choice to associate of affiliate with each other; friendship is concerned with positive feelings, often rendered as "love"; friends know each other on a personal level and have a sense of goodwill towards each other; engagement between friends should be characterized by gentleness; friends are loyal, particularly in times of adversity; friends desire justice for each other; friends do not abandon one another; friendship is characterized by hospitality; a friend is trustworthy; there is reciprocity, so that actions that demonstrate loyalty or generosity are to be met with comparable acts.[50] Notwithstanding some of the challenges and ambiguities that continue to be presented, this functional portrait of friendship illuminates a number of aspects of the relationship emerging between Yahweh and Moses, as will be evident in some of the analysis below.

It is also worthwhile at this point to note some of the correlations between the categories of masculinity which form the broader focus of this work, and the portrait of friendship just sketched out, in particular aspects of trustworthiness and loyalty which are common to both. As we have seen, Moses is short on friends in Israel. His position as an outsider means that he is socially isolated in many ways so that is in some way only in this relationship with Yahweh that he is able to give expression to the category of trustworthiness as a friends. In a similar fashion, Moses' familial relationships are in most respects abnormal. He does not uniformly receive the type of familial loyalty expected from those who are his kin, and the strange nature of his relationship with his siblings and spouse make it difficult to make a judgement on his own loyalty to them. But again, the relationship with Yahweh gives expression to this as he almost demands that Yahweh demonstrate that loyalty to him for the sake of their relationship. So the development of this relationship between Yahweh and Moses is important in so far as it illustrates Moses' qualities as a good friend, it also serves to build up the portrait of him as a man, as complicated as the aspects of this relationship prove to be! And it also begs the question: what kind of friend is Yahweh?[51]

MOSES AND YAHWEH AS FRIENDS

This expression, "as a man speaks to a friend" allows us to make sense of the conversation between Moses and Yahweh in Exod. 33:1–16. In verse 1, Yahweh has disowned the people and credits Moses with the task of delivering the people from Egypt.[52] In a similar fashion, he commands Moses to continue on with Israel, without Yahweh's presence. Moses' response is to recall the nature of the dialogue that has passed between them at various points, or more precisely, Moses uses Yahweh's declarations against him. In the first move Moses plays to their personal relationship and commitments Yahweh has made to him.[53] In doing so, Moses engages the issue of honor and reliability. What would it mean if Yahweh didn't match his word in relation to Moses? Affirming his belief that he has found favor in Yahweh's eyes, Moses presses and asks to know Yahweh's ways, and for Israel to be considered Yahweh's people. This emphasis on the special place of Israel ("your" people) recalls the offer made by Yahweh in Exodus 19 in which Israel were described as Yahweh's treasured possession.

This personal line of argument is met with a personal response. Yahweh responds to Moses' requests, promising to be with him and provide peace (Exod. 33:14). But Yahweh ignores Moses' comments concerning the status of the people of Israel. The emphasis is entirely on the person of Moses, rather than the distinctive character of the people.[54] And it is at this point that Moses presses. It is not sufficient for Yahweh's presence to be only with him. Were that the case, Moses' place as Yahweh's favored one would be lost, and the people of Israel would no longer be distinct (Exod. 33:16). Indeed, without Yahweh, Israel will cease to exist. It is, in Durham's reckoning, the ultimate either/or question,[55] and reveals the genius of Moses' rhetorical work through this section.

The result of this line of argument by Moses is full assent from Yahweh. He commits to all that Moses has requested, and reaffirms that Moses has won his favor and is known by name. Moses, having won these concessions, requests to see Yahweh's glory, a significant step from his previous request to know Yahweh's ways. This appears to be a request for a greater knowledge of Yahweh's character,[56] which is revealed as goodness, and the proclamation of the divine name in the face of Moses (Exod. 33:19). The theophany which follows (Exod. 34:6–7) demonstrates the way in which Moses has been able to convince Yahweh to alter direction and demonstrates the shift which has taken place within the dynamics of their relationship.

This exchange is predicated on the notion of friendship between Moses and Yahweh. Moses. Several of Olyan's categories appear here, and Moses insists that Yahweh hold to them, demanding that Yahweh prove himself as a good friend. Moses is concerned for the reputation of his friend which he has worked to develop; he has been loyal to Yahweh and now asks for it in return; he seeks an ever-closer knowledge of his friend; he asks Yahweh to be mindful of his own position as Yahweh's friend and to proclaim it. That is to say, the mutuality of their relationship is such that they are now friends. In each of these ways we see that Moses and Yahweh's relationship is qualitatively different. They are now friends, and this reality bears upon the way they engage with each other.

NUMBERS 11–14: FRIENDLY DISPUTES, FRIENDLY SOLIDARITY, FRIENDLY ADVICE

Numbers 11–14 contains a series of episodes that demonstrate the ways in which the relationship between Moses and Yahweh has developed into something akin to friendship. It is worth noting that the language that they use towards each other maintains a certain formality in so far as Moses continues to refer to Yahweh as "my lord" and Yahweh to Moses as 'my servant." Nonetheless, in this sequence of stories their dialogue and actions demonstrate publicly the growth of their relationship. As Leveen notes, these episodes signal a challenge on the "special relation[ship]" shared by Moses and Yahweh,[57] moving first from the people of Israel, and now to Moses' own family. In each instance, they respond in a manner which demonstrates a particular aspect of their growing friendship.

Numbers 11 is the first instance of the "murmuring motif"[58] within the book of Numbers. This motif appears at various points throughout the narrative which makes up Exodus and Numbers and has a common form: the people complain about a particular circumstance (lack of water [Exod. 17; Num 20], or food [Exod. 16; Num 11] or leadership [Num 12, 16]); the complaint is heard by Yahweh who punishes the people for their complaint; the people petition Moses to intercede; Moses intercedes and Yahweh relents. Commentators have noted that Moses' role throughout these episodes is that of intercessor, largely imagined as a prophetic function.[59] While that is clearly the case, the tone and language Moses adopts in Numbers differs greatly from that in Exodus 16 and 17, or even in the aftermath of the golden calf incident in Exodus 32. In those instances Moses pleads with Yahweh for relief for the people of Israel. In Num 11, the emphasis has shifted and Moses speaks not as intercessor, but in complaint.[60] And he speaks not on behalf of Israel, but solely himself.

The NRSV renders Num 11:10b "Then the LORD became very angry, and Moses was displeased." While this is accurate in relation to Yahweh, the MT suggests this is an understatement in relation to Moses: ובעיני משה רע (in the eyes of Moses, it was evil). But Yahweh and Moses are angry about different things. Yahweh is angry about the people's complaint. Very quickly we discover that Moses is angry about Yahweh. As we have noted already, the tone and language of the outburst is significantly different to Moses' speech elsewhere and points to the changed nature of their relationship. Rather than a measured approach, Moses lambasts Yahweh with accusations of mistreatment: "Why have you treated your servant so badly? Why have I not found favour in your sight . . .?" This idea of finding favor has already featured in the discussion here, but Moses reprises it for rhetorical purposes. Everything is Yahweh's fault,[61] his resentment clear in every utterance. Moses' language suggests that this is a conversation between partners, a relationship more characterized by equality than a power differential. As we have seen, the language of servant and lord persists but in this light it may have an ironic twist to it. Moses is clear that he has been wronged and moves quickly to create a metaphor whereby Israel is a suckling child and Moses either a mother or wet-nurse despite his emphatic claim that he is neither responsible for Israel's birth, not capable of sustaining them.[62] For Moses we can see here a failure by Yahweh in relation to the categories of friendship Olyan identifies. Moses claims to have been deceived, that Yahweh's claim of favor have been dishonest. The notion of mutual goodwill[63] is absent in Moses' accusations against Yahweh, leading to what is here, a quite candid conclusion: "If this is the way you are going to treat me, put me to death at once—if I have found favour in your sight—and do not let me see my misery" (Num 11:15). While we earlier saw the expression "as a man speaks to a friend" in a different scenario, the language here also suggests a relationship of some intimacy. Moses feels

betrayed and takes it personally which is a thing we would expect of a trust-
ing relationship. His comfort in speaking with such candour demonstrates the
closeness of their bond and so suggests that this is a disagreement between
friends. Yahweh's response in alleviating some of Moses' responsibilities
suggest that in some sense Moses was correct in his claim, or perhaps that
Yahweh simply wants to make his friend feel better. Whatever the case, Yahweh responds in two ways: the development of a leadership structure that
relieves Moses of sole responsibility, and the provision of meat to eat. However, Yahweh's anger finds expression here as the prodigious amount of quail
that is provided serves to bring about a "very great plague" and the people are
forced to bury their dead before leaving that camp (Num. 11:34–35).

As we noted in chapter 1, Numbers 12 tells a story of sibling jealousy.
Aaron and Miriam, the siblings of Moses, speak against him on account of
his marriage to a Cushite woman. Moses had previously married Zipporah,
a Midianite (Exod. 2:21) so it would appear that the nature of the complaint
is not to do with the Cushite woman being a foreigner.[64] Instead, it appears
to be a way of raising the substantive issue: the lack of recognition of their
own prophetic authority. As they ask: "Has the LORD spoken only through
Moses?" (Num. 12:2) Moses does not raise his voice in contest with his
siblings which the narrator (or as Gafney suggests, "Moses' publicist")[65]
explains by reference to Moses' superlative humility (Num. 12:3). Yahweh
intervenes, calling the three siblings to the tent and speaking plainly about
Moses' special place, both in relation to Yahweh and amongst the community:
"With him I speak face to face, and he beholds the form of the LORD. Why
then were you not afraid to speak against my servant Moses? (Num. 12:8–9).
The language of particularity and face-to-face encounter echo the assertion
of Exodus 33:11. Yahweh has responded in order to halt the slandering of his
friend. It is an act of loyalty in defense if one who has proven himself loyal
and so Moses' favor in the eyes of Yahweh is demonstrated in a fashion which
is beyond dispute. The words of Yahweh are coupled with punishment, as
Miriam is struck leprous in an instant. Aaron pleads with Moses, who in turn
pleads with Yahweh for her to be restored, which is agreed but only following
a seven-day exclusion (Num. 12:14). The exclusion mirrors the legal texts of
Lev 13:4 and 14:3 for leprosy, though it is noteworthy here that the reason for
her exclusion is not explained by way of her leprosy, but rather her shame.
Her punishment is likened to a daughter being spat in the face by her father
(Num. 12:14), a well-attested act of disgrace.[66]

While it is true that Yahweh acts as a friend in this instance, we can also
make a comparison between Yahweh and Moses here. When challenged by
his family, Moses is silent. This failure to act is similar to his inaction in Num.
25 when it is Phinehas who responds and earns Yahweh's praise while Moses

stands by, tacitly condemned for his failure to show zeal (Num 25:10–13). One way of understanding this is to imagine a lack of potency or vitality on the part of Moses in defending his own honor, a lack which is compensated for by the excess of vitality demonstrated by Yahweh's response in acting in a fashion restorative for Moses. What appears as friendly solidarity can also been understood as paternal protection and so a defense of honor on the part of Yahweh.

Numbers 13–14 tells the famous story of the first scouting of Canaan in which Joshua and Caleb emerge as Israelite heroes. What is relevant to our discussion here is the reaction of Yahweh to the faithlessness of the other scouts who spread "evil reports" on their return. The Hebrew noun דבה can also mean defamation,[67] which speaks to the inaccuracy of the reports offered. The people of Israel recoil at the reports and complain again to Moses and Aaron, saying they would have rather died in Egypt or the wilderness than be cut down in the so call Promised Land, and so resolve to return to Egypt (Num 14:2–3). As we have come to expect, Yahweh is incensed and determines to destroy the Israelites, sparing only Moses. Moses' response mirrors the approach he took in Exodus 33, appealing to the potential reputational damage Yahweh would suffer in the eyes of the nations:

> The Egyptians will hear about it . . . the nations who have heard about you will say: "It is because the LORD was not able to bring this people into the land he swore to give them that he has slaughtered them in the wilderness". . . .Forgive the iniquity of this people according to the greatness of your steadfast love. (Num 14:13–19)

Moses plays to Yahweh's reputation, but also to Yahweh's own self-description in the theophany of Exodus 34. What manner of god (or man) is Yahweh if he acts contrary his own description of himself? Moses' wisdom and ability to persuade Yahweh to change course demonstrates itself here, so too his fidelity to Yahweh and his cause. Still, Yahweh resolves to punish the offenders, bringing a plague that killed off the guilty scouts (Num. 14:38). Moses, perhaps understanding the limit of his influence, stays quiet.

These three stories demonstrate the depth of affection between Moses and Yahweh. In the first, a perceived breach of trust leads to a conflict which is resolved in order to reconcile a meaningful relationship. In the second, a friend responds to an insult levelled against his friend, and in the third, a friend intervenes in a course of action that would have been to the other's detriment. This friendship has also been a site of masculine performance, engaging categories of honor, wisdom, persuasion and loyalty, shared in these stories in equal measure between Moses and Yahweh. But in our final story, the friendship is damaged and the true hegemonic male of the story is laid bare.

STRIKING OUT—DISASTER AT MERIBAH

Our final scene is the story told in Numbers 20:2–13. It is a part of the cycle of murmuring stories that punctuate the narrative of Moses' life and parallels a story told in Exodus 17:1–7.[68] The form of the murmuring story runs it expected course, with the people lamenting a lack of water for themselves and their livestock. This is not an illegitimate complaint, and its veracity is attested in the text: "Now there was no water for the congregation" (Num. 20:2). So while the murmuring motif may appear at times to be vexatious, in this instance that is not the case. Moses and Aaron petition Yahweh for assistance who responds by instructing Moses to take his staff and *command the rock before their eyes to yield its water* (Num. 20:8). Moses takes the staff, insults the thirsty congregation (Listen, you rebels, shall we bring water out of this rock?) before dramatically *striking* the rock twice and enjoying the spectacle and adulation of the people as water gushed forth (Num. 20:10–11). Moses' sequence of actions here mirrors the events of Exodus 17 (though he fails to insult the people there), and therein lies the problem. The command of Yahweh in Exod. 17:6 is explicit: "Strike the rock, and water will come out of it." But this is altered in Numbers, as noted above where the instruction to Moses includes no violent force, but rather a vocal command.

Moses has certainly "played the man" to this point, and that perhaps was his greatest mistake. In elevating himself and turning Yahweh's provision of water into a personal performance, Moses has overstepped the mark.[69] There is no divine condemnation of the people for their request, but rather, a willingness to meet their physical need. The taunt of the Israelites is Moses' response, one quite at odds with Yahweh's legitimation of their request.[70] By turning the instruction to command the rock into an opportunity for taunting rhetoric and then striking the rock with a dramatic flourish Moses makes himself the centre of the miracle and the provider of Israel's needs. He taunts his opponents and then with the striking of his rod brings forth water from a rock, at once become the potent provider. Moses presents himself as "the man."

Quickly, though, his hubris is vanquished. Rather than bringing a plague upon Moses' so-called rebels—as we would expect at this point in the murmuring motif—it is Moses who falls victim to Yahweh's wrath. Yahweh's words, understood through the framework of friendship considered above, demonstrate an acute failing by Moses: "Because you did not trust in me to show my holiness before the eyes of the Israelites" (Num. 20:12a). The memory of this event in Psalm 106:32–33 includes an evaluation of Moses' speech as "rash," suggesting that it is in Moses' words that he failed, whether by the insulting of the Israelites, or the implied claim that it was he, Moses, that was providing the water from the rock.[71] In doing so, Moses demonstrates an arrogance at the expense of Yahweh, a distinct failure in loyalty and a failure to give his friend the honor he is due. In speaking rashly and striking the rock, Moses unwittingly strikes against himself, and the result is a disaster: "you shall not bring this assembly into the land I have given them" (Num. 20:12b).

Interpreters have long struggled with the severity of the consequence meted out against Moses, given what appears to be a minor offense. As we have seen, Yahweh and Moses' relationship had blossomed into a significant friendship, a reality recognisable through the triumvirate of stories considered in Numbers 11–14. But if we consider their relationship through the concept of hegemonic masculinity, it is perhaps little surprise that at some point a terminal fracture would appear. While it is true that at points along the way Moses has assisted Yahweh, those instances have largely been done in private in an attempt to dissuade Yahweh from destroying the people of Israel. Conversely, Yahweh's defense of Moses' honor had been a far more public affair, as in the instance with his siblings in Numbers 12 and his cousin in Numbers 16. Indeed, throughout the narrative in Numbers Moses has seemingly become increasingly weary, battered down by his responsibilities, his frustrations spilling over at numerous points. Leveen notes that the last attack comes from the least likely source[72]—God—but perhaps in light of our discussion here, Yahweh's intervention comes as no great surprise at all. Having struggled to control his family, the people, and finally himself, Yahweh's intervention demonstrates that even amongst those that sit and speak face-to-face there is a power differential. Moses' success in his relationships with other men has always relied upon this power which he here seems to have attributed to himself, but which is here revealed as always belonging to Yahweh.

THE DEATH OF MOSES—DEUTERONOMY 34

Despite the decision to deny the entry of Moses into the land, it is important to note that the position of Moses—described in Deut. 33:1 as the *man of God*—is one that still exceeds other great figures of Israelite memory, a point made clear in the report of his death in Deuteronomy 34. Moses ascends Mt Nebo and is shown the land that he will not inhabit. The language reverts to that which we have known before: Moses is called the servant of Yahweh as he dies on Yahweh's command (Deut.. 34:5). The language of servant serves as a reminder of the nature of Moses and Yahweh's relationship which was tested and finally fractured when Moses assumed to usurp Yahweh's position. Moses is not exonerated, but the death report here signals the enduring place of Moses in the tradition:

> Moses was one hundred twenty years old when he died; his sight was unimpaired and his vigor had not abated. . . .Never since has there arisen

a prophet in Israel like Moses, whom Yahweh knew face to face. (Deut. 34:7–10)

This eulogy directly contradicts Moses' own assertions regarding his well-being in Deuteronomy 31 when he says quite plainly that he is "no longer able to get about" (Deut. 31:2). In his death, legendary motifs are developed[73] which form an *inclusio* with the stories of his miraculous survival at birth. Tellingly, the intimacy of Moses and Yahweh is highlighted in the report, so too the singular place Moses holds in memory. There will be other prophets, but none like Moses.[74] And at the end of his life, there is Yahweh, laying his servant in the ground (Deut. 34:6). Moses dies alone, away from his family and away from those who benefitted from his leadership amongst them. Yahweh's presence in his death validates his life and work,[75] building upon the hagiographic descriptions of him and the extended period of mourning to give witness to the singularity of the man, Moses.

CONCLUSION

From their first encounter at the burning bush to the death of Moses in the presence of his lord, the story of Moses and Yahweh is unique in the scriptural record. Moses, initially attempting to present himself as unworthy and inca-pable grows into a remarkable prophet of Yahweh, both to the people of Israel and Pharaoh. Yahweh elevates Moses in manifold ways, and Moses in turn rises to the challenge. Indeed, so great is Moses' growth that for a time, this appears to be almost a relationship of equals, a friendship, as we have seen in various ways throughout our analysis of the story. In the end though, it is Yahweh's agency that wins out. It is Yahweh's decision to exclude Moses, it is Yahweh's power which prevails, and in doing so, reveals that it has always been Yahweh's hand which supported Moses' growth and Moses' demonstrations of power. The events of Numbers 20 were not a singular thing, but rather the crystalliza-tion of a pattern which had emerged across the length of the story. The bond[76] which had grown between Yahweh and Moses was broken, and the nature of their relationship forced to change.

Despite this 'unmanning', the singularity of Moses' relationship with Yah-weh—as complicated and troubling as it sometimes is—is enshrined in the tradition. It is this relationship which stands behind his ascent to becoming "the man, Moses," even while it is in this relationship that his masculinity is most diminished. It is with Yahweh that Moses bonds and demonstrates his skills in speech, wisdom and persuasion. But it is with Yahweh that Moses' potency is revealed as lacking, his agency undermined. It is Yahweh who buries Moses: in the end, a thoroughly appropriate conclusion.

NOTES

1. Howard Eilberg-Schwartz, *God's Phallus and Other Problems for Men and Monotheism* (Boston: Beacon Press, 1994), 142.
2. D. M. Gunn and Danna Nolan Fewell, *Narrative in the Hebrew Bible*, Oxford Bible Series (Oxford: Oxford University Press, 1993), 89.
3. David J.A. Clines, "Final Reflections on Biblical Masculinity," in *Men and Masculinity in the Hebrew Bible and Beyond*, ed. Ovidiu Creangă (Sheffield: Sheffield Phoenix Press, 2010), 239.
4. A representative list would include, "The Most High Male: Divine Masculinity in the Bible," in *Hebrew Masculinities Anew*, ed. Ovidiu Creangă (Sheffield: Sheffield Phoenix Press, 2019); Stephen D. Moore, *God's Gym: Divine Male Bodies of the Bible* (New York: Routledge, 1996); Francesca Stavrakopoulou, *God: An Anatomy* (London: Picador, 2021); Eilberg-Schwartz, *God's Phallus and Other Problems for Men and Monotheism*; Barbara Thiede, *Male Friendship, Homosociality, and Women in the Hebrew Bible: Malignant Fraternities*, Routledge Studies in the Biblical World (London: Routledge, 2021). It is worth noting that some of these works pre-date Clines' 2010 assessment, but continue to inform the ongoing work in this area.
5. For the sake of clarity, Yahweh and God will be used here synonymously.
6. Thomas B. Dozeman, *Exodus*, The Eerdmans Critical Commentary (Grand Rapids: W.B. Eerdmans, 2009), 117.
7. John I. Durham, *Exodus*, Word Biblical Commentary (Waco: Word, 1987), 30.
8. See Thomas Römer, *Dark God: Cruelty, Sex, and Violence in the Old Testament*, trans. Sean O'Neill, 3rd ed. (Mahwah: Paulist, 2013), 27. Römer points out that Yahweh is often associated with angels or messengers and these figures, in the Old Testament, are always male figures.
9. Durham notes that the angel, Yahweh, the fire as well as the use of the term Elohim create four designations of a singular reality. The interchange between symbol, messenger and God need to be understood in this context. Durham, *Exodus*, 31. As Dozeman notes, the divine messenger is often indistinguishable from God. Dozeman, *Exodus*, 125.
10. *Exodus*, 121.
11. For more on the phenomenon of names in the biblical materials, see Anthony Rees, "[Re]Naming Cozbi: In Memoriam, Cozbi, Daughter of Zur," *Biblical Interpretation* 20, no. –2 (2012).
12. Victor P. Hamilton, *Exodus: An Exegetical Commentary* (Grand Rapids: Baker Academic, 2011), 50.
13. R.S. Wafula, "The Exodus Story as a Foundation of the God of the 'Fathers,'" in *Postcolonial Commentary and the Old Testament*, ed. Hemchand Gossai (London: Bloomsbury, 2019), 14.
14. Dozeman, *Exodus*, 128.
15. Wafula, "The Exodus Story as a Foundation of the God of the 'Fathers.'"
16. Kenneth Ngwa helpfully outlines ways in which the adoption motif is re/deconstructed through the narrative. See Kenneth Ngwa, "The Story of Exodus and

Its Literary Kinships," in *The Oxford Handbook of Biblical Narrative*, ed. Danna Nolan Fewell (Oxford: Oxford University Press, 2018), 129.

17. Wafula, "The Exodus Story as a Foundation of the God of the ‚Fathers,'" 14.

18. Carol L. Meyers, *Exodus*, New Cambridge Bible Commentary (Cambridge: Cambridge University Press, 2005), 56.

19. Noteworthy here is the continued use of distance between Moses and Israel. Moses suggests language that would speak of "your ancestors," rather than including himself within the people of Israel.

20. Dozeman, noting the imperfect form, renders "I will be who I will be." See, Dozeman, *Exodus*, 116.

21. See, ibid., 132.

22. Durham, *Exodus*, 37.

23. Ibid., 38.

24. Ibid.

25. Meyers, *Exodus*, 60. Meyers notes that the image of Yahweh's hand occurs twenty-seven times in the book of Exodus and becomes a part of the vocabulary associated with redemptive acts.

26. Dozeman, *Exodus*, 140. Dozeman further comments that the snake may represent healing, pointing to Moses' crafting of a snake in Numbers 21.

27. Ibid. Similarly, Dozeman points to the healing of Miriam in Numbers 12, suggesting foreshadowing in these signs of significant moments in Moses' life.

28. Durham, *Exodus*, 49.

29. Dozeman, *Exodus*, 142.

30. Ibid.

31. Römer, *Dark God: Cruelty, Sex, and Violence in the Old Testament*, 69.

32. Eilberg-Schwartz, *God's Phallus and Other Problems for Men and Monotheism*, 160.

33. Ibid., 161.

34. See, Römer, *Dark God: Cruelty, Sex, and Violence in the Old Testament*.

35. Thiede, *Male Friendship, Homosociality, and Women in the Hebrew Bible: Malignant Fraternities*, 87.

36. Eilberg-Schwartz, *God's Phallus and Other Problems for Men and Monotheism*, 142.

37. Anthony Rees, "Unmanning Moses," *St Mark's Review* 2017, no. 1 (2017).

38. Hamilton, *Exodus: An Exegetical Commentary*, 167.

39. Durham, *Exodus*, 146.

40. Hamilton notes that this description of Moses is the same as the description of Mordecai in the book of Esther. See, Hamilton, *Exodus: An Exegetical Commentary*, 167.

41. Durham, *Exodus*, 148.

42. Gerhard von Rad, *Moses*, trans. Stephen Neill, 2nd ed. (Eugene: Wipf and Stock, 2012), 5.

43. Dozeman, *Exodus*, 425.

44. On the significance of place, see Edward W. Soja, *Thirdspace: Journeys to Los Angeles and Other Real-and-Imagined Places* (Cambridge: Blackwell, 1996).

45. Durham, *Exodus*, 261.

46. Indeed, it is a feature of the story that even beyond the events of this chapter, Moses' position as leader is always one that is subject to challenge.

47. Meyers, *Exodus*, 262.

48. von Rad, *Moses*, 11.

49. Saul M. Olyan, *Friendship in the Hebrew Bible*, The Anchor Yale Bible Reference Library (New Haven: Yale University Press, 2017), 7.

50. Ibid., –6.

51. Stuart Lasine, "Characterizing God in His/Our Image," in *The Oxford Handbook of Biblical Narrative*, ed. Danna Nolan Fewell (Oxford: Oxford University Press, 2016), 465.

52. This disowning of Israel by both Moses and Yahweh is a feature of the narrative. At times each of them attempt to force the other to take responsibility for them.

53. Though as Durham notes, at no point in Exodus is there a passage in which Yahweh has expressed these sentiments. See, Durham, *Exodus*, 447.

54. Dozeman, *Exodus*, 729.

55. Durham, *Exodus*, 448.

56. Dozeman, *Exodus*, 730.

57. Adriane Leveen, *Memory and Tradition in the Book of Numbers* (New York: Cambridge University Press, 2008), 86.

58. See Susan E. Hylen, "Murmur," in *The New Interpreter's Dictionary of the Bible*, ed. Katherine Doob Sakenfeld (Nashville: Abingdon, 2009); George W. Coats, *Rebellion in the Wilderness: The Murmuring Motif in the Wilderness Traditions of the Old Testament* (Nashville: Abingdon Press, 1968).

59. Carolyn Pressler, *Numbers*, Abingdon Old Testament Commentaries (Nashville: Abingdon, 2017), 90.

60. Ibid., 93.

61. Katharine Doob Sakenfeld, *Journeying with God: A Commentary on the Book of Numbers*, International Theological Commentary (Grand Rapids: Wm. B. Eerdmans, 1995), 72.

62. For an exploration of the maternal imagery here see Anthony Rees, "Moses: Mother of Israel?," in *Making Sense of Motherhood: Biblical and Theological Perspectives*, ed. Beth Stovell (Oregon: Wipf and Stock, 2016).

63. Olyan, *Friendship in the Hebrew Bible*, 5.

64. For a brief discussion of the ambiguity of these circumstances see Sakenfeld, *Journeying with God : A Commentary on the Book of Numbers*, 80–1.

65. Wilda Gafney, *Womanist Midrash: A Reintroduction to the Women of the Torah and the Throne*, 133.

66. Baruch A. Levine, *Numbers 1–20: A New Translation with Introduction and Commentary*, 1st ed. (New York: Doubleday, 1993).

67. David J.A. Clines, *The Concise Dictionary of Classical Hebrew* (Sheffield: Sheffield Phoenix Press, 2009), 72.

68. For an extensive treatment that concludes that these two passages represent two traditions of a single event see, Jacob Milgrom, *Numbers: The JPS Torah Commentary*, ed. Nahum M. Sarna, JPS Torah Commentary (Philadelphia: Jewish Publi-

cation Society, 1990), 448ff. Milgrom also considers the nature and consequence of Moses' sin by reference to significant Jewish interpreters *Numbers: The JPS Torah Commentary*, ed. Nahum M. Sarna, JPS Torah Commentary (Philadelphia: Jewish Publication Society, 1990

69. See, Rees, "Unmanning Moses."

70. Pressler, *Numbers*, 179.

71. Philip J. Budd, *Numbers*, Word Biblical Commentary (Waco: Word Books, 1984), 219.

72. Leveen, *Memory and Tradition in the Book of Numbers*, 53.

73. Richard D. Nelson, *Deuteronomy: A Commentary*, 1st ed., The Old Testament Library (Louisville: Westminster John Knox 2002), 396.

74. Robert Alter, *The Five Books of Moses : A Translation with Commentary* (New York: W.W. Norton & Co., 2004), 1059.

75. Don C. Benjamin, *The Social World of Deuteronomy: A New Feminist Commentary* (Eugene: Cascade Books, 2015), 191.

76. David J.A. Clines, "David the Man: The Construction of Masculinity in the Hebrew Bible," in *Interested Parties: The Ideology of Writers and Readers of the Hebrew Bible* (Sheffield: Sheffield Academic Press, 1995). The notion of the bonding male is explored here. See also Rees, "Unmanning Moses."

Conclusion

Moses is a character with many roles, amongst them; leader, prophet, family-man. Throughout the course of this book we have seen each of these roles, each putting different aspects of his character on display. As the leader of Israel Moses acts as an intermediary between their god, Yahweh and the people. This work requires sensitivity as he deals with a capricious and an equally capricious deity. It requires wisdom, strength and at times, significant courage. During the period in Egypt Moses suffers with the people of Israel as they are punished by a merciless Pharaoh blind with power and paranoia. Despite his own confusion and doubt (Exod. 5:22) he stays the course and is ultimately vindicated by the miraculous events at the sea (Exod. 14). In the wilderness Moses stares down rebellions in the camp including from amongst his own family and despite those who would rise against him, Moses stands up to a deity who has proven himself dangerous, a deity who thinks nothing of smiting humans for their willingness to complain. Moses speaks with Yahweh "face-to-face," and in doing so protects the people of Israel. No wonder then he is remembered as Israel's greatest prophet.

As a part of that role Moses also serves as a prophet to Pharaoh, the un-named King(s) of Egypt. Again, this role demands much of Moses. He is called on to proclaim great calamity which strike at people both innocent and defenseless. He enters into the presence of great power to speak words of judgement, putting his own life at risk. As he speaks with Yahweh "face-to-face," so too he speaks with Pharaoh. In some respects, we could conclude that Moses is less successful in these encounters than those with Yahweh, though this is due to the repeated hardening of Pharaoh's heart and in no way connected to Moses' skill with words. In the end, it is Pharaoh who pursues Moses and the Israelites and comes to a watery end in the Sea and Moses who survives to lead the people out of slavery and towards the promised land.

Moses' public success as leader and prophet is not always matched by success within his own family. Notably, his brother and sister raise public objections against him in Numbers 12. His relationship with Aaron is at times marked by significant closeness and a bond formed through shared trial and tribulation, but it is true also that their relationship s punctuated by episodes of significant frustration and misunderstanding. Moses' relationship with his wife, Zipporah, and his two sons is by no means a significant one in his life. Indeed, any relationship he shares with them is the result of his father-in-law, who re-unites them after a lengthy period of separation. Here, conflicting categories of masculinity converge: if the womanless life is a marker of masculinity, Moses shines here as a banner example. However, if protection and provision of one's family is significant, then we might need to judge Moses a little differently.

However, this book has not been about the roles of Moses, but his perfor-mance of masculinity through them. In this investigation we have considered his relationships with other male characters understanding the social aspect of "performance." This consideration has allowed for a comparison utilising various categories of masculinity, the sum of those being understood as hege-monic masculinity. I set out to argue that in each of these human relationships Moses emerges as a superior man and so is to be understood as a performer of hegemonic masculinity.

In his relationship with Aaron, Moses demonstrates the characteristic of the bonding male. This demonstrates itself in his defense of Aaron in Numbers 16 and his ceding to his request to spare Miriam in Numbers 12. But Aaron's loyalty is clearly lacking in relation to Moses, as is seen by his failure in Exo-dus 32 and his role in the rebellion of Numbers 12. These failures in solidarity also present as failures in wisdom. These are Aaron's decisions and prove to be costly for him and others, as opposed to Moses who is presented as acting in solidarity and in ways which are beneficial to all. And most tellingly, Aaron is introduced to the story as a good speaker, and yet his speaking role ends up being significantly less that that of Moses. It is Moses who speaks to the people, to Yahweh and to Pharaoh. So while Moses' relationship with Aaron is significant, it is not a relationship of equals. Moses emerges as the better man at every point.

The relationship between Moses and his father-in-law is the most con-structive human relationship in his life. As we see in the other relationships, time and time again it is Moses who performs masculinity more successfully, whether in wisdom, persuasion, honor and so on. Yet in each of these cat-egories, his father-in-law proves to be Moses' match. Indeed, we might even venture to say that Moses' performance of these categories is enhanced by the example of his father-in-law. There are categories which differentiate Moses from his father-in-law: we never see Jethro act in violence; we know he has seven daughters but know nothing of his wife or sons (those who would represent a legitimate heir); we know nothing of his physical appearance. It is probably sufficient to say that in these respects, Moses' father-in-law is not an exemplar of hegemonic masculinity. Nonetheless, we need also stress that Moses' performance of masculinity seems powerfully influenced by his father-in-law, or perhaps better, his father-in-law facilitates Moses' masculine performance, in a fashion which honors the contribution he makes to Moses' life. This is not a bonding of the type Moses experiences with Aaron, yet we do see in Moses' response to his father-in-law some of these traits, such as the desire to honor him by giving him the lead role in the celebrations of Exodus 18, and by heeding his subsequent advice. In this we see also Jethro's capacities for wisdom and persuasion in full-effect, even while they serve no great benefit to him.

The two Pharaohs which are part of Moses' life form a remarkable contrast with him. Moses does not know the first Pharaoh, and yet this king exerts an enormous influence in his life. The Pharaoh is impetuous, paranoid and despite wielding immense political power, is continually subverted. Humble midwives resist his inhumane demands to put Hebrew boys to death (Exod. 1:17–21), and his own daughter adopts Moses and raises him as her son. As an adult Moses' life is again threatened by Pharaoh, but ultimately, the Pharaoh's political power proves impotent and he is unable bring his plan to pass. Moses escapes and establishes a new life in Midian. The second Pharaoh becomes known to Moses through their series of confrontations in Exodus 7–11. The second Pharaoh is more developed than his predecessor, and at times appears willing to heed Moses' calls for the relief of the Israelites. But the Pharaoh is revealed as a cruel and stubborn individual, hardening his heart to Moses' words (and having his heart hardened by Yahweh), the result being a series of calamities brought upon his kingdom and those within it. His is a failure of wisdom, and as king, of honor if we understand his role to include the protection of his people. He leads his Kingdom into ruin and his military to their demise at the sea. Conversely, Moses leads Israel through the sea to safety, watching his opponent perish and then walking away. It is Moses who prevails at every step.

The rebellion of Moses' cousin Korah in Numbers 16 is something of a highpoint for Moses, even while the story ends in significant tragedy. Korah emerges as a confident, defiant individual, capable of mustering support and confronting Moses with what appears to be a reasonable argument. And yet, as we have seen, the demise of Korah is swift, and the narrator seems to delight in particular aspects of the story. Rather than usurping Moses or even winning a concession from him, the earth opens up and consumes Korah and his family, a thing prophesied before Moses just seconds before it took place

(Num. 16:31–32). Moses then emerges as a man of wisdom and potency, while Korah is presented as foolish and dishonorable. Further, the name Korah seems to mock him, hinting at baldness and so marking him as weak and lacking in beauty.

If the events of Numbers 16 represent a highpoint, it is reasonable to say that those of Numbers 25, coming in the shadows of the events at Meribah in Numbers 20, represent a low point for Moses. In the midst of a grieving community Moses witnesses the arrival of an Israelite man and his Midianite wife but does not respond. Given the context of mourning—a response to Israel's failure with the Moabite women (Num. 25:1–5)—the actions of the Israelite elite Zimri and his wife Cozbi (the daughter of a prominent Midianite), are seemingly intended to be understood as a grave failure, a point understood by cultic guard Phinehas, who quickly responds and slays the two of them with a single thrust of his spear (Num 25:8). Phinehas is lauded by Yahweh for his actions, thereby constituting a tacit rebuke of Moses for his failure to act. Phinehas is said to have acted with Yahweh's "zeal," a zeal which manifests itself here with a particular type of violence in the face of Moses' own passivity. In a strange way, Phinehas' violent act constitutes a commitment to Yahweh's honor and demonstrates his own physical potency whereas Moses' indecision points his declining faculties of both body and mind.

In the final chapter we saw that as strong as Moses' performance of hegemonic masculinity is in relation to other humans, he is ultimately undone in his relationship with Yahweh. Moses' unmanning[1] at the hands of Yahweh comes as a result of his failings at Meribah in Numbers 20, though as we have seen, that was a breaking point rather than a singular event. Moses' struggles were particularly evident in Numbers 11 when in trying to articulate his frustration with Yahweh he turned to feminine metaphors of conception and nursing to illustrate his confusion. Nothing is less masculine than feeling like a woman (!) and even while Moses' argument is that he is not those things, his invocation of them is suggestive of his own sense of being feminized. Moses' own words betray him: in this relationship it is Yahweh who excels in potency and strength, Yahweh who charts the course and sees things through to their end. It is Yahweh that determines that Moses will not enter the Promised Land and will die on the wrong side of the river.

THE CONCEPTUAL VALUE OF HEGEMONIC MASCULINITY

While it has perhaps been unfair to compare Moses to Yahweh, as we noted, Yahweh is presented as a character in the narrative, a "paper person" to use Barthes' terminology,[2] and aspects of the relationship have stood up to the analysis offered here. There is enough similarity for this to have been a viable exercise. Indeed, there were times when Moses appeared to hold the upper hand with Yahweh and to influence Yahweh by appeal to Yahweh's potential failure in the masculinity categories. None the less, it is perhaps no surprise that Moses would come off second best by this comparative approach, and so any evaluation of the value of the concept should appropriately that that comparison aside.

The analysis of Moses' relationships with the other characters does, in the end, benefit from the concept of hegemonic masculinity. By thinking through the categories germane to each relationship, a clearer picture of the narrator's presentation of the characters is possible and valuable comparisons can be made. Not surprisingly, the value it most keenly seen in the relationships that span a great length of time. As Olsen notes of Clines' study of Moses, a small sample of chapters (three out of 137 in the Moses tradition) is almost certainly too restrictive.[3] As a result we may want to exercise caution in our assessment of Korah and Phinehas who here only constitute a single chapter in the broader narrative. The concept of hegemonic masculinity allows us to assess particular aspects of their characterization, but they are hardly developed characters, or to use Forster's terminology, "round."[4] The physical actions of Korah and Phinehas provide the means by which we gain most information: Korah leads a group of rebels, he speaks powerfully and is unafraid to openly challenge Moses and Aaron. Phinehas acts quickly—and violently—in the face of what he perceives as wrong-doing. In each case, this direct characterization leads us to particular inferences about their character.[5] In both cases, categories of masculinity help us to build particular understandings of these individuals. And yet, as Olson notes, the sample size is too small. Korah is literally swallowed up in the course of his narrative and makes no further appearance. Phinehas does reappear in the narrative (Numbers 31, Joshua 22 and Judges 20), though in each instance his role is similar to the one established in Numbers 25: namely, protection of the cult and religious orthodoxy. Phinehas is a man of violence at every point. This is an insufficient set of data to make an informed judgement. Nonetheless, the two characters do serve a function and that is in the way in which Moses is contrasted against them at these particular points. Korah and Phinehas may not provide sufficient data to make a decision regarding them, but they do help to illustrate certain aspects of Moses' own performance. As Margolin notes, these embedded stories allow us to reflect on Moses, the main character, through the contrast made between them.[6]

In relation to Korah we can see the way in which this contrast serves to build up Moses' masculinity. It is Moses who ends the encounter with his honor enhanced, having stared down Korah and his rebels and publicly humiliated them to the point of their death. It is Moses' words that prevail. Korah and his rebellions serves as a vehicle to enhance Moses, and the narrator's choice of name for Korah, playing with the notion of baldness, serves to demean him further. Phinehas on the other hand emerges in a stronger position through the events of Numbers 25, or more to the point, Moses' standing is damaged. Moses' potency is waning, through the failure of his mind and body to act. Yahweh's blessing of Phinehas stands as a condemnation of Moses who has failed on a matter of loyalty, just as he had in Numbers 20. But with such a narrow view of Phinehas, this is far less a comment on his hegemonic masculinity than it is on Moses'. In these instances it is clear that hegemonic masculinity has proven to be a useful concept, though more in relation to an assessment of Moses than the other characters.

The studies of Moses' father-in-law, Aaron, and Pharaoh offer a far more significant body of material to work from. Jethro presents as a hospitable and wise figure in Moses' life. As we have seen, it is he who influences Moses to the greatest extent and is a figure whom Moses honours in a range of ways. And yet this counselling role seems to be the purpose of Jethro through the narrative. Several of the categories of masculinity are absent in his characterization, in particular violence (Clines' primary category), the production of *legitimate* heirs along with his physical appearance, of which we know nothing. So to describe Jethro as a performer of hegemonic masculinity would again be to say too much. However, we are able to affirm that he performs particular categories of masculinity with great effect, and serves as facilitator of Moses' own growth in masculinity.

Of the other human characters within Moses' life it seems clear that Aaron is the most developed. He is introduced as an eloquent speaker, a thing confirmed at various points, though not always in ways that are positive. He has children, he works together with Moses in ways that demonstrate wisdom and commitment to him. In Numbers 16:41–50, in the face of a rebellion against Aaron and Moses he acts with great courage and conviction, holding back the wrath of Yahweh from consuming the Israelites. However, unlike the presentation of Jethro, Aaron's characterization features moments of significant failure, most notably in Exodus 32 where he fails to resist the people of Israel's request for a golden image of god, and in Numbers 12 when he stands with Miriam against Moses. Yahweh's endorsement of Moses, coupled with the community's ongoing affirmation of Moses as their leader points to Aaron's falling short of hegemonic masculinity, and his failures again serve to highlight Moses' strengths. Aaron gains his own rewards. The High Priesthood flows from his line, through Phinehas. And yet at his death (Num. 20:22–29) there is no great narrative flourish similar to the report of Moses' death. The people of Israel mourn for the loss of a significant figure, but there is no assessment of his life in the fashion of Deuteronomy 34.

Moses' greatest adversary is the Pharaoh, or more precisely, Pharaohs. As we noted, there is a strategy of collapse employed in the characterization of the two Pharaohs in Moses' life so that they share certain characteristics which allow them to be considered together. If power is a key marker of masculinity, then the Pharaohs are exemplary. As the king of the Egypt and leader of an empire, the Pharaoh stands as a man with incomparable influence. That power is performed with significant violence in both cases: the first oversees an oppressive regime which abuses its slaves. His irrational paranoia leads to a series of policies which account to what we would call attempted genocide.[7] The second Pharaoh is defiant in the face of Moses' demands. His stubbornness ushers in a series of disasters that destroy his kingdom and its life. In both cases, power does not equate with potency, and is not coupled with wisdom. Despite their immense power, the Pharaohs are to be evaluated as failed men,[8] and in relation to Yahweh, fake-gods. Their failure, similarly to those of Aaron, mean we are able to assess them as failures in relation to hegemonic masculinity, failures which serve to highlight Moses' success, and crucially in this instance, those of Yahweh.

If we take the sum of these comparative analyses and couple them with the other aspects of Moses' masculinity explored in chapter one, we can reasonably assert that Moses stands as an example of hegemonic masculinity within the narrative of his life, though we might temper this by noting a decline in his performance across time. The scriptures attempt to deny his growing frailty, as we have seen, but they contradict Moses' own assessment of himself. If Haddox is right, that hegemonic masculinity includes matters of bodily integrity,[9] Moses' self-claimed fragility is a strike against him.

Perhaps, then, the example of Moses points to the fantasy of the concept. If Israel's greatest prophet, the towering figure of the biblical tradition falls short, is the concept really viable? We must note here that the Moses considered here is a paper person, a literary character, and so too the other protagonists we have considered. The humanity so often revered in his presentation, precisely at the moments of his failures, points to the unattainable standard the concept holds up. If a reconfigured hegemonic masculinity is to be possible, it will need to take seriously the notion of the flawed hero.

MAN(LY) PROBLEMS

The contingent nature of hegemonic masculinity is also demonstrated through our discussion. As we noted, hegemonic masculinity is conditioned by culture. Cultures produce subjects and those subjects perform their culturally prescribed roles. If we were to create a suite of categories for hegemonic masculinity in our Western world, it is unlikely those we have considered here would be adopted *en masse*. The categories considered here are coloured by the patriarchal world from which they emerge. This is by no means to suggest that the era of patriarchy has been closed, but we might expect that the significant gains in female agency and changes to social structures and expectation might be accompanied by a shift in what constitutes hegemonic masculinity. Hopefully, the hegemonic male can become the one who empowers the women in his life, not solely imagining himself as a protector of them. Indeed, perhaps given the hetero-normative nature of this construction, the hegemonic male might be the one who gives value to every relationship in his life, resisting the very idea of the instrumental relationship. In doing so, hegemonic masculinity can differentiate itself from its close cousin, toxic masculinity.[10]

Hegemonic masculinity may have proven a useful tool for analysis of biblical texts and relationships between characters, but that analysis has only served to demonstrate the embodied problem of hegemonic masculinity, demonstrated as it is through homosocial relationships. These performances are replete with competition, the nature of which is dangerous to those who compete, but also to vulnerable members of society whose lives are impacted by the system. Such problems have been noted before, with questions regarding the constructive contribution biblical masculinity studies might offer.[11] This study has revealed much which objectionable and to continue to uncritically hold up such figures as masculine models is a failure. Clines is right: a refusal to speak out about it is a dereliction of our moral duty.[12]

FUTURE DIRECTIONS

This study has proceeded along purely literary lines, with little if any engagement with questions of history. As noted in the introduction, the final form of Moses' story is perhaps the work of many hands over a long period of time. Historically oriented critics have, with varying degrees of certainty, identified textual strata which make up the extended narrative we have considered here. Echoing Dennis Olson,[13] there is certainly scope to explore the representation of Moses' within these traditions where they can be reasonably established. This may serve to further nuance the finding of my work here.

Further, this study has had little interest in the way in which Moses is received in the religious traditions that value him. As a key figure in the three great mono-theistic faiths,[14] Moses is an immensely significant figure in the religious life of a large part of the human family. The appropriation of Moses as a model figure in Jewish, Christian and Islamic traditions represents a major opportunity afforded by this initial exploration. What of Moses' character is worthy of emulation? What aspects of his character have been developed in the development of the traditions? What aspects of Moses are we right to resist? Fruitful work awaits those who might take up these questions.

Finally, I hope the value of this extended study of Moses is understood to be of value. Olson's comment regarding Clines' reading of Moses is valid: characterization of major figures unfolds over larger textual units and as such, studies of those characters are benefitted from a more extended consideration. This is by no means intended as a criticism of Clines or other colleagues that have waded into the sea of masculinity studies, nor a diminishment of the gains made by them. This work would be impossible without those efforts. It is simply to point to the possibilities afforded by longer studies such as these as the discourse matures.

THE MAN, MOSES

This work has relentlessly sought to keep Moses at its centre. There is no need nor means for the continued elevation of Moses: his revered memory is secure in the sacred books of billions. Their memory of him reveals that despite inevitable human failing, and here we might add male failure, Moses was an uncommon character, one who transcended human expectations and yet fell foul of them time and time again. The Moses found in the pages of the Old Testament may fail to meet our contemporary notions of the ideal man, that idea we have called hegemonic masculinity. We need not judge him too harshly for that. As for Moses, so for us: human expectation is a fickle thing and none of us, even the most heroic, live to our most highly held ideals all the time. A realization of our own reality should allow us to re-think Moses, to re-think masculinity. Yes, Moses was violent. Yes, Moses failed in a range of relationships. Much of that was despicable and we are right to name it as such. But that constitutes but a first step. We must, as Koosed implores, must find reasons for hope, or perhaps better, a plan for hope, which enables boys and men to resist "the coercive power of the patriarch and the denigrating crush of slavery"[15] in the unleashing of liberation.

The memory of Moses included in his story is not naïve regarding his flaws, but they look past them. Not dwelling on his short comings, the assessment of his life in the reporting of his death points to the enduring value and place of this man; the man, Moses.

NOTES

1. See Anthony Rees, "Unmanning Moses," *St Mark's Review* 2017, no. 1 (2017). On the unmanning of Ezekiel see Chapter 4 of Rhiannon Graybill, *Are We Not Men?:*

Unstable Masculinity in the Hebrew Prophets (New York: Oxford University Press, 2016).

2. Roland Barthes, *Image, Music, Text*, trans. Stephen Heath (New York: Hill and Wang, 1977).

3. Dennis T. Olson, "Crossing Boundaries: Moses the Man, Masculinities and Methods," *Hebrew Bible and Ancient Israel* 5 (2016): 156.

4. For a brief overview see Jerome T. Walsh, *Old Testament Narrative: A Guide to Interpretation*, 1st ed. (Louisville: Westminster John Knox Press, 2009), 24.

5. Uri Margolin, "Character," in *The Cambridge Companion to Narrative*, ed. David Herman (Cambridge: Cambridge University Press, 2007), 77.

6. Ibid.

7. Colin Martin Tatz, *With Intent to Destroy: Reflecting on Genocide* (London: Verso, 2003).

8. Brian DiPalma, "De/Constructing Masculinity in Exodus 1–4," in *Men and Masculinity in the Hebrew Bible and Beyond*, ed. Ovidiu Creangă (Sheffield: Sheffield Phoenix Press, 2010).

9. Susan E. Haddox, "Is There a 'Biblical Masculinity'? Masculinities in the Hebrew Bible," *Word & World* 36, no. 1 (2016).

10. bell hooks, *The Will to Change: Men, Masculinity, and Love* (New York: Atria Books, 2004).

11. David J.A. Clines, "Final Reflections on Biblical Masculinity," in *Men and Masculinity in the Hebrew Bible and Beyond*, ed. Ovidiu Creangă (Sheffield: Sheffield Phoenix Press, 2010), 239.

12. Ibid.

13. Olson, "Crossing Boundaries: Moses the Man, Masculinities and Methods."

14. Alongside the works noted in the Introduction, see Mahsheed Ansari and Hakan Coruh, "The Prophets as Archetypes of Peace in the Qua'ran: The Use and Nonuse of Isrā'īliyyāt Sources in the Story of Mūsa," in *Things That Make for Peace: Traversing Text and Traditon in Christianity and Islam*, ed. Anthony Rees (Lanham: Lexington, 2020).

15. Jennifer Koosed, "Moses, Feminism and the Male Subject," in *The Bible and Feminism: Remapping the Field*, ed. Yvonne Sherwood (Oxford: Oxford University Press, 2017), 237.

Bibliography

Ackerman, Susan. "Why Is Miriam Also among the Prophets? (and Is Zipporah among the Priests?)." *Journal of Biblical Literature* 121, no. 1 (Spr 2002): 47–80.

Albertz, Rainer. "Ambivalent Relations between Brothers in the Hebrew Bible." In *With the Loyal You Show Yourself Loyal*, edited by T. M. Lemos, Jordan D. Rosenblum, Karen B. Stern and Debra Scoggins Ballentine. Ancient Israel and Its Literature, 29–44. Atlanta: SBl Press, 2021.

Alter, Robert. *Ancient Israel: The Former Prophets: Joshua, Judges, Samuel, and Kings: A Translation with Commentary.* 1st ed. New York: W. W. Norton & Co., 2013.

———. *The Five Books of Moses : A Translation with Commentary.* New York: W. W. Norton & Co., 2004.

The Ancient Egyptian Book of the Dead. Translated by Andrews Carol and R. O. Faulkner. New York: MacMillan, 1985.

Ansari, Mahsheed, and Hakan Coruh. "The Prophets as Archetypes of Peace in the Qua'ran: The Use and Nonuse of Isrā'īliyyāt Sources in the Story of Mūsa." In *Things That Make for Peace: Traversing Text and Traditon in Christianity and Islam*, edited by Anthony Rees, 25–40. Lanham: Lexington, 2020.

Arnold, B. T., and John H. Choi. *A Guide to Biblical Hebrew Syntax.* Cambridge: Cambridge University Press, 2003.

Ashcroft, Bill, Gareth Griffiths, and Helen Tiffin. *Post-Colonial Studies: The Key Concepts.* 2nd ed. New York: Routledge, 2007.

Assmann, Jan. *From Akhenaten to Moses: Ancient Egypt and Religious Change.* Cairo: American University in Cairo Press, 2014.

Bal, Mieke. *Narratology: Introduction to the Theory of Narrative.* 3rd ed. Toronto: University of Toronto Press, 2009.

Barrett, Frank J. "The Organizational Construction of Hegemonic Masculinity: The Case of the Us Navy." In *The Masculinities Reader*, edited by Stephen M. Whitehead and Frank J. Barrett, 77–99. Cambridge: Polity Press, 2001.

Barthes, Roland. *Image, Music, Text.* Translated by Stephen Heath. New York: Hill and Wang, 1977.

Benjamin, Don C. *The Social World of Deuteronomy: A New Feminist Commentary.* Eugene: Cascade Books, 2015.

Bird, Sharon R. "Welcome to the Men's Club: Homosociality and the Maintenance of Hegemonic Masculinity." *Gender and Society* 10, no. 2 (1996): 120-32.

Bodner, Keith. *The Rebellion of Absalom.* London: Routledge, 2014.

Boer, Roland. *The Sacred Economy of Ancient Israel.* Library of Ancient Israel. Edited by Douglas A. Knight. Louisville: Westminster John Knox, 2015.

Brenner-Idan, Athalya. *The Israelite Woman: Social Role and Literary Type in Biblical Narrative.* Cornerstones. 2nd ed. London: Bloomsbury, 2015.

Britt, Brian M. *Rewriting Moses: The Narrative Eclipse of the Text.* Journal for the Study of the Old Testament Supplement Series. London: T & T Clark, 2004.

Brittan, Arthur. "Masculinities and Masculinism." In *The Masculinities Reader*, edited by Stephen M. Whitehead and Frank J. Barrett, 51–5 Cambridge: Polity Press, 2001.

Budd, Philip J. *Numbers.* Word Biblical Commentary. Waco: Word Books, 1984.

Burgh, Theodore W. "Music." In *The Interpreter's Dictionary of the Bible*, edited by Katherine Doob Sakenfeld, 166-75. Nashville: Abingdon, 2009.

Butler, Judith. *Gender Trouble: Feminism and the Subversion of Identity.* Routledge Classics. New York: Routledge, 2006.

Camp, Claudia V. *Wise, Strange and Holy : The Strange Woman and the Making of the Bible.* Journal for the Study of the Old Testament. Supplement Series. Sheffield: Sheffield Academic Press, 2000.

Childs, Brevard S. *The Book of Exodus: A Critical, Theological Commentary.* Old Testament Library. Louisville: Westminster John Knox, 2004.

Christensen, Duane L. *Deuteronomy 21:1–34:12.* Word Biblical Commentary. Nashville: Thomas Nelson, 2002.

Claassens, L. Juliana M. *Mourner, Mother, Midwife: Reimagining God's Delivering Presence in the Old Testament.* Louisville: Westminster John Knox, 2012.

Clines, David J. A. "Being a Man in the Book of the Covenant." Chap. 1 in *Read the Law: Essays in Honour of Gordon J. Wenham*, edited by J. G. McConville and Karl Möller, 3–9. London: Bloomsbury, 2007.

Clines, David J.A. *The Concise Dictionary of Classical Hebrew.* Sheffield: Sheffield Phoenix Press, 2009.

———. "Dancing and Shining at Sinai: Playing the Man in Exodus 32–34." In *Men and Masculinity in the Hebrew Bible and Beyond*, edited by Ovidiu Creangă. The Bible in the Modern World, 54-63 Sheffield: Sheffield Phoenix Press, 2010.

———. "David the Man: The Construction of Masculinity in the Hebrew Bible." In *Interested Parties: The Ideology of Writers and Readers of the Hebrew Bible*, 212-43. Sheffield: Sheffield Academic Press, 1995.

———. "Final Reflections on Biblical Masculinity." In *Men and Masculinity in the Hebrew Bible and Beyond*, edited by Ovidiu Creangă, 234–9. Sheffield: Sheffield Phoenix Press, 2010.

———. "The Most High Male: Divine Masculinity in the Bible." In *Hebrew Masculinities Anew*, edited by Ovidiu Creangă, 61–82. Sheffield: Sheffield Phoenix Press, 2019.

Coats, George W. *Moses: Heroic Man, Man of God*. Journal for the Study of the Old Testament Supplement Series. Sheffield: JSOT Press, 1988.

———. *Rebellion in the Wilderness: The Murmuring Motif in the Wilderness Traditions of the Old Testament*. Nashville: Abingdon Press, 1968.

Collins, John J. "The Zeal of Phinehas: The Bible and the Legitimation of Violence." *Journal of Biblical Literature* 122, no. 1 (2003): 3–21.

Connell, R. W. *Masculinities*. 2nd ed. Cambridge: Polity Press, 2005.

Connell, R. W., and James W. Messerschmidt. "Hegemonic Masculinity: Rethinking the Concept." *Gender & Society* 19, no. 6 (2005): 829–59.

Davies, Eryl W. *Numbers: The Road to Freedom*. Phoenix Guides to the Old Testament. Sheffield: Sheffield Phoenix, 2015.

DiPalma, Brian. "De/Constructing Masculinity in Exodus 1–4." In *Men and Masculinity in the Hebrew Bible and Beyond*, edited by Ovidiu Creangă, 36–53. Sheffield: Sheffield Phoenix Press, 2010.

DiPalma, Brian Charles. "Scribal Masculinity and the Court Tales of Daniel." In *Hebrew Masculinities Anew*, edited by Ovidiu Creangă, 229–50. Sheffield: Sheffield Phoenix, 2019.

Downing, F. Gerald. "Honor." In *The New Interpreter's Dictionary of the Bible*, edited by Katherine Doob Sakenfeld, 884–5. Nashville: Abingdon, 2007.

Dozeman, Thomas B. "The Midianites in the Formation of the Book of Numbers." In *The Books of Leviticus and Numbers*, edited by Thomas Römer, 26–84. Leuven: Uitgeverij Peeters, 2008.

Dozeman, Thomas B. *Exodus*. The Eerdmans Critical Commentary. Grand Rapids: W.B. Eerdmans, 2009.

Durham, John I. *Exodus*. Word Biblical Commentary. Waco: Word, 1987.

Eilberg-Schwartz, Howard. *God's Phallus and Other Problems for Men and Monotheism*. Boston: Beacon Press, 1994.

Eller, Karen. "Numbers 25: A Reading by a Queer Australian." In *Terror in the Bible*, edited by Monica Jyotsna Melanchthon and Robyn J. Whitaker, 47–63. Atlanta: SBL, 2021.

Flood, Michael. "Men, Sex, and Homosociality How Bonds between Men Shape Their Sexual Relations with Women." *Men and Masculinities* 10, no. 3 (04/01 2008): 339–59.

Frevel, Christian. *Desert Transformations : Studies in the Book of Numbers*. Forschungen Zum Alten Testament. Tübingen, Germany: Mohr Siebeck, 2020.

Gafney, Wil. "A Queer Womanist Midrashic Reading of Numbers 25:1–18." In *Leviticus-Numbers*, edited by Athalya Brenner and Archie C.C Lee. Texts@Contexts, 189–98 Minneapolis: Fortress, 2013.

Gafney, Wilda. *Womanist Midrash : A Reintroduction to the Women of the Torah and the Throne*.

George, Mark. "Masculinity and Its Regimentation in Deuteronomy." In *Men and Masculinity in the Hebrew Bible and Beyond*, edited by Ovidiu Creangă, 64–82. Sheffield: Sheffield Phoenix Press, 2010.

Goldingay, John. *The First Testament: A New Translation.* Downers Grove: IVP, 2018.

Goldstein, Elyse. *Revisions: Seeing Torah through a Feminist Lens.* Toronto: Key Porter, 1998.

Grafius, Brandon R. *Reading Phinehas, Watching Slashers: Horror Theory and Numbers 25.* Lanham: Lexington Books / Fortress Academic, 2018.

Graybill, Rhiannon. *Are We Not Men?: Unstable Masculinity in the Hebrew Prophets.* New York: Oxford University Press, 2016.

———. "Elisha's Body and the Queer Touch of Prophecy." *Biblical Theology Bulletin* 49, no. 1 (2019): 32–40.

———. "Jonah 'between Men': The Prophet in Critical Homosocial Perspective." In *Hebrew Masculinities Anew*, edited by Ovidiu Creangă, 10–28. Sheffield: Sheffield Phoenx, 2019.

Greenberg, Moshe. *Understanding Exodus: A Holistic Commentary on Exodus 1–11.* Second edition ed. Eugene: Cascade Books, 2013.

Gunn, D. M., and Danna Nolan Fewell. *Narrative in the Hebrew Bible.* Oxford Bible Series. Oxford: Oxford University Press, 1993.

Haddox, Susan E. "Favoured Sons and Subordinate Masculinities." In *Men and Masculinity in the Hebrew Bible and Beyond*, edited by Ovidiu Creangă, 2–19. Sheffield: Sheffield Phoenix Press, 2010.

———. "Is There a 'Biblical Masculinity'? Masculinities in the Hebrew Bible." *Word & World* 36, no. 1 (2016 2016): 5–14.

———. "Masculinity Studies of the Hebrew Bible: The First Two Decades." *Currents in Biblical Research* 14, no. 2 (February 1, 2016 2016): 176–206.

Hamilton, Victor P. *Exodus: An Exegetical Commentary.* Grand Rapids: Baker Academic, 2011.

Harrison, James B. "Men's Roles and Men's Lives." *Signs* 4, no. 2 (1978): 324–36.

Hays, Christopher. "Live by the Sword, Die by the Sword: The Reinvention of the Reluctant Prophet as Moviemoses." https://www.academia.edu/10037402/Live_By_the_Sword_Die_By_the_Sword_The_Reinvention_of_the_Reluctant_Prophet_as_MovieMoses_.

Higginbotham, Carolyn. "Egypt." In *The New Interpreter's Dictionary of the Bible*, edited by Katherine Doob Sakenfeld, 206–26. Nashville: Abingdon, 2007.

———. "Pharaoh." In *The New Interpreter's Dictionary of the Bible*, edited by Katherine Doob Sakenfeld, 48–85. Nashville: Abingdon, 2009.

hooks, bell. *The Will to Change: Men, Masculinity, and Love.* New York: Atria Books, 2004.

Hugenberger, G.P. "Phinehas." In *International Standard Bible Encyclopedia*, edited by Geoffrey W. Broimley. Grand Rapids: William B. Eerdmans, 1986.

Hylen, Susan E. "Murmur." In *The New Interpreter's Dictionary of the Bible*, edited by Katherine Doob Sakenfeld, 166. Nashville: Abingdon, 2009.

John Coleman, Darnell, and Darnell Colleen Manassa. *The Ancient Egyptian Neth-erworld Books.* [in English] Writings from the Ancient World. Atlanta: SBL Press, 2018.

Josephus, Flavius. "The Antiquities of the Jews." Translated by William Whiston. In *Complete Works of Flavius Josephus.* Grand Rapids: Kregel, 1960.

Junior, Nyasha, and Jeremy Schipper. "Mosaic Disability and Identity in Exodus 4:10; 6:12, 30." *Biblical Interpretation* 16 (2008): 428–41.

Kalmanofsky, Amy. "Moses and His Problematic Masculinity." In *Hebrew Masculinities Anew*, edited by Ovidiu Creangă, 173–89. Sheffield: Sheffield Phoenix Press, 2019.

Kimmel, Michael S. "Masculinity as Homophobia: Fear, Shame and Silence in the Construction of Gender Identity." In *The Masculinities Reader*, edited by Frank J. Barrett and Stephen M. Whitehead, 266–87. Cambridge: Polity Press, 2001.

Kirova, Milena. *Performing Masculinity in the Hebrew Bible.* Hebrew Bible Monographs. Sheffield: Sheffield Phoenix Press, 2020.

Kirsch, Jonathan. *Moses: A Life.* 1st ed. New York: Ballantine Books, 1998.

Koosed, Jennifer. "Moses, Feminism and the Male Subject." In *The Bible and Feminism: Remapping the Field*, edited by Yvonne Sherwood, 225–239. Oxford: Oxford University Press, 2017.

Kugler, Robert. "Priests and Levites." In *The New Interpreter's Dictionary of the Bible*, edited by Katherine Doob Sakenfeld, 596–613. Nashville: Abingdon, 2009.

Lasine, Stuart. "Characterizing God in His/Our Image." In *The Oxford Handbook of Biblical Narrative*, edited by Danna Nolan Fewell, 465–77. Oxford: Oxford University Press, 2016.

Lemos, T. M. *Violence and Personhood in Ancient Israel and Comparative Contexts.* Oxford: Oxford University Press, 2017.

Leneman, Helen. *Moses: The Man and the Myth in Music.* Sheffield: Sheffield Phoenix Press, 2014.

Leveen, Adriane. *Memory and Tradition in the Book of Numbers.* New York: Cambridge University Press, 2008.

Levine, Baruch A. "Korah, Korahites." In *The New Interpreter's Dictionary of the Bible*, edited by Katherine Doob Sakenfeld, 547–8. Nashville: Abingdon, 2008.

———. *Numbers 1–20 : A New Translation with Introduction and Commentary.* 1st ed. New York: Doubleday, 1993.

———. *Numbers 21–36 : A New Translation with Introduction and Commentary.* 1st ed. New York: Doubleday, 2000.

Lipka, Hilary. "Shaved Beards and Bared Buttocks: Shame and the Undermining of Masculine Performance in Biblical Texts." In *Being a Man: Negotiating Ancient Constructs of Masculinity*, edited by Ilona Zsolnay. Studies in the History of the Ancient near East, 176–97. London: Routledge, 2017.

Lutzky, Harriet C. "The Name "Cozbi" (Numbers 15, 18)." *Vetus Testamentum* 47, no. 4 (1997): 546–49.

MacDonald, Malcolm. *Schoenberg.* The Master Musicians. Rev. ed. New York: Oxford University Press, 2008.

Măcelaru, Marcel V. "Saul in the Company of Men: (De)Constructing Masculinity in 1 Samuel 9–31." In *Biblical Masculinities Foregrounded*, edited by Ovidiu Creangă and Peter-Ben Smit, 51–68. Sheffield: Sheffield Phoenix, 2014.

Macwilliam, Stuart. "Ideologies of Male Beauty and the Hebrew Bible." *Biblical Interpretation* 17 (2009): 265–87.

Margolin, Uri. "Character." In *The Cambridge Companion to Narrative*, edited by David Herman, 66–79. Cambridge: Cambridge University Press, 2007.

Matthews, Victor Harold, and Don C. Benjamin. *Social World of Ancient Israel, 125–587 Bce.* Peabody: Hendrickson, 1993.

McEntire, Mark. "Cozbi, Achan, and Jezebel: Executions in the Hebrew Bible and Modern Lynching." *Review & Expositor* 118, no. 1 (2021): 21–31.

Melanchthon, Monica Jyotsna, and Robyn J. Whitaker. *Terror in the Bible : Rhetoric, Gender, and Violence.* International Voices in Biblical Studies. Atlanta: SBL Press, 2021.

Meyers, Carol L. *Exodus.* New Cambridge Bible Commentary. Cambridge: Cambridge University Press, 2005.

Milgrom, Jacob. *Numbers: The JPS Torah Commentary.* JPS Torah Commentary. Edited by Nahum M. Sarna. Philadelphia: Jewish Publication Society, 1990.

Moore, Stephen D. "Final Reflections on Biblical Masculinity." In *Men and Masculinity in the Hebrew Bible and Beyond*, edited by Ovidiu Creangă, 240–55. Sheffield: Sheffield Phoenix, 2010.

———. *God's Gym : Divine Male Bodies of the Bible.* New York: Routledge, 1996.

Morgan, David H. "Family, Gender and Masculinities." In *The Masculinities Reader*, edited by Stephen M. Whitehead and Frank J. Barrett, 223–32. Cambridge: Polity Press, 2001.

Murphy, Kelly J. *Rewriting Masculinity : Gideon, Men, and Might.* Oxford: Oxford University Press, 2019.

Nelson, Richard D. *Deuteronomy :A Commentary.* The Old Testament Library. 1st ed. Louisville: Westminster John Knox 2002.

Ngwa, Kenneth. "The Story of Exodus and Its Literary Kinships." In *The Oxford Handbook of Biblical Narrative*, edited by Danna Nolan Fewell, 125–36. Oxford: Oxford University Press, 2018.

Nissinen, Marti. "Biblical Masculinities: Musings on Theory and Agenda." In *Biblical Masculinities Foregrounded*, edited by Ovidiu Creangă and Peter-Ben Smit, 271–85. Sheffield: Sheffield Phoenix, 2014.

Olson, Dennis T. "Crossing Boundaries: Moses the Man, Masculinities and Methods." *Hebrew Bible and Ancient Israel* 5 (2016): 151–68.

Olyan, Saul M. *Disability in the Hebrew Bible: Interpreting Mental and Physical Differences.* Cambridge: Cambridge University Press, 2008.

———. *Friendship in the Hebrew Bible.* The Anchor Yale Bible Reference Library. New Haven: Yale University Press, 2017.

Organ, Barbara E. "Pursuing Phinehas: A Synchronic Reading." *Catholic Biblical Quarterly* 63, no. 2 (2001): 203–18.

Palmer, Alan. *Fictional Minds.* Frontiers of Narrative. Lincoln: University of Nebraska Press, 2004.

Perdue, Leo G., Joseph Blenkinsopp, John J. Collins, and Carol Meyers. *Families in Ancient Israel.* Family, Religion, and Culture. 1st ed. Louisville: Westminster John Knox, 1997.

Philo. "On the Life of Moses, I." Translated by C.D. Yonge. In *The Works of Philo: Complete and Unabridged.* Peabody: Hendrickson, 1993.

———. *The Works of Philo: Complete and Unabridged.* Translated by Charles Duke Yonge. New Updated ed. Peabody: Hendrickson, 1993.

Pilch, John J. "Baldness." In *The New Interpreter's Dictionary of the Bible*, edited by Katherine Doob Sakenfeld, 386. Nashville: Abingdon, 2006.

———. "Leprosy." In *The New Interpreter's Dictionary of the Bible*, edited by Katherine Doob Sakenfeld, 635–7. Nashville: Abingdon, 2008.

Pitkanen, Pekka. *A Commentary on Numbers: Narrative, Ritual, and Colonialism.* Routledge Studies in the Biblical World. London: Routledge, 2018.

Pixley, Jorge. "Exodus." In *Global Bible Commentary*, edited by Daniel Patte, 17–29. Nashville: Abingdon, 2004.

Pleck, Joseph. "The Theory of Male Sex-Role Identity: Its Rise and Fall,1936 to the Present." In *In the Shadow of the Past: Psychology Views the Sexes*, edited by Miriam Lewin, 205–25. New York: Columbia University Press, 1983.

Powery, Emerson B. "Kiss." In *The New Interpreter's Dictionary of the Bible*, edited by Katherine Doob Sakenfeld, 536. Nashville: Abingdon, 2008.

Pressler, Carolyn. *Numbers.* Abingdon Old Testament Commentaries. Nashville: Abingdon, 2017.

Propp, William Henry. *Exodus 1–18: A New Translation with Introduction and Commentary.* The Anchor Bible. 1st ed. 2 vols. New York: Doubleday, 1999.

Rapp, Ursula. "Zipporah: The Vanishing of a Wife." In *Torah*, edited by Imtraud Fischer, Mercedes Navarro Puerto and Andrea Taschel-Erber. Bible and Women, 313–28. Atlanta: SBL Press, 2011.

Rees, Anthony. "Moses: Mother of Israel?" In *Making Sense of Motherhood: Biblical and Theological Perspectives*, edited by Beth Stovell, 16–26. Oregon: Wipf and Stock, 2016.

———. "Numbers 25 and Beyond: Phinehas and Other Detestable Practice(r)s." In *Leviticus-Numbers*, edited by Athalya Brenner and Archie C. C. Lee. Texts@Contexts, 163–78. Minneapolis: Fortress 2013.

———. "[Re]Naming Cozbi: In Memoriam, Cozbi, Daughter of Zur." *Biblical Interpretation* 20, no. 1–2 (2012): 16–34.

———. *[Re]Reading Again: A Mosaic Reading of Numbers 25.* Playing the Texts. London: Bloomsbury, 2015.

———. "Unmanning Moses." *St Mark's Review* 2017, no. 1 (2017): 63–74.

———. "What Gleams Must Be Good: Reading Arnold Schoenberg's Moses Und Aron." *The Bible and Critical Theory* 15, no. 2 (2019): 141–55.

Reif, Stefan C. "What Enraged Phinehas: A Study of Numbers 25:8." *Journal of Biblical Literature* 90, no. 2 (1971): 200–06.

Römer, Thomas. *Dark God: Cruelty, Sex, and Violence in the Old Testament.* Translated by Sean O'Neill. 3rd ed. Mahwah: Paulist, 2013.

Sakenfeld, Katharine Doob. *Journeying with God: A Commentary on the Book of Numbers.* International Theological Commentary. Grand Rapids: Wm. B. Eerdmans, 1995.

Schoenberg, Arnold. *Moses Und Aron.* Munich: Art Haus Musik, 2006. videograbación, 1 videodisco (134 min.): son., col.; 4 3/4 plg. + 1 folleto (37 p.) ; 18 cm., 101259 Arthaus Musik.

———. "Moses Und Aron: Oper in Drei Akten." Mainz: B. Schott's Söhne, 1957.

Schuele, Andreas. "Heart." In *The New Interpreter's Dictionary of the Bible*, edited by Katherine Doob Sakenfeld, 764–6. Nashville: Abingdon, 2007.

Scott, Ridley. *Exodus: Gods and Kings.* Melbourne: Informit, 2014.

Seebass, Horst. "The Case of Phinehas at Baal Peor in Num 25." *Biblische Notizen,* no. 117 (2003): 40–46.

Segal, Alan F. "Dead, Abode of The." In *The New Interpreter's Dictionary of the Bible*, edited by Katherine Doob Sakenfeld, 63–5. Nashville: Abingdon, 2007.

Shectman, Sarah. *Women in the Pentateuch : A Feminst and Source-Critical Analysis* Sheffield: Sheffield Phoenix Press, 2009.

Shields, Mary E. "Marriage, OT." In *The New Interpreter's Dictionary of the Bible,* edited by Katherine Doob Sakenfeld, 818–21. Nashville: Abingdon, 2008.

Sicherman, Max. "The Political Side of the Zimri-Cozbi Affair." *Jewish Bible Quarterly* 36 (/ 2008): 22–4.

Sivan, Helena Zlotnick. "The Rape of Cozbi (Numbers XXV)." *Vetus Testamentum* 51, no. 1 (2001): 69-80.

Soja, Edward W. *Thirdspace: Journeys to Los Angeles and Other Real-and-Imagined Places.* Cambridge: Blackwell, 1996.

Stackert, Jeffrey. *A Prophet Like Moses: Prophecy, Law, and Israelite Religion.* Oxford: Oxford University Press, 2014.

Stavrakopoulou, Francesca. *God: An Anatomy.* London: Picador, 2021.

Stone, Ken. *Sex, Honor, and Power in the Deuteronomistic History.* Journal for the Study of the Old Testament Supplement Series. Sheffield: Sheffield Academic Press, 1996.

Tatlock, Jason R. "Phinehas." In *The New Interpreter's Dictionary of the Bible*, edited by Katherine Doob Sakenfeld, 516. Nashville: Abingdon, 2009.

Tatz, Colin Martin. *With Intent to Destroy: Reflecting on Genocide.* London: Verso, 2003.

Thiede, Barbara. *Male Friendship, Homosociality, and Women in the Hebrew Bible: Malignant Fraternities.* Routledge Studies in the Biblical World. London: Routledge, 2021.

Thomas, Bronwen. "Dialogue." In *The Cambridge Companion to Narrative*, edited by David Herman, 80–93. Cambridge: Cambridge University Press, 2007.

Vanzant, Michael G. "Midian, Midianites." In *The New Interpreter's Dictionary of the Bible*, edited by Katharine Doob Sakenfeld, 79–81. Nashville: Abingdon, 2009.

von Rad, Gerhard. *Moses.* Translated by Stephen Neill. 2nd ed. Eugene: Wipf and Stock, 2012.

Wafula, R.S. "The Exodus Story as a Foundation of the God of the 'Fathers.'" In *Postcolonial Commentary and the Old Testament*, edited by Hemchand Gossai, 0–26. London: Bloomsbury, 2019.

Walsh, Jerome T. *Old Testament Narrative: A Guide to Interpretation.* 1st ed. Louisville: Westminster John Knox Press, 2009.

Whitehead, Stephen M., and Frank J. Barrett. "The Sociology of Masculinity." In *The Masculinities Reader*, edited by Stephen M. Whitehead and Frank J. Barrett, 1–26. Cambridge: Polity Press, 2001.

Willis, Timothy M. "Clan." In *The New Interpreter's Dictionary of the Bible*, edited by Katherine Doob Sakenfeld, 679. Nashville: Abingdon, 2006.

———. "Family." In *The New Interpreter's Dictionary of Te Bible*, edited by Katherine Doob Sakenfeld, 427–30. Nashville: Abingdon, 2007.

———. "Name, Naming." In *The New Interpreter's Dictionary of the Bible*, edited by Katherine Doob Sakenfeld, 217–9. Nashville: Abingdon, 2009.

Wilson, Kevin A. "Kohath, Kohathite." In *The New Interpreter's Dictionary of the Bible*, edited by Katherine Doob Sakenfeld, 546. Nashville: Abingdon, 2008.

———. "Reuel." In *The New Interpreter's Dictionary of the Bible*, edited by Katherine Doob Sakenfeld, 785. Nashville: Abingdon, 2009.

Wilson, Stephen. "Biblical Masculinities and Multiple Masculinities Theory: Past, Present and Future." In *Hebrew Masculinities Anew*, edited by Ovidiu Creangă, 19–40. Sheffield: Sheffield Phoenix Press, 2019.

Wilson, Stephen M. *Making Men: The Male Coming-of-Age Theme in the Hebrew Bible.* New York: Oxford University Press, 2015.

Zornberg, Avivah Gottlieb. *Moses: A Human Life.* Jewish Lives. New Haven: Yale University Press, 2016.

Index of Biblical Sources

About the Author

Anthony Rees is senior lecturer in Old Testament at Charles Sturt University. He is the author of *[Re]Reading Again: A Mosaic Reading of Numbers 25* (Bloomsbury, 2015) and *Voices of the Wilderness* (Sheffield Phoenix Press, 2015), and editor of *Things that Make for Peace: Traversing Text and Tradition in Christianity and Islam* (Lexington, 2020). He previously taught at Pacific Theological College in Fiji.